Political Theories of Decolonization

Political Theories of Decolonization

Postcolonialism and the Problem of Foundations

MARGARET KOHN

AND

KEALLY MCBRIDE

OXFORD
UNIVERSITY PRESS

OXFORD
UNIVERSITY PRESS

Oxford University Press, Inc., publishes works that further
Oxford University's objective of excellence
in research, scholarship, and education.

Oxford   New York
Auckland   Cape Town   Dar es Salaam   Hong Kong   Karachi
Kuala Lumpur   Madrid   Melbourne   Mexico City   Nairobi
New Delhi   Shanghai   Taipei   Toronto

With offices in
Argentina   Austria   Brazil   Chile   Czech Republic   France   Greece
Guatemala   Hungary   Italy   Japan   Poland   Portugal   Singapore
South Korea   Switzerland   Thailand   Turkey   Ukraine   Vietnam

Published by Oxford University Press, Inc.
198 Madison Avenue, New York, NY 10016

www.oup.com

Library of Congress Cataloging-in-Publication Data
Kohn, Margaret.
Political theories of decolonization : postcolonialism and the problem
of foundations / Margaret Kohn and Keally McBride.
     p.   cm.
Includes bibliographical references and index.
ISBN 978-0-19-539957-8; ISBN 978-0-19-539958-5 (pbk.)
1. Decolonization. 2. Postcolonialism.
I. McBride, Keally D. II. Title.
JV152.K65   2011
325'.301—dc22   2010018456

Printed in the United States of America
on acid-free paper

For our children,
Noah and Zach,
Celeste and Theo,
and the promise of making the world anew

CONTENTS

ACKNOWLEDGMENTS

A coauthored book such as this one accumulates more than the usual indebtedness. When we began this project, we acknowledged that there needed to be two of us in order to even begin taking on the large task of examining theories of decolonization from different periods and locations. Again and again, we found that two of us were not up the job in every particular, and so we relied on the kind assistance of our colleagues whose historical knowledge, regional expertise, linguistic acumen, and personal experiences greatly enriched our inquiry.

Jim Reische and Rogers Smith provided the earliest encouragement of the endeavor as we applied for grants. Angela Chnapko at Oxford University Press provided firm support for the endeavor, encouraging us to continue to work through our methodological difficulties. Anonymous reviewers for the Press provided invaluable feedback, allowing us to clarify our arguments and the goal of the book.

We would also like to thank our production editor, Joellyn Ausanka, and copy editor, Mark LaFlaur, for their careful work on this manuscript, especially their guidance on the spelling of Arabic and Persian words and names, which are based on the *Oxford Dictionary of Islam*. We also gratefully acknowledge Dayanita Singh for allowing us to reproduce her beautiful image as the cover of this volume.

Both of us have presented papers, separately and jointly, that allowed many individuals to contribute to the development of our inquiry. We would like to thank George Ciccariello-Mayer, Joan Cocks, Kennan Ferguson, Farah Godrej, Leigh Jenko, Uday Mehta, Anthony Parel, Jeff Paris, Darren Walhof, and Matt Whitt. Kevin Bundy, Marianne Constable, Shirin Deylami, Roxanne Euben, Ramin Jahanbegloo, Courtney Jung, James Martel, Dean Mathiowetz , Eduardo Mendieta, Carole Pateman, Manfred Steger, Ronald Sundstrom, Brian Weiner, and John Zarobell read portions of the manuscript and provided critical responses.

The University of San Francisco and the University of Toronto provided research support, and we have had the benefit of research assistance by Paola Vu, Zachary Scalzo, Angie Martinez, and Keith Calara. Thanks also to the students in our graduate seminars at the University of San Francisco, the University of Florida, and the University of Toronto for their ideas and input.

We also benefitted from the support of our colleagues, including Simone Chambers, Rebecca Kingston, Paul Kingston, Antoinette Handley, Ronnie Beiner, Cliff Orwin, Melissa Williams, Joe Carens, Mohammed Fadel, Annick Wibben, Elisabeth Friedman, Corey Cook, Stephen Zunes, Robert Elias, James Taylor, Anne Bartlett, Lois Lorentzen, Jeff Paris, and the Political Theory workshop and the Criminal Law Roundtable at the University of Chicago.

This collaboration has been a partnership that has been rewarding, allowing us to enrich both our friendship and our understanding of the world and the dynamics of political change. However, we need to acknowledge the tremendous collaborative effort by our other partners. Thank you, Ryan and John, for all that you did while we were writing this book.

Political Theories of Decolonization

Introduction

Political Theory and Decolonization

This book was inspired by the observation that postcolonial political theories had not found their way onto the syllabi of standard courses in political theory with much frequency. This is particularly remarkable considering how many of the more vibrant issues in contemporary political thought—such as global justice, multicultural citizenship, and human rights—would be enriched by postcolonial perspectives.

Even more, it is clear that the legacy of colonialism and the movements for independence continue to significantly shape political regimes around the globe. Anticolonial movements critiqued and revolted against the unequal distribution of power in the world. They were less successful at generating alternative, more equitable modes of distributing power, which is what decolonization, understood as truly ending the disparities of colonialism, would entail. Decolonization is unrealized, but not necessarily unrealizable. This means we have an arguably pressing responsibility to reconsider its aspirations. Decolonization, the dream of self rule, is the most recent incarnation of the long-standing project to achieve political freedom and therefore deserves a prominent place in the discipline of political theory. Political theories of decolonization provide extended ruminations about the challenges of founding a new polity that is more just, and they have the potential to deepen how political theorists understand core concepts such as freedom, equality, sovereignty, and the rule of law.[1]

COLONIAL CRITIQUE AND POLITICAL THEORY

Some of the recent scholarship in political theory has focused on the treatment of colonialism in the writings of canonical thinkers such as Locke, Burke, Mill,

Diderot, Tocqueville, Smith, and Kant.[2] These works reveal the extent to which colonialism and imperialism dominated the minds of great thinkers as the colonial project was taking place. While these recent studies provide fascinating insights into colonial issues in Enlightenment thought, they tend to overlook the voice of the colonized, instead focusing on close textual readings of canonical thinkers. This scholarship engages the topic of colonialism without drawing upon thinkers who spoke to these issues from the experience of being colonized. However, our decision to focus on the insights that emerge when "the empire writes back" is not primarily motivated by the desire to diversify the political theory canon. After studying the writings of canonical figures such as Tocqueville and Mill we simply felt that there had to be more thoughtful—and more up-to-date—reflections on colonialism. This book emphasizes that there was and continues to be a lively and illuminating debate about the problems of colonialism, decolonization, and postcoloniality by those very people who have experienced it.

We advance what initially may appear to be a difficult claim: even though every colonial context did produce different responses and strategies of resistance, there is a set of texts that can be identified as "postcolonial political thought" that address shared concerns and thematics. We will present thematic arguments, bringing out particular commonalties in postcolonial texts across different locations and times. This is not to deny the importance of specific historical and geographical contexts, but rather to point out that particular problems reoccur, despite differences in time and location. Other disciplines have wrestled with the designation of authors, texts, and movements as postcolonial and have fruitfully compared different localities and moments in history.[3] In all of these chapters, we present contextual information about these thinkers, but also draw upon the disciplinary methods of political theory to point out thematic continuities. Our research has found that many postcolonial thinkers were part of transnational networks and intellectual communities. For example, the Peruvian Marxist José Mariátegui wrote an essay criticizing Gandhi, and the Islamic theorist Ali Shariati translated the work of Frantz Fanon. Many of these thinkers shared ideas and strategies and saw the struggle to end colonialism as part of an international movement. The nonaligned movement that proclaimed itself at the Asian-African Conference in Bandung, Indonesia, in 1955 originated in Brussels in 1923 where anticolonial leaders from around the world met to strategize together, as will be discussed in the following chapter. We read these texts as both historical products and ideas that provide insight into other times and places. This approach is appropriate to our stated task: to present a series of essays that demonstrate what the intellectual histories of decolonization and postcolonialism offer to the endeavors of political theorists.

The central theoretical issue in this book is the problem of foundations, a recurring theme in the history of political thought. Machiavelli and Rousseau turned to the "foreigner founder" in order to solve the paradox that good institutions form virtuous citizens, but only virtuous citizens will adopt and animate good institutions. Inspired by his conviction that the Roman Empire brought civilization to the barbaric British Isles, John Stuart Mill turned this foundational story into a deeply problematic theory of civilizational advance. He argued that a benevolent foreign dictator such as Charlemagne, the Mughal emperor Akbar, or the British East India Company could inculcate obedience and introduce the rule of law, setting the stage for civilizational advance and, eventually, self-government. The colonized, not surprisingly, had a different view of the "benevolence" of their rulers and the desirability of European civilization. But the problem of foundations proved to be an enduring challenge.

By now it is widely recognized that many colonial subjects were divided subjects. Many figures both internalized and resisted European values that described their people as having no value.[4] Less widely understood is the political side of this paradox. The postcolonial state was also structured by colonial ideas and institutions that were designed to enforce subordination and exploitation. This meant that the postcolonial state was a divided state. Some postcolonial writers such as Ho Chi Minh and Frantz Fanon looked to the future, hoping that participation in the revolutionary struggle would turn colonial subjects into citizens. Others such as Gandhi, Afghani, and even Mariátegui looked to the religious traditions and institutions of the past to mobilize resistance and legitimize alternatives to the economic and political structures of the colonial state.

Historical distance now provides the opportunity to understand postcolonialism as a political phenomenon with distinct problems, dynamics, instabilities, and legacies. Historical accounts of the birth and death of "Third Worldism" have been published.[5] And while we can point to twentieth-century decolonization as a historically specific episode, political problems of decolonization continue to haunt regimes today.[6] A central dynamic of postcolonial political thought is the difficult transition from providing opposition to an established regime to articulating the principles, institutions and methods of self-determination. In questions of economy, education, law, and citizenship, we can see this same dynamic played out over and over again. How do movements and leaders evolve from being critics of colonial regimes and instigating revolutionary political change to being able to establish a stable, political alternative?

If the critique of colonialism as a systematic denial of freedom was clearly accomplished, the other central aspiration of postcolonial political theory—that of helping to establish stable systems of self-determination—has been only a tentative achievement. Postcolonial thinkers offered radical critiques of global power imbalances that still resonate today, but they also developed strategies for accomplishing independence that were more difficult to realize. To understand the contemporary global political climate, we need to examine the particular structures and dilemmas of postcolonial political thought and action.

METHODOLOGICAL ISSUES

This study differs from the approaches that predominate in most of what is usually labeled "postcolonial theory." In literary studies, postcolonial theory has tended to emphasize the relationship between knowledge and power. There has been intense scholarly interest not only in the literary production of former colonies but also in the theoretical issues raised by academic attempts to represent non-European societies.[7] The two most influential texts in this strand of postcolonial theory are Edward Said's *Orientalism* and Gayatri Spivak's "Can the Subaltern Speak?"[8] The scholarly literature inspired by these seminal works is enormous and, while it has influenced us in many ways, the literature concerning the relationship between knowledge and power is not the focus of this book. Other aspects of postcolonial thought to have inspired a great deal of attention are the analysis of discourse as an instrument of power and the history of colonial governmentality.[9] Some historians have argued that postcolonialism is the paradigm of our time, and have taken this to heart through the development of new fields of scholarship, such as Atlantic Studies, that place formerly nationalist accounts of history in a colonial context.[10] Recent historical work displays how postcolonial ideas can shift modes of inquiry and lenses of analyses in long-established fields rather than simply add new areas and figures into consideration.[11]

This project is not a work of comparative political theory, in that we are not presenting these theorists as somehow representative of distinct cultural perspectives.[12] These postcolonial texts, though of course influenced by and in some ways emblematic of different cultural perspectives, relate to the issues of power, domination, and the possibilities of self-determination in relationship to hegemonic powers. They also engage in a historically specific project of critiquing colonial power and theorizing alternatives. Given that the modern European legitimating narrative of the social contract had been discredited by the experience of colonialism, intellectuals sought other, alternative foundations, including land, religion, and the transformative experience of fighting for freedom. These texts were developed in reaction to colonial powers, and many (though not all) of the authors were deeply influenced by Western political theories. Still other texts were written by reformers who were critical of many dimensions of their own societies. Given this syncretic character, we do not read them as representatives of any particular system of political thought. The project does have a comparative dimension, but only in the broader sense that we draw comparisons between thinkers as we point out their similarities and differences.

We felt that a comprehensive examination of texts of postcolonial political thought would encourage more political theorists and teachers to consider what these texts can add to our understanding of political life, as well as illuminate how many of the central questions of political theory are imaginatively explored by postcolonial thinkers. While existing scholarship has helped us to understand European canonical works differently and to appreciate the difficulties in speaking for and about others, there are many other questions and issues of politics that remain to be explored. What ideas and assumptions have informed the process of founding a new regime out of the remnants of colonialism and reinvented traditions? What views of civilization have been advanced as alternatives to the "civilizing mission" of the colonial powers? How have critical, counterhegemonic ideas been institutionalized, or have they been? Comparative politics scholars have studied the trajectory of postcolonial state formation, but political theorists have been slow to add analyses of how the experience of colonialism and the struggle against it radically reconfigured the ideals of law, universality, and citizenship in ways that continue to shape regimes after they have attained independence.[13] We think that a theoretical exploration of the texts of decolonization and postcolonialism will greatly enhance our capacity to understand political change.

It can also serve as an important supplement to the dominant approach to the topic of global justice, which focuses on developing and defending normative arguments for a more cosmopolitan approach to moral obligation. Postcolonial political theories tend to cast the developed world in the role of exploiter rather than savior and point to the tension between the moralistic justifications of colonialism and its actual practices. Understanding the dynamics of colonization and decolonization across different contexts provides an additional vocabulary for analyzing contemporary politics. The logics of neoliberalism and processes of globalization often dominate our vocabulary for understanding the world beyond a national framework. Seeing the dynamics of decolonization and postcolonialism in various guises around the world provides lenses or conceptual frameworks that can complement analyses of the undeniably important role of development, security, and global justice. While globalization has captured headlines in accounts of the developing world, many of the critiques and analyses of globalization find their roots in virtually forgotten anticolonial texts by Jalal al-e Ahmad, Amílcar Cabral, Ho Chi Minh, and José Mariátegui.[14] Therefore we present this collection of essays in the spirit of expanding the scope of questions and issues presented by postcolonialism in the field of political theory.[15]

There are significant obstacles that have hindered the study of postcolonial political theory in North America. Some important texts are unavailable in translation, and only a small number of political theorists have mastered non-European language skills. Acquiring literacy in the history and culture of former colonies is also a challenge to scholars trained in European political theory. But these challenges are not insurmountable. Many postcolonial texts were written in Spanish, English, or French because the authors were educated in the colonial school system and wanted to reach a transnational audience. Also, even when the relevant texts must be read in translation, it is possible to take advantage of the academic division of labor between area studies and theory. Figures such as Afghani, Dussel, Mariátegui, and Al-e Ahmad have been the subject of extensive scholarly scrutiny and there are excellent historical works, translations, and interpretive pieces that can help alert new readers to controversies in translation and issues of textual interpretation.

Another obstacle, however, is that the theoretical language itself can become a source of paralysis. All the concepts presented in this book—such as the West, Europe, the Third World, postcolonialism—are all themselves highly contested notions. Although we use some of these terms, we recognize their limitations and political implications. The issue of naming has been very controversial in postcolonial studies because it is one of the foremost acts of representation. Employing a label not only defines the domain of inquiry in a particular way, but it also conjures the intended and unintended traces of other historical uses.[16] As Anne McClintock points out, the term "postcolonial" is problematic because it suggests a linear, progressive history; it obscures the varied colonialisms of different countries and periods; and it establishes a binary between two periods that are often intertwined through forms of neocolonialism.[17] While we would not want to imply that we are living in a world in which colonialism can be understood entirely in the past tense, we do believe that scholars working in this area have made it clear that using the term does not mean that power disparities no longer exist. As Diana Brydon observed in the introduction to her edited collection of postcolonial works, "Postcolonialism matters because decolonization is far from complete and colonial mentalities, including the inequities they nurture, die hard."[18]

In this book we use the word postcolonialism as a broad term that encompasses the critique of colonialism, the movements for national liberation, and the ongoing struggles with the legacies of colonialism. Defined in this way, postcolonialism does not mark the end of colonialism but rather the emergence of the world it created. We also use the narrow term "political theories of decolonization" to describe the intellectual history of the movements that fought for political independence from colonial power. The debates about terminology reflect the seriousness with which postcolonial theorists in other fields have taken the issue of power and language. We think it is time for political theorists to engage this material more themselves even though these contested debates about representation can make the challenges of cross-cultural translation and dialogue seem daunting.

OUTLINE OF THE BOOK

In the imaginations of political theorists, societies spring from the minds of philosophers such as Plato, or emerge from compacts, agreements, and declarations as in social contract theory. We know that this is not the case in the real world, and some figures, such as Machiavelli, acknowledge that conquest and war are what give rise to polities. Postcolonial theorists offer a wealth of rumination on the problems of founding within the context of power struggles.

The problem of founding is that it never happens on an empty canvas: there is a history that precedes it. How postcolonial populations and governments relate to the past, and how they try to overcome the past to create a present and future of self-determination, is one of the most fateful elements of postcolonial politics today. Three chapters of the book (1, 2, and 5) examine three different kinds of foundational strategies that emerged in the movements of decolonization during the twentieth century. These strategies are a rebuke to colonial ideologies and are a form of "colonial critique." One response is to create a unified precolonial cultural identity to serve as a point of reference and a conceptual foundation in the development of a new regime, as in the case of the negritude movement. Another response is to turn to religion to provide unity. Other thinkers focus on the indigenous population's relationship to the land as a measure of self-rule and a source of autonomy. The solutions to the problem of founding presented in these texts offer insight into the attempt to create commonality among citizens—a commonality that transcends their shared experience of subordination to colonial rule.

The first chapter, "Postcolonial Political Theory and the Problem of Foundations," examines the historical origins of the international political movement that started the process of decolonization in the twentieth century to show why foundational stories are particularly important in the postcolonial context. It then examines the development of negritude in detail, looking at two different varieties of that movement as conceived by Léopold Senghor and Aimé Césaire. This example allows us to see how negritude is a political response to the experience of French colonialism and how it was used to break away from the claims of universalism that circulated in the French empire.

The problem of postcolonial foundations may initially seem to be the exclusive concern of countries that directly experienced foreign military and political control by occupation. Yet European influence was also a concern throughout the Ottoman Empire, in China, and in Iran, where the state's autonomy was undermined by European economic and military initiatives. Intellectuals in these countries tried to understand the reasons for their relative weakness and debated whether the solution was Westernization, some sort of hybrid form of modernization, or more faithful adherence to traditional practices and norms. Chapter 2, "Westoxification/Detoxification? Anti-Imperialist Political Thought in Iran" focuses on anti-imperialist themes in the work of Iranian writers. Even though postcolonial approaches to Islamic thought are rare, we think that there are important commonalities between strands of Islamic political theory and other critiques of imperialism and colonialism. Islamic modernists were engaged in a project that pervaded the colonial world, that of reimagining and recasting traditional sources as alternatives to the institutions and practices imposed by the colonial powers. The anti-imperialist dimension of Islamic modernism is particularly pronounced in the work on Jamal al-Din al-Afghani (Sayyid ad-din al-Afghani). For Afghani, Islam is a necessary source of unity, identity, and mobilization against imperialism. These same ideas reappear in slightly different form in the writings of Ali Shariati and Jalal Al-e Ahmad, two twentieth-century intellectuals who influenced the Iranian Revolution (1978–79). Their critique of "westoxification"—the disease of Western civilization—provided a rhetorical link between different groups that opposed the Shah for different reasons.

Three other chapters of the book (3, 4, and 6) move from the rupture with colonial rule and ideologies to the difficulties of establishing a postcolonial form of politics. Chapter 3, "Self-Determination Reconsidered," argues that our understanding of revolution can be enhanced by examining twentieth-century movements for independence. These movements wanted to do more than just replace foreign rulers with indigenous elites who would ensure the smooth functioning of existing forms of exploitation. Reconfiguring Confucian ideas about virtue, Ho Chi Minh saw revolution as a process of self-cultivation and transformation for both leaders and citizens. Frantz Fanon has a similar emphasis upon the liberatory aspects of struggle, but he becomes apprehensive about the manipulation of the masses by nationalist leaders. How are we to regard democratic revolutions of independence that did not create governments with democratic accountability? This chapter starts to unpeel the difficulties of establishing democracy in postcolonial regimes.

Chapter 4, "Colonialism and the State of Exception," focuses on law as one dimension of the problem of transition into the postcolonial regime. Martial law was frequently declared in the colonies, particularly as popular resistance to exogenous powers swelled. But it remained controversial since it seemed anti-thetical to the claim that colonialism was a civilizing mission bringing the rule of law to barbaric places. Mill, Burke, and Tocqueville all debated martial law; while they were in broad agreement about the acceptability of the colonial state, they disagreed about the legitimacy of exceptional measures. Ngugi wa Thiong'o and Achille Mbembe, on the other hand, argue that the real issue is the state itself, not the exception. For Ngugi, the State of Emergency in Kenya (1952–59) revealed the deeper logic of colonial governance. Their approach to the concept of the state of exception illuminates some of the problems of founding a new state out of the violent vestiges of the old order.

Chapter 5, "Grounds of Resistance," delves into the unique importance of land claims in postcolonial political thought. The chapter examines critiques of colonialism based on the relationship between a people and the physical terri-tory they inhabit. This emphasis proves to be useful in critiquing neocolonial forms of economic development, as both Amílcar Cabral and, more recently, the Zapatista movement have done. Introducing land as a central element of their political analysis is one readily apparent innovation that theories of decol-onization offer to the field of political theory.

One legacy of colonialism was the economic penetration of capitalism into less developed regions. Whether as a source of raw materials or low-wage labor, a market for industrial products, an outlet for unemployed people from the colonizers' homeland, core countries have sought ways to profit from their dominance over the periphery. Marxism provided a language for de-scribing economic inequality and understanding the struggle against it. For this reason it exerted a powerful influence on national liberation movements and critics of the postcolonial state. Yet the value of Marxist theory was limited by its developmental theory of historical progress and the erasure of race/culture. Chapter 6 "The Philosophy of Liberation," traces some of the ways in which the Marxist idea of proletarian revolution has been radically reworked in the postcolonial context. The Peruvian Marxist José Mariátegui used the method of historical materialism but he identified the indigenous people as a potentially revolutionary subject and challenged the assumption that all societies follow the same stages of economic development. Enrique Dussel's philosophy of liberation departs even farther from Marxism. He insists that each structure of domination, not only capitalism, must be assessed from the perspective of those who bear the burdens rather than those who enjoy the benefits. In the philosophy of liberation, the subject of emancipation is not the proletariat but a diverse group that may include the indigenous person, the campesino, the slum-dweller as well as the worker; an alliance between them is a political and ethical necessity rather than an eco-nomic one.

The conclusion, "Gandhi and the Critique of Western Civilization," focuses on the most famous critic of colonialism. Unlike most of the other theorists in this book, Mohandas (Mahatma) Gandhi is the subject of an extensive secondary literature in the field of political theory.[19] While building on this work, we try to show the similarities between Gandhi's critique of Western civilization and the arguments advanced by Ahmad and others. We read Gandhi's *Hind Swaraj* (Indian Home Rule) as a paradigmatic work of colonial critique that demystifies colonial ideology and inverts the dominant hierarchy by celebrating the values that colonialism denigrates. Gandhi's vision of the independent Indian state, however, was controversial. M. N. Roy, a contemporary critic, scathingly denounced Gandhi's self-sufficient peasant villages as nostalgic nonsense based on Orientalist fantasy rather than anything approaching an objective description of rural life. M. N. Roy also dismissed the popular view that spirituality, locality, and simplicity constituted the heart of "India's message." So, instead of concluding with a neat summary of "the postcolonial message," we end with a cautionary reminder. There is no postcolonial message or program as such, but there are multiple and sometimes contradictory postcolonial messages.

When we started this book we hoped to understand the subjugated knowledge embedded in the forgotten intellectual history of the struggles for decolonization. This project seemed to hold out the possibility of a different way of thinking about political theory, including core concepts such as rights, democracy, and property. There are a number of terms and ideas that reappear in this literature with great frequency, such as decentralization, solidarity, communal self-sufficiency, economic justice, and positive freedom. None of these ideas are unfamiliar to mainstream academic political theory, but the thinkers and political figures in this book write about them with urgency and anger and link them together in unfamiliar ways.

Critics of colonialism also attempted to break apart the assemblage that linked ideas of freedom and justice to culturally specific symbols and used this assemblage to justify practices of domination and exploitation. But the task of founding a new postcolonial polity proved more difficult than many anticipated. It was impossible to go back to the world that colonialism destroyed; new economic conditions and political forces made that infeasible.

An important question is how exactly postcolonial theories present a challenge to liberal democratic norms, because they seem to have been relatively unsuccessful in creating social stability, regimes that respect human rights, or in many cases even governance that is adequate. It is tempting to look at the disarray of many postcolonial countries and say that what they lack is stronger support for a liberal democratic framework.

Postcolonial political thought is a response to practices of expropriation and domination that were carried out often in the name of liberal ideals. These ideals became thoroughly discredited because of political practices on the part of colonizers, so much so that many theorists of decolonization rejected the liberal framework entirely.[20] A number of recent studies have concluded that the link between liberal ideas and colonial practice was not an aberration; they have suggested that liberal theory was formulated in part as *a way of legitimizing* colonial expropriation and domination. But the political ramifications of the convergence of liberal ideology and illiberal colonial practices are most clearly demonstrated by the rejection of the ideals and administration of colonizing powers by movements of revolution and independence. The issue is not only which ideals are being embraced, but also how these ideals interact with political practices. Postcolonial political thought is one response to the disjuncture between the ideals and actions of colonizing powers.

For this reason, Michael Freeden's book *Ideologies and Political Theory*[21] is useful in understanding what the study of postcolonial ideologies can offer political theory as a field. Most helpfully, Freeden rejects the notion that political ideologies are somehow false, while political philosophy aims at uncovering timeless truths. Instead, we need to understand that political ideologies are lenses that not only shape but create perceptions, actions, and, hence, reality. Studying these ideologies should not lead to a simplistic endorsement or rejection of them. Instead, a more nuanced interaction is required, and the contexts created by colonial history means that this interaction will largely be experienced as a clash between liberal democratic and postcolonial ideological positions. Postcolonial political ideologies were intended to challenge colonial power and perceptions. They still do.

Postcolonial Political Theory and the Problem of Foundations

Moments in which new regimes are founded are of particular interest to political theorists. How did the interruption of a political order come about? How is the legitimacy of the new regime asserted and grounded? Will stability occur as a result of the change, or will change (or disorder) become endemic to the country? Ultimately, stories, fables—or even noble lies if you prefer—have been the most reliable method for explaining a polity's emergence and bestowing legitimacy upon its authorities. These stories are strategic and retrospective, inventing a past that serves the present. They provide a foundation for polities by making claims about the past, yet they also shape the present and the future. We can trace the tension between the aspiration to change the course of history and the constraints that inevitably encroach upon human action by examining these narratives. This is a central aspect of theories of decolonization: the desire to change the course of history and assert self-determination, accompanied by a need to nonetheless reckon with the historical legacies of colonialism.

Political theorists and historians often think about myths and stories that emerge post facto to explain the foundation of a new regime. These stories exclude some details and invent others, and are often fragmented or contradictory, as has been detailed in Rogers Smith's *Stories of Peoplehood* and Eric Hobsbawm's *The Invention of Tradition*.[1] Foundational accounts create a coherent lens for interpreting the past, present and future of a regime or collective. Fighting over these narratives has been common in both political theory and public debate, with some people trying to include forgotten characters or revise the story line to be more historically accurate, and other parties holding on to an already established story or attempting to resurrect a forgotten one.

Understanding the effects of exclusion and the shaping of history as a reflection of past political ideologies has been one theme common in political theory.

At times, it seems that these tales are solely constructed to consolidate the interests of the powerful. Historical events are ruthlessly clipped and shaped to provide support for present-day objectives, and narratives such as Manifest Destiny, or "la mission civilisatrice," provided ideological cover for less than savory activities. So another goal of political theorists has been to trace how different stories about the past are used to shape present and future political outcomes. This chapter moves a step back in time to add one more element to this project by examining how the colonial past shaped the founding stories of decolonization. While the rest of this book examines the trajectories of postcolonial regimes that were established in part by these foundational stories, the goal of this chapter is to establish the setting in which theories of decolonization were developed. Here, we argue that the stories—and politics—that accompanied colonization ultimately influenced the stories and politics that accompanied decolonization.

While this may seem a relatively obvious point, it is important to understand how this dynamic has political implications. In short, the tale of colonization was one of progress being delivered to darker areas of the globe: colonization would bring all peoples into the trajectory of European notions of historical progress. Marx argued, "Indian society has no history at all, at least no known history. What we call its history, is but the history of the successive intruders who founded their empires on the passive basis of that unresisting and unchanging society."[2] In other words, colonizers brought history to India, and naturally having a history is the first step in being able to progress through it. John Locke asserted, "In the beginning all the world was America," that is, undiscovered and lacking (European) civilization.[3] The assertion was that some day, the colonized peoples would be able to take up the white man's burden as their own task, and the weight of governing the globe could be transferred onto newly trained shoulders. They could take over the endeavor of historical progress once colonialism started it.

Of course the moment of transfer seemed to recede infinitely into the distance. The narrative of progress through colonization was problematic for a number of different reasons that have become evident to us today. What is less apparent is how movements of decolonization were nonetheless structured by the need of the colonized to repudiate this narrative. Indigenous leaders needed to take up self-determination, but not on the terms of progress and liberalism as defined by the colonizers. Instead, self-determination needed to be a break from the colonial past, not a natural outcome of their period of tutelage by the Europeans. Why? In the most general terms, it is important to recognize how the terms of self-determination and liberalism, and the tools of modern governance including the rule of law, constitutional government and bureaucracy,

were deeply tainted by their association with the brutalities of colonial administration. From the perspective of those who had endured colonial rule, the
claims of civilization seemed greatly exaggerated. This perspective is best
captured by Gandhi's response to an inquiry into his perspective on English
civilization, to which he replied, "I think it would be a good idea."

More specifically, the early movements for national self-determination were
met with staunch opposition and violent repression. There was vehement disagreement as to whether the indigenous people had progressed through their
colonial tutelage sufficiently to take over governance. At a specific historical
moment the narrative of progress could have been supported by actual political
change, but the gradualist vision advocating for transfer of power was violently
defeated, as we will explain. For these reasons, foundational narratives of decolonization bear little resemblance to the ones more familiar to audiences that
have been accustomed to thinking of the French, American, and Russian revolutions as paradigmatic. All of these revolutions could be presented as an inevitable (or at least triumphant) result of human freedom in achieving historical
progress according to the dictates of agreed-upon principles. In contrast, many
of the foundational narratives that emerge at the moment of decolonization are
stories that seem to look backward, not forward.

One can get a sense of the difficulty of creating a postcolonial founding narrative by thinking of these narratives as a play. Imagine a script that includes a
scene where the characters decide to disregard what the playwright has written.
Now imagine a staging of this play where the actors decide to stop following the
script and improvise. How can one tell if the new action is just part of the narrative as planned by the playwright, or whether actors have truly gone renegade?
The script of colonialism included a final scene whereby power would be transferred over to "the native." In reality, this scene never arrived. But when the time
came to *seize* self-determination and become authors of their own historical narrative, it needed to be on entirely different terms in order to signal a break from
the colonial regime instead of serving as its natural conclusion, or even worse,
the ultimate justification for the colonial project. Writing a narrative based on
oppositional values became essential to the practice of self-determination. This
fact helps us to reflect upon what the term "self-determination" truly means in
this context: it means to determine one's world according to terms chosen by
oneself, or by a people collectively. As such, it falls firmly into the tradition of
political theory that seeks to remake the world through imaginative capacity: the
freedom to make a world, a polity, not merely respond to the world as it is.

For purposes of comparison, let us start by taking a closer look at the problem
of founding in a former colony that many of us are familiar with: the United States.
Jacques Derrida examined the Declaration of Independence and the signatures
upon it, trying to decode the grounds on which the United States was founded.

> How is a state made or founded, how does a State make or found itself? And an independence? And the autonomy of one which both gives itself, and signs, its own law? Who signs all these authorizations to sign?[4]

His efforts are reminiscent of a story in which a child asks an elder about a story explaining that a turtle carries the world on its back. What is the turtle standing on? Another turtle. And that one? "There are turtles all the way down" is the final reply. Similarly, Derrida looks at the Declaration and starts to unpeel the layers of authority it purports to represent.

> Here then is the "good people" who engage themselves and engage only themselves in signing, in having their own declaration signed. The "we" of the declaration speaks "in the name of the people." But this people does not exist. They do *not* exist as an entity. They do *not* exist, *before* this declaration, not *as such*. If it gives birth to itself, as free and independent subject, as possible signer, this can hold only in the act of the signature. The signature invents the signer.[5]

The signature upon the Declaration that creates and somehow independently confirms the entity that signs it is the perfectly appropriate foundation for a polity that is contractual at its core. In both the founding moment and continuing practice, contractualism is the primary mechanism that transforms the constraint of individuals into a marker of his or her freedom.[6]

This contractual capacity is not, however, a strong element in more recent postcolonial foundational narratives. Contractualism is a comparatively ahistorical foundational narrative. In contrast, more recent postcolonial foundational narratives do not start with a flat assertion of self-determination in the present. Instead, an explanation for past subordination accompanies the claim to future self-determination. All foundings must create a break with the past, and all foundings bear traces of that past, as Machiavelli, for instance, so clearly articulated. Derrida's reading does not account for the violence of foundings that is so vigorously denied in the contractual narrative in the United States. The Declaration of Independence bears the marks of racial anxiety wrapped into a potent combination with colonial contestations, as when slave rebellion and Indian resistance is explained as a plot by the Crown against colonists.[7] A close reading of the Declaration of Independence belies the claim that the truths it offers are self-evident since it offers a litany of abuses heaped upon the colonists by the crown as a justification for the act of rebellion. Even the contractual narrative, at first glance so neat and tidy, is not free of bruises suffered on the trajectory toward its signing.

The task of many political theorists has been to expose the layers of subordination, exclusion, and even genocide that are ignored in the foundational stories of settler societies such as the United States.[8] In polities where the colonized are the majority in the new independent state, foundational stories *must* acknowledge practices of racism, violence, and subordination. The task for political theorists therefore is not to unpeel the layers of the narrative to reveal the struggle underneath it. Rather, we investigate how these stories are used to create a foundation for a polity in spite of its immediate experience of violence, exploitation, and subordination.

The stories presented here are a selection of postcolonial founding narratives that have been developed. And while these stories describe and thereby change historical trajectories, they are nonetheless a product of their historical juncture. The strategies presented here offer a glimpse into the problem of founding in the twentieth century, in a world with superior methods of resource extraction, a devastatingly effective racialized caste system, and well-disseminated systems of Orientalist knowledge that denigrated indigenous traditions and beliefs. In this postcolonial world, is not the claim to independence and the ability to generate a new system of politics all the more difficult and crucial? The problem of foundations is not so far away from our own time, after all. The leaders in the movements for decolonization were forced to confront the same dilemma that many historical figures have faced: on a template of oppression and subordination, how does one draw an image of freedom and self-determination?

FOUNDING MOMENTS AND POSTCOLONIAL POLITICAL ACTION

Hannah Arendt wrote about politics and freedom as occurring in the space "between past and future" in her book of the same title.

> Seen from the viewpoint of man, who always lives in the interval between past and future, time is not a continuum, a flow of uninterrupted succession; it is broken in the middle, at the point where "he" stands; and "his" standpoint is not the present as we usually understand it but rather a gap in time which "his" constant fighting, "his" making a stand against past and future, keeps in existence.[9]

At its most basic, the struggle to achieve postcolonial politics is precisely this exercise of using the present as an opportunity to create a new future and end the past: as such it is precisely the activity of political action as defined here by Arendt.

In a speech at the University of Cairo in 1967, Léopold Senghor argued in favor of the Organization of African Unity. But he began by demonstrating the problem at hand: "To base solely on anti-colonialism the joint organization that we plan to build is to give it a very fragile foundation. For it is not the colonial past that characterizes us as Africans. We share it with all the other peoples of Asia and America. It belongs to the past—at any rate, it will belong to the past tomorrow. It lies behind us now that our task is to build our future."[10] Senghor is leading into his definition of negritude and the argument for it as the basis of a Pan-African federated government, but his stuttering over the past and future is just as indicative of his vision of politics. Because he has taken it as his task to help build a future for himself and for the rest of Africa, this means that colonialism will now be the past. His current assertion of self-determination will turn the present into the past: "it will belong to the past tomorrow." The collective conception of the present must be differentiated from the collective perception of the past in order to serve as a foundation for the claims of political independence. The revolution must then not only build the future, but also redefine the past in building the foundation for postcolonial political systems.

All of the following chapters in this book address the problem of founding new regimes out of the colonial contexts, so it is appropriate that we begin by examining the structure of the postcolonial foundational narrative. There are two aspects to providing a new foundation for postcolonial political regimes: the first is to provide a convincing break between the past and the future through decisive action in the present. In Arendt's terms, this is the struggle of freedom: the ability to act today and potentially change the future allows the same person to define or characterize the past as history. After all, if you are colonized the past and present offer no glimpse of self-actualization. Action is required to provide a break with the past and present, and to change the trajectory of the country's future. The second aspect of this foundational task is to reinterpret the past in such a way that it may help in the present and future struggle for self-rule—or, at the very least, not hinder it. The past must be transformed into a stage for what is to come so as not to be a stigma or burden.

Many postcolonial theorists have taken pains to understand the transition toward self-rule and to see how that which came before taints or drives what is currently emerging, as Tocqueville did in *The Old Regime and the French Revolution* (1856). Nationalism was clearly the dominant response to the problem of foundations, and has been extensively explored and critiqued most notably by Partha Chatterjee.[11] Rabindranath Tagore warned against the dangers of embracing nationalism—a tradition with no indigenous roots—as the model for Indian independence.[12] Similarly, Frantz Fanon wrote about the dangers of nationalist consciousness in *The Wretched of the Earth*.

Less noted are the other responses to this problem of foundations. One narrative creates a sense of shared identity to use as a basis for pride and unification, such as Aimé Césaire and Senghor's development of the concept of negritude. As the speech by Senghor quoted above indicates, he believed that Africans had a common experience and identity that transcended the experience of colonization. He hoped that negritude would provide unity among colonized populations, a sense of pride in the past, and a basis for the culture that would flower after revolution.

Another strategy is a turn to religion to provide for unity, offer a plan for the future, and create an explanation of the colonial past. As we shall explore in Chapter 2, understanding Islamism as a postcolonial foundation helps explain its vitality and influence.

These stories are shaped by the material and cultural legacies of the past, but they also shape what is to come, and therefore they are emblematic of the capacity of human beings to restructure and change their world. After presenting the history of early attempts in nationalist movements to follow the script provided by the colonizing powers, in what has been termed "anti-colonial liberalism" we will then move to examine the structure of one of the foundational stories that accompanied movements of decolonization, negritude.

NARRATIVES OF PROGRESS, COLONIALISM, AND EARLY ANTICOLONIALISM

The political tension between the idea of historical progress and human agency is familiar to many political theorists. It is particularly evident in the debates over Marxist political action at the end of the nineteenth century: will the revolution be produced by historical contradictions, or do you need political actors to come and make history? This question and the different strategies suggested by its answer has plagued Marxist politics. To understand how one narrative of progress came to be regarded as a disabling one that foreclosed the range of human action, as opposed to the triumphalist belief in the human capacity to continually improve the world, one needs to examine the historical record.

The narrative of progress and gradual transfer of power created tensions very early in the British colonial project. For one thing, if the goal was to create self-rule by the colonial subjects, how would colonial administration go about setting that up? An example of this conundrum is the statement by Sir Thomas Munro, then governor of Madras, "On the Ultimate Aim of British Rule in India" (1824). He argued that the British needed to think about their rule as permanent "until the natives shall at some future age have abandoned most of their superstitions and prejudices and become sufficiently enlightened." But just because they were not capable today of self-rule did not mean, in his estimation, that they should be excluded from all aspects of governance. Munro argued for using colonial subjects as police, and said that this inclusion could help them on their path toward self regulation. "With what can we talk of our paternal government if we exclude the natives from every important office, and say, as we did until very lately, that in a country containing 150,000,000 inhabitants no man but a European shall be entrusted with so much authority as to order the punishment of a single stroke of rattan?"[13] The idea that imposing rule from elsewhere would create the capacity to self-regulate was as troubling in the colonial context as it was domestically, as evidenced by the lengthy debates over how to relate the tutelage of children to adult self-governance, and what the age of reason truly was. As late as 1943, Herbert Morrison, Labour party leader, responded to the idea of giving African colonies their independence as an aberration akin to "giving a child of ten a latch-key, a bank account and shot-gun."[14]

Even more progressive voices exhibit confusion about the relationship between colonial rule and its ultimate aim of self governance. For instance, Lord Macaulay asserted after spending three years in India as head of the Indian Law Commission that if Indians seized the mantle of self-rule in India, it would be "the proudest day in English history." Naturally, he continued to assume that such events were appropriately marked as a British accomplishment and hence as an episode of British history and, not a break from it. Macaulay was not alone in presuming self-rule as the concluding act of colonialism, though he did have a large role in articulating exactly what such a devolution of the British empire would look like. His scheme contained racial components, and he believed colonies that were predominantly white, such as Canada, would be able to achieve self-rule sooner than those that were not.

This narrative of progress toward self-rule was brought to the forefront of world politics during the First World War. In January 1917, Woodrow Wilson issued a proclamation that foresaw peace coming from a rejection of the system of secret alliances that had dragged nations into war. "No peace can last, or ought to last, which does not recognize and accept the principle that governments derive all their just powers from the consent of the governed, and that no right anywhere exists to hand peoples about from sovereignty to sovereignty as if they were property." Though Wilson had countries such as Poland in mind when he made the statement, Erez Manela's *The Wilsonian Moment: Self-Determination and the International Origins of Anticolonial Nationalism* establishes how colonized peoples around the globe responded to Wilson's pronouncement as a signal that the time for self-rule had arrived. Wilson appeared to be stepping onto the world stage in an all-powerful position, and it was assumed his professed belief in self-determination—the phrase originates from this historical moment—could not be resisted by intransigent colonial powers. It was, perhaps naively, assumed that if necessary American military power would give the persuasive edge to Wilson's beliefs in universal self-determination. Movements stirred in Egypt, India, China and Korea, and hopeful nationalist advocates such as Nguyen Tat Thanh (who eventually renamed himself Ho Chi Minh) sought an audience with the president himself in order to press his case for independence before the man he saw as an ally to his nationalist cause.[15]

Unfortunately, Wilson presumably was thinking of European countries when he made the statement. His well-known racism (the Virginia-born president resegregated the federal workforce while he was president and was an enthusiastic audience for D. W. Griffith's film *The Birth of a Nation*) may have simply caused a blind spot. It was inconceivable to him that other races would assume that such universal principles applied to them. Whether this was the case or whether it was a more calculated ploy to disrupt the international system ultimately does not matter for the purposes of this argument. What is crucial is that nationalist leaders and movements did respond to Wilson's rhetoric, and made a play for the transfer of power to commence.

In 1918, Sa'd Zaghlul, a nationalist leader from Egypt, attempted to open discussions with the British government about independence, citing Wilson's principles as evidence that the British government could no longer submit the Egyptian people to a government against their will. When he was denied his audience, Zaghlul wrote directly to Wilson hoping he would represent the Egyptian nationalists' interests at the Peace Conference in Paris. "No people more than the Egyptian people has felt strongly the joyous emotion of the birth of a new era which, thanks to your virile action, is soon going to impose itself upon the universe."[16] Wilson, recognizing the delicate nature of interfering with the internal struggles of the British Empire, declined to respond to repeated entreaties from the Egyptians. Their polite petitions to join the League of Nations, supported by evidence of Egypt's long history, indigenous body of knowledge, law, and overall cultural enlightenment were buried at the Paris Peace Conference.[17]

When this tactic failed, the Wafd party started what is now called the 1919 Revolution. What began as peaceful public demonstrations against British rule became violent as the British tried to suppress the movement altogether. In the spring of 1919, eight hundred Egyptian civilians were killed, including many women whose participation in the uprising was highlighted as an indicator of their cultural enlightenment. The killing of women in particular was cited as evidence of the brutality of the British rule. Wilson recognized the establishment of the British protectorate, a new form of colonial administration that was established in response to the revolution. The rhetoric of self-determination that had been touted as part of the peace process now looked to be a ruse, a velvet glove obscuring an iron fist. One participant in Wafd recalled the bitter disappointment that resulted when their movement was denied recognition by the world: "Here was the man of the Fourteen Points, among then the right to self-determination, denying the Egyptian people its right to self determination and recognizing the British protectorate over Egypt. . . . Is this not the ugliest of treacheries?! Is it not the most profound repudiation of principles?!"[18]

Similar episodes played out around the world, including early nationalist demonstrations in India that resulted in the Amritsar massacre of 1919. But these episodes did not have to be repeated in every locale for anticolonial leaders to learn their lesson from the experiences of others.

The first major international gathering of anticolonial leaders occurred just eight years later in Brussels in 1927. Here leaders such as Sukarno, Nehru, Messali (founder of Algeria's Étoile Nord-Africaine) and leaders from Iran, South Africa, and Palestine, having been spurned by the Paris Peace Conference, joined together to form their own international organization. As Vijay Prasad notes, "Brussels scorned and repudiated Versailles."[19] It was clear that they would have to define self-determination on their own terms now that the dominant powers of the world had rejected their claims to this supposedly universal principle.

Interestingly, the narrative of historical progress continued to be invoked by the fading powers at the end of their colonial regimes. It was a face-saving pretense to assert that the end of formal colonialism was actually its continuation, such as in 1950 when the British Colonial Office declared, "The transfer of power is not a sign of weakness or of liquidation of the Empire, but is, in fact, a sign and source of strength."[20] The British took a long bow to conclude their starring role as they engaged in what they euphemistically called "the transfer of power." That this transfer took place on terms very different than the colonizers had once envisioned suggests that indeed the empire was crumbling under its own weight, not just as the result of a siege. Yet the challenge to European colonial power perhaps made it all the more important to insist upon the continuation of their overarching narrative. If they could no longer control all the actors and purse strings, at least they could dictate the story that helped mask their slipping predominance. The French government coined the term, "le courant de l'histoire," or the tide of history, to explain the inevitable independence of Algeria.[21] Such a framing device of course makes political choices appear as inevitable outcomes, but it also has the effect of erasing the political actions of the Algerians who brought independence about. The inescapable arc of history, not the FLN (Front de Libération Nationale), determined the fate of Algiers.

Given this context, it is not surprising that narratives of postcolonial foundings search for their origins in times, spaces, and identities that are clearly distinct from the colonial episode. Moderate nationalist movements in the early twentieth century made claims based upon the dominant narratives of progress and by adopting the tools of liberal governance as their own, but were denied the opportunity by colonial powers not ready to relinquish their positions. At the 1955 Bandung conference, the delegates endorsed the right to self-determination as well as a broader human rights agenda. Subsequent narratives of decolonization used terms that were often in sharp repudiation of the liberal ideas that accompanied conquest and became influential. They value identities, religious beliefs, and territorial connections that had been specifically devalued or denied by the colonizing powers. The content of the narrative had to provide a clear break with the narratives of progress in order to make it clear that the tools of political action had indeed changed hands.

NEGRITUDE AS POSTCOLONIAL FOUNDATION

Negritude is difficult to characterize because it has led many lives. It has been variously invoked as a cultural movement, psychological posture, political platform, biological certainty, and cosmic force. In fact, one could argue that its adaptability to any number of causes may be the key to its political impact during the twentieth century. At its most basic, negritude is the assertion of the value of black identity and culture, and a direct repudiation of the racism that accompanied colonialism and that continues to inflect general perceptions of identity and behavior today. Because racism has not expired, we would expect to see that negritude will continue to serve as a political, social and cultural tool. Today the revaluation of racial identity often appears as an element in protests against a "homogenizing" globalization and also to invoke a common purpose and outlook in diasporic identities. Kwame Anthony Appiah called negritude the oppositional moment of "a classic dialectic," which emerges as a response to the unfilled hopes of simple equality and a challenge to the pervasive claims of racial inferiority.[22]

But to appreciate the political significance of negritude, one must understand how it emerged as an oppositional strategy, specifically in relation to the universalist aspirations of French colonialism. French colonialism had the formally stated goal of assimilation. The idea was that through education and acculturation, the inhabitants of French territories would ultimately become French citizens. This aspect of French colonial policy, which it must be emphasized was a stated ideal rather than actual practice in most cases, provided the context for the emergence of negritude. First, the professed French practice of linking cultural acquisition to citizenship, even in the context of colonialism, provided a clear example of the political utility of a fictional, transhistorical community. In fact, early claims to full French citizenship in Senegal were made on precisely these grounds, as political representatives from Senegal held the French government to their stated rhetoric. Second, a closer examination of the origins of negritude in the surrealist cultural movement below reveals that the founders of the philosophy, Césaire and Senghor, were products of the process of assimilation. Ironically, French policies for assimilation spawned the ideology of African specificity. Frantz Fanon summarized this historical progression neatly: "It is the white man who creates the Negro. But it is the Negro who creates negritude."[23]

However, the connections between negritude and surrealism are not just a sign of the educational assimilation of Senghor and Césaire. The two movements deeply influenced one another, as we will explore in detail below. Negritude is a belief in a shared essence of blackness, including a structure of being, modes of perception, and cultural practices. To demonstrate this vision and explain it, proponents of negritude used philosophy, literature, art, poetry, and theater. But their goals were political since they primarily aimed to redefine blackness in celebratory terms. Surrealism was also a cultural movement with political goals. However, rather than having racially specific aspirations, surrealists used cultural interventions to try to disorient their audiences. This disorientation would lead the public to question aspects of reality that they took as given. Both movements, negritude and surrealism, were driven by the idea that cultural products can have political effects by insisting that reality is not necessarily at it appears, and therefore one should not take the perceived order as given or unchangeable. The membership and tools of the two groups overlapped, but the goals of each movement were distinct.

Understanding how negritude emerged as a strategy that specifically responded to French colonialism requires a closer look at French practices in regard to citizenship and race. In Senegal, the official stance was that full citizenship would be offered to inhabitants of French colonies who adopted French culture, but in practice this was rarely the case. Léopold Senghor, one of the leading figures of the negritude movement, was born in the Medina and therefore was not eligible for citizenship. He had to be made a French citizen through a special exemption so he could stand for his master's examination in philosophy at the Sorbonne (only citizens were allowed this privilege at the time). This gave him acute insight into the way that assimilation into French citizenship was the false promise of colonialism.

While the official stance might have been that full citizenship would be offered to inhabitants of French colonies who attained learning, in practice this was rarely the case. Instead, the mainland viewed those who administered the colonies with suspicion, irrespective of their background, regarding as "pied noirs" those whose feet became blackened through their contact. In 1848, the new government set up a series of communes in Senegal, and through this small opening in French political history provided the means by which thousands of native Senegalese could claim full French citizenship.

Senegal contained four communes within the country (Gorée, Dakar, Rufisque, and Saint-Louis), while the section of Senegal that fell outside of the communes was called the Medina. Two of these communes, Gorée and Saint-Louis, were under full French control at the time of the 1848 revolution. At this time, assimilation became a genuinely, if briefly, pursued goal of colonial administration. France banned slavery, gave citizenship to the inhabitants of the communes, and provided the right to elect a deputy to the Assembly in Paris. As France incorporated the other two communes into their administrative control in the 1860s, they extended the same rights to these territories as well.[24] In 1848, this policy added 4,500 new citizens to the French voting rolls; by 1906 this number had increased to 10,000. Within Senegal this population was known as *originaires*. In the 1880s France extended its control to the rest of the country, and inhabitants of the Medina were placed under a protectorate and became subjects of France rather than citizens. So in Senegal, there were three different classes of citizens and subjects: Senegalese outside the communes were subjects, *originaires* inside the communes were French citizens, and creoles who were products of European settlers and Senegalese inhabitants were afforded French citizenship based upon their half-French parentage. The creoles took care to distinguish themselves from the *originaires* by emphasizing their connection to French culture.[25] In theory, French culture was to provide the unifying element in citizenship; in practice, however, assimilation and citizenship were not necessarily related. Instead, race and hereditary status played the most significant role.

Because France did not actually tie assimilation to citizenship in Senegal, it should be no surprise that the *originaires* did not assimilate. Despite fifty years of full French citizenship, the policy had failed to create citizens assimilated to French culture; in the communes, Islam was still the predominant faith. French administrators were horrified by the situation. Having full-fledged French citizens who were not culturally French, then as now, made it more difficult to embrace the principle of universalism so loudly proclaimed in France. One inspector general, V. Verrier, found the combination of French citizenship and cultural difference in Senegal alarming and proposed that citizenship be revoked and awarded only to white inhabitants and Africans who could prove their assimilation.[26] Such a dramatic reversal of political privileges was considered unwise, however there was some success in modifying claims for full citizenship, and *originaires* ceased to carry the privileges of French citizenship outside of the communes.[27] In effect, French policy shifted and linked the rights of citizenship to the *territory* of the communes rather than to the inhabitants thereof—the soil could be claimed as acculturated even if the people could not. The other fateful element of this decision was that a previously enfranchised elite was mobilized to fight to retain or regain previous entitlements.

Out of this context, Blaise Diagne was the first black African to be elected as the Senegalese representative to the French Assembly, in 1914 and began to campaign for the full restoration of French citizenship to the *originaires*. Diagne was given a golden opportunity by the outbreak of World War I: France desperately needed Senegalese enlistments to reinforce their quickly overextended military. Diagne suggested to his constituency that they refuse to sign up unless their citizenship were restored. On October 19, 1915, the question was settled: *originaires* were full fledged French citizens and would therefore fight the nation's battles.[28] The pressure for conscripts was the underlying reason for the success of this campaign, but Diagne's rhetoric in appealing for citizenship for his countrymen is remarkable; he used the notion of a mystical, universal French identity as the basis for his political claims, a position he held throughout his career. In 1930, he made a speech to the French Chamber of Deputies in which he professed: "I belong to those who believe that France's traditional posture . . . can only find its resolution in unity both of conception and doctrine, a unity of the spirit between France and the peoples or races scattered across her overseas territories."[29] Assimilation to French ideals of universal citizenship, the theory behind French colonial conquest though not the practice of its colonial administration, had proven to be the way to gain citizenship ultimately. In effect, Diagne held the French government to its own rhetoric. More important for the purpose of this discussion, invoking shared cultural heritage was demonstrated to have clear political utility.

Blaise Diagne served in the French National Assembly for twenty years, until his death in 1934. One of the more minor of his many accomplishments was arranging for Léopold Senghor to be made a citizen so he could stand for his master's examination in philosophy at the Sorbonne, mentioned above. Senghor was in Paris, writing about themes of exoticism in Baudelaire, when he met Aimé Césaire. In 1933, they coined the term "negritude," though Césaire is generally credited with having used the term first. Both were poets and worked together on the journal *L'Étudiant Noir*. They were exemplary scholars in the French system, but their experiences in Paris made both of them acutely aware of their status as second-class citizens within French culture.

The intricate connection of negritude to French culture is best captured by the fact that both Césaire and Senghor wrote in French, which was the only choice to bring their message of a persisting African identity to a transnational audience. Senghor's work is peppered with quotes by Marx, Marcel Mauss, Jean-Paul Sartre, Henri Bergson, and Hegel, demonstrating his complex understanding of European philosophy at every turn and using it as the basis for his exploration of the African personality. Similarly, Césaire was influenced by emerging anthropological studies, frequently citing the ethnologist Leo Frobenius, historiography such as Spengler's *Decline of the West*, and Nietzsche's philosophy, in addition to current aesthetic theories.[30]

Though Senghor and Césaire were ultimately to part ways in their political journeys, they were unified in 1933 in breaking from the established literary and cultural scene of students from all corners of the French Empire, brought to Paris to be educated so they could both administer the colonies and bring French values to their home populations. There appears to have been only one issue of *L'Étudiant Noir*, but its impact was disproportionate to its brevity.[31] Césaire and Senghor took all the tools of French culture and knowledge at the time and used them to assert affiliation with an oppositional identity. In this way, they demonstrated their ability to assimilate, and pronounced their freedom in choosing not to.

French assimilationist policies laid the foundation for the realization of negritude in a number of other ways as well, by providing the cultural influence via surrealism, and through the educational system, which brought together intellectuals from various parts of the French empire who quickly recognized their common subordination. The policies of assimilation meant that the most talented of those from the reaches of the empire came to study in Paris, but it was this experience that provoked the clear recognition of the boundaries of such assimilationist policies. At the same time, recognition of both the diversity and the commonalties of the French colonial experience also gave birth to the idea of a unity of identity. Césaire comments on the collective discovery of negritude:

> It was simply that in Paris at that time there were a few dozen Negroes of diverse origins. There were Africans, like Senghor, Guineans, Haitians, North Americans, Antilleans. Etc. This was very important for me. . . . as well as an awareness of the solidarity among blacks. We had come from different parts of the world. It was our first meeting. We were discovering ourselves. This was very important.[32]

In an interview in 1967, Césaire pointed out that negritude was a way of rejecting assimilation without rejecting his education. The liberating aspects of surrealism allowed him to look beyond the appearance of things and find another reality. A key principle of surrealism was the significance of the collective unconscious; freeing the imagination was a crucial part of social liberation. For surrealists like André Breton and Louis Aragon, this meant liberation from bourgeois values, customs, and habits that restricted the range of human experience. For Césaire, this collective unconscious could also be a source of

resistance to colonial culture. He explained, "I said to myself: it's true that su-
perficially we are French, we bear the marks of French customs; we have been
branded by Cartesian philosophy, by French rhetoric; but if we break with all
that, if we plumb the depths, then what we will find is fundamentally black."[33]
Césaire also attaches the term "disalienation" to negritude, hypothesizing that it
is literally coming back into oneself in the midst of a racist regime. Negritude
refers back to an imagined past, a quality of African life that existed before
colonization, endured through colonization, and will succeed colonization.

One way of interpreting negritude is seeing it as a form of primitivism, a view
that is supported by the fact that Senghor begins his discourse on negritude by
presenting thirty pages of anthropological and archaeological evidence about
early inhabitants of the Continent.[34] Yet to see this only as a form of romanticism or a fantastical projection would be to ignore the nuances hidden in the
work and outlook of Césaire and Senghor. Their intellectual connection with
surrealism becomes very important in developing a more complete understanding of their invocation of the term "negritude."

Irving Markovitz wrote about negritude as a result of elite cultural assimilation: "Like the Greeks, the French had always proclaimed to the peoples of the
world that when they [the non-French] had achieved the level of French civilization, they would be equal. Negritude attempted to show that this level was
attained. It was a demonstration in abstraction, erudition and sensitivity."[35]
Markovitz proposes that the abstract elements of negritude made it primarily
cultural, and not truly revolutionary. But this evaluation ignores how abstraction is a necessary component of revolution: one must first be able to imagine
the world in a way that it does not currently exist. Negritude was an act of imagination, but its abstract basis provided its power: it provided the lens and inspiration for a complete revaluation of the current racial hierarchy. Defiled
Africanness could be proclaimed, and what was detested could become a point
of pride.

Césaire's connection with surrealism was much more long-standing and significant than Senghor's. André Breton wrote the introduction to the publication
of Césaire's, *Cahier d'un retour au pays natal* (Notebook of a Return to My Native Land), a work that is considered the epic poem of negritude. Moving back
to Martinique, in 1941 Césaire published a journal, *Tropiques*, for four years
that documents his continuing engagement with cultural revaluation as a form
of political liberation. The journal was a more or less official mouthpiece of the
surrealist movement and featured contributions from European surrealists as
well as figures from the Caribbean.

Suzanne Césaire, his wife, who was also an integral figure in the movement,
remarked that surrealism was the revolutionary element within negritude:
"Thus, far from contradicting, diluting, or diverting our revolutionary attitude

toward life, surrealism strengthens it. It nourishes an impatient strength within us, endlessly reinforcing the massive army of refusals."[36] Surrealism was important in two different ways to the Césaires' development of negritude. First, it was a way of seeing that allowed them to view reality from a different lens, thereby reinterpreting it. Surrealist art takes what is familiar and displaces it, for instance by changing its size or juxtaposing unfamiliar elements (a fur-covered teacup, say, or Dalí's melting watches). It brings awareness of how perception structures our sense of reality, and that a change in perception may let a different version of "the real" emerge. Influenced by Freud's work on the unconscious, surrealists also valued the "truth" in aspects of self, experience, and world that are often repressed or ignored. In Breton's *Surrealist Manifesto* (1924) he argued, "Under the pretense of civilization and progress, we have managed to banish from the mind everything that may rightly or wrongly be termed superstitious, or fancy; forbidden is any kind of search for truth which is not in conformance with accepted practices." Dreams are a medium through which we can access alternative truths, and Breton argued that new forms of reality, or surreality, would emerge as dream and reality become intertwined.

Césaire's literary work includes many dream sequences and references to dreaming. But along with the dream motif there is also a sense that his characters are slowly awakening, coming to recognize parts of themselves that they had forgotten. The change in their perception through the opening to experiences and voices that had been ignored or repressed allows them to come to a new vision of self. To consider how this process has political import, imagine Césaire, an educated, French-speaking surrealist artist and intellectual who also happens to be black. According to the dominant terms of the day, to become an intellectual, one renounced blackness; to embrace blackness was to ignore one's training. How can one accommodate the seeming impossibility of one's existence? Only by challenging the dominant terms of the day and by establishing alternative truths based upon experience could Césaire overcome the double alienation from his color and his intellectual tradition.

Césaire did not think that political revolution was more important than these personal shifts that could come about as the result of cultural perceptions and encouragement. From the beginning, both he and Senghor affiliated negritude with the left, but disagreed with doctrinaire communism that saw political revolution as antecedent to cultural shifts. Ultimately, he decided that surrealism alone would not provide the political change he sought, and this evolution is evident in the pages of *Tropiques*, which started to publish increasingly strident accounts of the economics and politics of colonialism until its last issue in 1945. At this time, Césaire ran for office, and was elected mayor of Fort-de-France, beginning decades of service as a public official in Martinique. After a relatively brief embrace of communism, Césaire split from the French Communist Party

(Parti communiste français) in 1956 with a well-publicized letter to Maurice Thorez, then leader of the PCF. In 1980, Césaire gave Colin Dayan an interview, recounting the fact he had never relinquished the view that surrealism and imagination were essential to anticolonialism. Dayan reports, "Resistance for Césaire is not just political, but psychic. Repression is not only a history of mutilation and torture. It is also the buried and forgotten. The revolution must be 'internal,' a complete overhauling of consciousness, what he called 'une rencontre bien totale.' "[37]

Frantz Fanon has provided the most devastating critique of negritude, arguing that it is just an inversion of the distortions of colonialism: "It seems then that the West Indian, after the great white error, is now in the process of living the great black mirage."[38] The importance of being grounded in reality was particularly important for Fanon, as we shall discuss in Chapter 3, "Self-Determination Reconsidered." However, to characterize Aimé Césaire's engagement with surrealism as an endorsement of fantasy altogether is to miss the revolutionary aspirations of Césaire specifically and the surrealist movement more generally. Walter Benjamin observed of surrealism: "Since Bakunin, Europe has lacked a radical concept of freedom. The Surrealists have one."[39] Césaire understood that one had to see, feel, and then understand that other worlds and selves are possible before one can begin to create them. Political freedom is about imagining alternatives, and what better source for these visions than the truth hidden inside one's self?

Léopold Senghor's development of negritude took a very different path, although it served a similar purpose for him in providing the foundation for understanding colonial subordination and the subsequent path toward political liberation. Negritude also provided a new way of understanding the experience of colonial subordination. Senghor's work had two very different aspects: the first was presenting historical research to provide for the empiricism of shared characteristics. The second, virtually forgotten element of what he did was to propose that negritude was also accompanied by a unique ontology and epistemology. In an essay translated as "The African Apprehension of Reality," Senghor characterizes this aspect of negritude by contrasting it with the European mode of being and knowing. Europeans use what he calls "objective intelligence" whereby one approaches the world in a spirit of distinction. "He first distinguishes the object from himself. He keeps it at a distance. He freezes it out of time and, in a way, out of space. He fixes it, he kills it."[40] European modes of being and knowing thus create separateness between viewer and the object viewed. The political ramifications of this mode of being in the world are that the European views the world as subordinate to the self: "he makes a means of it."[41]

In contrast, Senghor claims that the African embodies a sort of internal rationality, whereby connections between self and world are explored—the self is discovered through convergence with objects, space, and others around him. "Our subject abandons his *I* to sym-pathize and identify himself with the THOU. He dies to himself to be reborn in the *Other*. He does not assimilate, he is assimilated."[42]

This description provides an alternative explanation for the processes of subordination and objectification that characterized colonialism. Instead of it being a matter of will, power, inferiority or superiority, it becomes an ontological distinction between interiority and exteriority. The experience of subordination, of being assimilated, is a key to what defines African systems of thought and experience. It will persist even as the political situation changes.

It also suggests the ultimate contribution that Africans can make to the development of what Senghor calls the Universal Civilization. The unique form of African perception and being will come to complement the European form of knowledge. Their synthesis together will lead to the foundation of a universal culture. Senghor applies Hegelian dialectics to the experience of colonization and presents a new interpretation of the history of servitude, develops an argument for the shared strengths of Africans based upon this principle, and outlines a future role for Africans in world politics.

Senghor used negritude as a biological essence that in part provided the materialist underpinning for African socialism. Because a form of socialism existed in Africa long ago, and because Africans are still basically the same as they were before colonialism, naturally African socialism will need to be instated again. Rather than dialectical materialism, Senghor's version of negritude became a form of dialectical identities that would act as the engine of history, and the physical identities of all races would join together to create Universal History, combining into a sort of *geist* or world spirit that could integrate the simultaneous influence of all races.

There are two main critiques of negritude today. The first points out the movement's complicity in the French colonial structure, as a direct response to the experience of colonialism. In his intellectual history of negritude (2005), Gary Wilder argues that it can only be understood as an extensive response to the ideals of colonial humanism circulating in France between the world wars. "Negritude writers became implicated in the elaboration of colonial humanism even as they formulated an alternative black humanism." This dynamic does not lead him to conclude that the movement is bankrupt, but rather "politically inadequate."[43] Partha Chatterjee has leveled a similar disappointment in anticolonial movements that have adopted nationalist models:

Nationalism denied the alleged inferiority of the colonized people; it also asserted that a backward nation could "modernize" itself while retaining its cultural identity. It thus produced a discourse in which, even as it challenged the colonial claim to political domination, it also accepted the very intellectual premises of "modernity" on which colonial domination was based.[44]

The similarity with negritude is undeniable. Writers accepted many of the stereotypes about blackness that had circulated, in order to revalorize them.

The other primary criticism of negritude decries the essentialism of the movement. Although Césaire ultimately decided that blackness was not a physical, but rather a cultural essence, at its inception negritude was conveyed by blood. Critics suggest that even this cultural variant of negritude simplifies the variety of black experiences in general, creating an illusory uniformity. Isn't this another form of stereotyping that must be resisted?

In some ways, critics are similarly disappointed by the lack of pure oppositionality offered by the philosophies of negritude. For the first, negritude is deeply complicit in the colonial structure and therefore is not truly an alternative foundation. And critics of the identity politics of negritude assert that it is a form of warmed-over primitivism. In many regards, this critique also seems to be about a quest for purity and a desire to have identity recognized without coercion; in other words, to have a socially affirmed identity outside of social pressures.

But perhaps the search for purity in political foundations is misguided. Freedom and reaction cannot be mutually exclusive. Mistaken also is the assumption that a foundational moment is one that exists outside of the trajectory of history. Foundations are moments within history that change potential experience and trajectories, not some sort of hypothetical Archimedean point or thought experiment. The measure of a foundation needs to be whether it is a story that provides a space for imagination and then action.

Negritude is about the power of reinterpretation and alternative modes of perception that can lead to a radical break from the present and a new ability to reimagine the future. But as one *tsumo* (proverb) from Zimbabwe comments, "Observation is the cleverness of the cripple." In other words, action, not mere perception, is the real source of empowerment. Taken on these terms, it cannot be denied that negritude served as an inspiration for both perception and action. Senghor and Césaire are some of the few poets of the twentieth century to become political leaders for the majority of their lives.

These foundational narratives have become traveling narratives, still shaping the present and seeking to found a different future. The ideal of negritude is echoed in contemporary cultural and political movements that assert the power of diasporic identities and write postnationalist historical accounts such as Paul

Gilroy's *The Black Atlantic*. However, the founding story is but the first aspect of the problem of founding that we will explore. The story itself may be taken to establish a blueprint, but further examination of different cases of postcolonial politics reminds us that the material conditions in which the stories are told are also important. Foundations, even as they reinterpret history and change the future, cannot erase the past. If foundational stories demonstrate that politics is about imagining a different past and future, more detailed exploration of different cases of political movements of decolonization reminds us that both the legacy of colonialism and the struggle against it will continue to shape the new regimes. As Césaire observed, "The flotsam of any Ancien Régime has a strange staying power."[45]

Westoxification/ Detoxification

Anti-Imperialist Political Thought in Iran

More than thirty years have passed since the Iranian revolution of 1978–79. Historical perspective allows us to see the paradoxical elements of the event in sharper relief. The Iranian Revolution was dramatically televised, one of the first urban revolutions outside of Europe, and a mass social movement as opposed to a vanguardist operation. That such modern political forms would install clerical theocracy seems ironic, incomprehensible. Popular fury was harnessed to create the world anew and to take a sharp turn from what was widely acclaimed and accepted as the natural trajectory of modernization.

One astute observer of Islamic politics, the Pakistani writer, scholar and activist Eqbal Ahmad, compared the Iranian and French Revolutions as iconic for their respective ages: "(T)he Iranian was like the French, a unique and perhaps seminal revolution for the postcolonial era as the French had been for the industrial age."[1] What does it mean to say that the Iranian Revolution is seminal for the postcolonial era? Iran was never formally colonized, but the leaders ceded economic control to foreign companies and governments in exchange for financial and military aid. The Iranian revolution was seen as repudiation of western influence or imperialism, broadly conceived. In short, this claim demands that we reconsider whether the formal definition of colonization is sufficient for understanding the phenomenon of postcolonialism. More important, the Iranian revolution marked the beginning of a political movement with strong appeal that is not just a direct repudiation of a particular colonial ruler but is an original political formation that responds to conditions of continued European and American dominance after the era of formal colonization had ended.

That self-governance and self determination came to be seen as synonymous with the rejection of external sources as opposed to self-legislation demonstrates how thoroughly outside (read: Western, European, and American) influences had troubled the Iranian political tradition. As in all long-standing traditions, there were reformers and conservationists in a struggle to determine its future. The asymmetrical contact between what was essentially a pastoral society with western capitalist systems of expropriation during the nineteenth and twentieth centuries meant that Western influence became a third presence in the debate between reformers and traditionalists. Although it would be easy to conjecture that traditionalists would be more suspicious of outside influences than reformers, the example of Islamic anti-imperialism shows that there were no such clear lines of affiliation.[2] The Iranian revolution can be understood as the curious, but not unpredictable, outcome of this historical and intellectual engagement; social reformers joined forces with traditionalists, finding common ground in their desire to repel what they saw as the alien powers that had overpowered both of them.

The Iranian revolution took place during the Cold War, and support for the Shah was widely understood as part of a broader strategy for promoting the geopolitical interests of the United States. Today the connection between Islamism[3] and anti-imperialism is ignored by the mainstream media and dismissed by some influential academic commentators such as Bernard Lewis.[4] Political Islam is typically described as religious fundamentalism, and Islamist ideology is understood in the West as an atavistic desire to return to a premodern past, which makes it easy to overlook its salience as a distinctively contemporary political ideology. Debates over the *hijab* or the legitimacy of *sharia* reinforce this tendency to portray Islam and modernity as two opposite worldviews when in fact they are interrelated.[5]

In *A Fundamental Fear: Eurocentrism and the Emergence of Islamism* (1997), Bobby Sayyid tries to explain why the name Islam has been used as a banner for political protest and mobilization.[6] He suggests that an earlier generation of modernizing elites had blamed Islam for the region's economic and political weakness. When the modernization project, inspired by Europe and imposed with the help of elites, failed to bring about prosperity and autonomy, Islam was available as a potent signifier.[7] It already stood for everything opposed to the West: tradition rather than modernization; morality instead of materialism; order and stability rather than change and upheaval; purity in place of corruption; and pride rather than subordination.[8] Since Islam had not been an important source of institutional power or legitimation for (often secular) pro-Western regimes, it was available as a basis of critique and resistance. According to Sayyid, the Ayatollah Ruhollah Khomeini was particularly adept at mobilizing the ideal of Islam to constitute a new political, anti-imperialist subjectivity.[9]

This link between Islam and anti-imperialism, however, has a history that predates Khomeini.[10] In the late nineteenth century, Jamal al-Din al-Afghani promoted Islamic unity and orthodoxy as the only effective tool for combating the growing power of the West. In the 1960s, Jalal Al-e Ahmad, a leftist and secular member of Iran's intelligentsia, wrote despairingly of *gharbzadegi* or "westoxification," a term that became a popular metaphor for the debilitating effects of Western lifestyles, institutions, and values. Ali Shariati argued that a renewal of Islam was the only possible cure for westoxification. Al-e Ahmad, Shariati, and Khomeini all denounced westoxification, but they meant something very different by the term. The term itself, however, achieved a kind of unstable political alchemy, making very different approaches look as though they shared common goals.

This chapter focuses on four thinkers from Iran, which locates them outside the mainstream of Sunni Islam.[11] It would be equally interesting to explore the intellectual history of the Muslim Brotherhood and the New Islamists, focusing on the ideas of Hasan al-Banna, Sayyid Qutb, and Yusuf al-Qaradawi.[12] A critique of imperialism and the postcolonial Egyptian state also plays a role in their writings. But it is beyond the scope of this book to provide an overview of something as diverse, complex, and vast as modern Islamic political thought, so we decided to focus on one theme, the critique of westoxification. This allows us to show how very different thinkers came to understand the political significance of Islam in interrelated ways.[13] Although we use the term "Islamic political thought" to describe the work of thinkers who share a cultural/religious identity, we freely admit that they are just one strand of an extremely diverse intellectual tradition.

Even though postcolonial approaches to Islamic political thought are uncommon, we think that there are important commonalities between strands of Islamic political thought and other critiques of colonialism and imperialism. Jalal Al-e Ahmad's critique of "westoxification" shares many themes and rhetorical features with Gandhi's critique of Western civilization in *Hind Swaraj*.[14] Islamic theorists were engaged in a project that was going on throughout the postcolonial world, that of reimagining and recasting traditional sources as alternatives to the institutions and practices imposed by the colonial powers.

The four authors featured in this chapter do not form a single intellectual tradition in any obvious sense. They do not fall on the same side of the left-right divide, nor is it possible to group them together under the familiar labels such as religious or secular, fundamentalist or reformist. Al-e Ahmad was a secular leftist who translated French literature and quoted Camus, not the Quran. Khomeini, on the other hand, insisted that European authors and institutions had nothing to teach Dar al-Islam (the territory of Islam, the region where Islamic law holds sway).[15] It is precisely because of these differences that their similarities are all the more striking. They all turn to Islam as the answer and this tells us something important about the question. The question is related to the problem of foundations as formulated in earlier chapters: how to prevent the centrifugal tendencies of colonial and postcolonial modernity from destroying the existing society and replacing it with something that realizes neither the values of the old world nor the promises of the new? What is striking is how the traditional answers given in political theory—the social contract, the deliberative assembly—seem unsuited to answering this question.

AFGHANI'S ANTI-IMPERIALISM

Jamal al-Din al-Afghani (Sayyid Jamal ad-Din al-Afghani) was a prominent figure who lived in Turkey, Egypt, Iran, France, and Afghanistan, working as a political adviser, teacher, and writer. His thought influenced both the reformist and radical strands of political Islam.[16] He was an early mentor of Mohammed Abduh, who is considered one of the founding figures of liberal Islam.[17] Afghani's ideas were appealing to Muslim reformers because he extolled the virtues of Western science. He also insisted that rationalism and science were not Western imports but traditional elements of Islamic culture. This position, however, was viewed with suspicion and hostility by the more conservative elements of the religious establishment. In 1871 Afghani was exiled from Turkey because of a speech embracing Western science and defending philosophy as equal to prophecy.[18] Although this later position had roots in the Islamic philosophy of the tenth to thirteenth centuries, it was considered a heterodox view that had been repudiated by theologians.

Despite Afghani's activities as a reformer, he also inspired movements usually associated with the terms "radical" or "fundamentalist."[19] Afghani was a radical in so far as he embraced Islamic principles as a way of bringing about a distinctive political logic: modernization without Western hegemony. Over the course of Afghani's career, he increasingly emphasized the importance of Islam as a framework for mobilizing resistance to European imperialism in the Middle East. He tried to forge an alliance between anti-Western reformers and conservative figures in the Islamic religious establishment. He laid the intellectual foundations for a coalition that would ultimately prove pivotal to the success of the Iranian Revolution in 1979: an alliance between reformers and the *ulama* (or *ulema*, 'the learned,' Islamic scholars). Afghani was living in Iran in 1890 when the Iranian government granted a British company a monopoly on the purchase, sale, and export of all tobacco grown in Iran.[20] This concession directly affected the majority of the population and made the extent of foreign economic control apparent to everyone. Afghani, who had become a passionate anti-imperialist during his years living in British-occupied India, used religious appeals to convince Iranians to resist this economic domination by unbelievers. He wrote a letter to the head of the Shi'i *ulama*, who issued a fatwa (ruling) calling for a boycott of tobacco. This boycott was successful, and the shah was forced to rescind the British concession. Even though some scholars have concluded that Afghani's role may have been exaggerated,[21] it shows that he was correct in believing that Islamic identity could be a powerful force capable of motivating people to participate in the struggle against imperialism.

Afghani insisted that civilization and progress did not require uncritical assimilation of European models. The modern world, for Afghani, was a place where European science, military power, and economic development had undermined the political autonomy and threatened the cultural identity of the Islamic world. Modernity and imperialism were integrally linked, and it was difficult to separate European technical innovations and culture from the military domination and economic exploitation that were key elements of the new global system. To the subjugated people of the Middle East, the West signified not only a geographical entity (Europe) but also a religious system, a history of geopolitical rivalry, and a set of values. To its detractors, the values of Western civilization were primarily negative: materialism, hedonism, secularism, and excessive individualism. Others associated the West with science, rationality, critical thinking, and material progress.[22] Some political leaders and intellectuals responded by arguing that the only way to reassert political independence was to adopt the Western practices that had ensured military superiority.[23] This approach was realized most fully in Turkey under Kemal Ataturk, the first president of the Republic of Turkey (1923–1938), and was based on an integrated approach that included secularism, nationalism, and modernization.[24] Ataturk's approach was emulated to varying degrees by other Muslim nations in the early twentieth century, especially Reza Khan (Reza Shah Pahlavi) in Iran (ruled 1925–41). The dominant alternative was to reject Western civilization altogether and promote strict adherence to existing religious practices, prohibitions, and legal and educational institutions. Afghani was among a small but influential number of thinkers who articulated a third alternative. He insisted on the social function of religious orthodoxy while also defending rationalism and critical thinking.

At first Afghani's writing appears inconsistent because he defends both religious orthodoxy and enlightenment ideals. In some essays he criticizes Islam for stifling critical thinking and in others he defends an orthodox approach to religion as the only way to ensure morality and political stability.[25] The contradiction is resolved to some degree when we understand Afghani's reasons for promoting religion and science: his defense of religion is distinctly political. He does not say that faith in God or prayer will provide the solutions to terrestrial problems. Instead, he suggests that religion provides the social conditions that allow humans to work together to promote the common good. In Afghani's most famous work, "Refutation of the Materialists," he argues that religion promotes beliefs that have enormous social utility.[26] Religion teaches that earthly existence provides humans with the opportunity to perfect themselves in order to gain access to the afterlife. Furthermore, religion fosters a belief in the superiority of the community sharing one's faith. This helps strengthen the bonds among group members and also encourages a rivalry among groups that can stimulate greater accomplishments. According to Afghani, religion can also solve two challenges that beset any political community: free riding and corrupt government. The belief in the afterlife provides an incentive for all members of the community to follow the law and it also binds leaders to the same code of conduct followed by the governed.

Religious orthodoxy, however, can also lead to passivity and uncritical acceptance of authority. This is one of the reasons why Afghani insisted that "science" (i.e., rationalism) could contribute to civilizational development. Under the right circumstances, rationalism and critical thinking can be important ways of preventing stagnation—cultural, social, and economic. Scientific study is also necessary to produce technological innovations that are needed to strengthen the position of the Islamic world and counterbalance the growth of European domination. For Afghani then, religious orthodoxy and scientific rationality were not contradictory epistemologies but rather tools that could be used to advance the goal of strengthening the Islamic world and resisting the threat posed by British imperialism.[27]

WESTOXIFICATION

Jamal al-Din al-Afghani's work is intriguing because it traces his struggles to identify a position located somewhere between rationalism and revelation, tradition and innovation, reform and dissolution, Westernization and syncretism. He wanted to foster a form of modernism that was not simply derivative of Western cultural and economic patterns. He feared Western hegemony, whether it took the form of direct military occupation (Algeria, Egypt, India), economic control (Iran), or cultural dissolution. He worried that if Muslims allowed themselves to be governed by Europe, the Islamic world would suffer the disadvantages of modernity without reaping its benefits.

In the twentieth century a wide range of new groups responded to the challenges posed by European domination; these included secular nationalist and socialist parties as well as movements such as the Muslim Brotherhood that more forcefully rejected the influence of the West.[28] Before the 1960s, most Iranian intellectuals drew on secular rather than religious language when formulating their critique of political authoritarianism and economic inequality.[29] Even when they were critical of European imperialism, the nationalist or socialist rhetoric still implied a Western orientation. Jalal Al-e Ahmad's scathing critique of Western culture, *Gharbzadegi*, was something of a turning point in the language of anti-imperialism.

Jalal Al-e Ahmad (1923–1969) was a writer, teacher, and at one time an activist in the communist Tudeh Party. Al-e Ahmad was raised in a Shiite clerical family, but his early writings and political activities had a distinctively secular character. He wrote short stories that mocked traditional religious practices, criticized religious leaders, and participated in secular political organizations such as the Tudeh party.[30] Toward the end of his life, however, he turned toward Islam, which he felt was one of the few resources for inspiring resistance to westoxification.[31]

Al-e Ahmad popularized the concept of *gharbzadegi* in a book manuscript written in 1962 and circulated widely through the Iranian underground, published in English as *Occidentosis: A Plague from the West*. The term is usually translated as westoxification, occidentosis, or west-struckness, connoting both 'dazzled' and 'sickened.' For Al-e Ahmad, *gharbzadegi* has two dimensions: the negative influence of the West and the complicity or active promotion of Western identities and lifestyles on the part of Iranians. Before examining this argument, it is critical to understand what Al-e Ahmad means by East and West. He explains:

> All I will say here is that "East" and "West" are no longer geographical or political concepts to me . . . for me, they are economic concepts. The West comprises the sated nations and the East, the hungry nations. To me, South Africa is part of the West. Most of the nations of Latin America are part of the East, although they are on the other side of the world.[32]

This definition is similar to the distinction between "developed" and "less developed countries," terms that are frequently employed in academic studies and among international aid and development agencies. For Al-e Ahmad, the West stands, above all else, for industrial capitalism and the bourgeois ideology that it spawned.

In *Gharbzadegi*, Al-e Ahmad develops four arguments that are similar to other Marxist and postcolonial critiques. First, he advances a version of dependency theory. He notes that the world is divided into two poles of "wealth and poverty, power and impotence, knowledge and ignorance, prosperity and desolation" and this division, far from diminishing, is increasing because the global economic system is structured to benefit the West.[33] Al-e Ahmad also notes that the problem would not be solved if the less developed countries somehow miraculously managed to catch up and achieve levels of prosperity similar to that in the West. Given the alienating character of modern life in Western societies, Westernization has a dystopian dimension. Al-e Ahmad notes the uniformity of dress and habits in the West and the highly regimented nature of assembly line production and white collar employment.[34] Although Al-e Ahmad seldom uses the term "capitalism,"[35] he describes a mode of production in which machinery and efficiency do not serve to promote the human good but become ends in themselves.

Although Al-e Ahmad's distinction between East and West is rooted in political economy, his project is ultimately an exercise in the critique of ideology. By consuming Western products, Iranians are participating in a system that leads to both economic dependence and cultural dissolution. In consuming commodities, the Iranian bourgeoisie fails to recognize the underlying social relations of production that such consumption is reinforcing. In other words, westoxification is a form of commodity fetishism, but its effects are amplified by the geography of uneven development. For Marx, the commodity form disguised the way that surplus value was created through the expropriation of workers' labor time; for Al-e Ahmad, the commodity now mystifies the neoimperial relationship between countries. Western nations benefit both by acquiring raw materials (oil, for example) at advantageous prices and by creating a market for surplus goods.

Given the neo-Marxist character of Al-e Ahmad's analysis, it is not initially clear how Islam plays a role in his analysis. In *Gharbzadegi* he does not explicitly endorse Islam or sharia law as the solution to westoxification, but he does include a few oblique references that have intrigued and puzzled his readers. For example, he writes with admiration about the great Mirza of Shiraz who destroyed the tobacco concession by issuing a fatwa.[36] He explains that "the clergy was the last citadel of resistance against the Europeans."[37] He also eulogizes Fazlullah Nuri (Shaykh Nuri), an Iranian Shiite cleric who was executed in 1909 because of his opposition to the Constitutional Revolution. Al-e Ahmad states, "I look on that great man's body on the gallows as a flag raised over our nation proclaiming the triumph of occidentosis after two hundred years of struggle."[38] This is a somewhat shocking passage for a leftist to write, given that Nuri was an archconservative and monarchist who opposed the constitutional reforms that brought parliamentary government to Iran because he came to see the reforms as a threat to Islamic law. Al-e Ahmad argues that the clergy has been a consistent opponent of westoxification, and the implication seems to be that Islam may be the only viable cure for the disease.

Despite these laudatory passages, however, Al-e Ahmad was no apologist for the clerical establishment. In *Gharbzadegi* he characterizes religious leaders as "obsessed with trivia."[39] His distance from the religious establishment is clearest in the following excerpt:

On the other hand, religion, with all its customs and institutions, relies as well as it may on superstitions and retreats to the shopworn customs of the past. In the twentieth century, religion relies on the criteria of the Middle Ages.[40]

For Al-e Ahmad, the problem is not Islam per se but in the reactionary, defensive position taken by the religious establishment in response to the growing influence of the West. This reactive posture has the effect of alienating westernized elites from their own culture (which is rooted in Islam) and insulating the Islamic community from dynamic, reformist forces. This bifurcation was cemented during the Persian Constitutional Revolution (circa 1905 to 1911) when "rule in accordance with Islamic law and constitutionalism emerged as the two contradictory concepts of religion and irreligion."[41] In this passage, Al-e Ahmad seems nostalgic for this period when "Islam/government based on Islamic law/religion" still had the necessary social scope to be a barrier against the influence of machines and the West."[42]

The shift from a largely pro-Western to anti-Western orientation may also reflect the changing political situation in Iran. After the CIA-backed coup d'état that removed Iranian premier Mohammad Mosaddeq (1951–53) from power, the regime of Mohammad Reza Shah Pahlavi (Shah of Iran from 1941 to 1979) was widely considered a proxy for American and European interests. The Shah passed laws requiring Western dress, banning the chador, and adopting Western educational reforms. This meant that the economic inequality and political repression of the Pahlavi regime became deeply associated with Western culture. The critique of westoxification was a way of describing everything that was wrong with the status quo, and this description privileged a certain type of answer, one that drew on traditions that predated the colonial era. According to Iran scholar Nikki R. Keddie,

> The main appeal of an idealized distant past, however, whether Islamic or pre-Islamic, was and is that a great variety of values may be read into it, while the evils of the present can be ascribed to deviation from the true Iranian or true Islamic essence. In a period when all society was at least formally Islamic, it was natural for many thinkers to blame problems on Islam and the Arabs. . . . As Iran became more modern and Westernized, the evils of indiscriminate Westernization became more obvious . . . it was natural for many after 1960 to blame evils on Western ways and to turn for salvation to an idealized Islamic past.[43]

The bifurcation of westernized elites and religious population was also part of the problem. This cultural divide made it difficult for anti-Shah intellectuals to form an alliance with the common people. Al-e Ahmad tentatively concluded

that Islam might be part of the solution; Shariati and Khomeini made this argument more forcefully. Both recognized and embraced the political potential of
Islam but had different visions of the meaning of Islamic government.

ALI SHARIATI

Al-e Ahmad's political theory is not Islamic in so far as he does not rely on
Islamic sources in order to evaluate the legitimacy of different forms of political
authority or practices. But it was one important piece of the broader discourse
of the Islamic revolution in Iran. *Gharbzadegi* temporarily sutured together two
very different ideologies: Islamism and socialism. United in their opposition to
westoxification, these two powerful political movements could overlook their
differences. Ali Shariati, the most famous theorist associated with the Iranian
Revolution, also played a pivotal role in laying the foundation for this alliance
by developing a progressive and political approach to Islam. This side of the
Iranian revolution is largely forgotten because of the way that Islamists subsequently consolidated power. But when anti-Shah protestors marched in the
streets, they carried the pictures of another figure next to the iconic images of
the Ayatollah Khomeini. These were pictures of Ali Shariati.

Ali Shariati (1933–1977) was educated by his father, a well-known Shia
ulama. He won a scholarship to the Sorbonne, where he completed a doctorate
in sociology. In France he was exposed to the ideas of anticolonial thinkers such
as Frantz Fanon and Jean-Paul Sartre, and he became involved with an Islamic
group that opposed the Shah. When he returned to Iran in 1964 he was arrested
for his political activities. After his release, he held a series of posts as a university professor and lecturer at *Husayniya-yi Irshad*, an innovative Islamic cultural center. In his lectures he articulated a distinctive approach to Islam as well
as a non-Marxist, yet radical, critique of economic domination and exploitation. Although he was careful to express his critique of the Shah's regime in
allegorical terms, he was still perceived as a threat to the regime. After another
jail term, he was released on the condition that he leave the country. He died in
England a few months later.

The main theme that runs through Shariati's writing is that Islam is an important resource that must be mobilized in order to resist Westernization. In order to
play this important political role, however, Islam itself has to be reformed and
revitalized. Shariati developed these arguments in two speeches titled "From
Where Shall We Begin" and "Machinism."[44] "From Where Shall We Begin" is a
lecture Shariati delivered at the Aryamehr University. He argues that the problems endemic to Islamic countries in particular and traditional societies in general are exacerbated by the gulf that exists between elites and the common man.

The popular culture in these countries is distinctively Islamic but the elites have assimilated Western secular values, which makes them unable to communicate effectively with the people. Traditional religious leaders are the only sector of the intelligentsia that has maintained a connection with the people. This gives them potentially great influence, but this influence is seldom exercised to bring about social change.

Shariati organized his lecture around the question "what is a free-thinker?" By "free-thinker" he seems to mean something like "critic" or "reformer." He emphasizes that there is no such thing as a "universal" critic because the primary task of the critic is to identify and understand the social problems of a given time and place. Jean-Paul Sartre's critique of consumption and materialism, he explains, does not apply to underdeveloped societies of Africa and Asia. But nor was Shariati particularly impressed by the diagnoses that indigenous intellectuals provided to help cure Iran's ills. Liberation movements such as women's equality and the reactionary politics of cultural conservatives (for example the book burning movement of the 1940s) were both "a smokescreen to cover up the real causes of a nation's misery and corruption."[45] Shariati's speeches were often attended by agents of the Shah's secret police (SAVAK), so it is not surprising that he never fully explains the real source of Iran's misery. Instead, he emphasizes the need to demystify the relationship between "the looted and the looter," "the exploiter and the exploited."[46]

The answer to the question in the title of Shariati's lecture—"from where shall we begin?"—is Islam. He insists that the social reformer and critic must "search for his people's common ideas."[47] "His language must be comprehensible," his solutions "proper and relevant to his period." By this he means that they should be expressed in the language and metaphors of Islam. In this lecture, Shariati considers some possible objections to his emphasis on religion as a resource for political critique. He notes that the process of reforming feudalism and fostering equality in Europe did not take an explicitly religious form. He responds by suggesting that Islam, unlike Christianity, has more scriptural resources for resisting oppression. It is more concerned with creating a just, stable political order on earth and is not hampered by the legacy of accommodation to "Caesar." But his main argument is very similar to Afghani's. He emphasizes that the need for unity between indigenous elites and the masses is more urgent in the context of foreign domination. Islam is the common language and culture that makes communication and political mobilization possible.

Despite this call for a resurgent Islamic identity on the part of westernized elites, Shariati did not uncritically embrace existing religious institutions and leaders. He spoke openly of "the present corrupting role of religion among the masses"[48] and denounced religious dogmatism as a heinous crime.[49] He stated that westernized elites who did not establish a connection with the people would remain trapped in their very limited role as technicians tending the Western "machine" while the masses would continue to passively accept their exploitation. Shariati insisted that dialectical tensions do not inevitably lead to revolution or social change. Critical intellectuals must make these tensions visible; they must also articulate meaningful alternatives and inspire an ethos of courage and resistance if they are to bring about change.

If Islam is the bond that can potentially suture the rift that was exposed and deepened by imperialism, how does Shariati understand Islam? Shariati's approach to Islam was syncretic. He endorsed concepts such as democracy and explained them in terms of Islamic models and sources. For example, he departed from traditional Islamic political theory, emphasizing that the Quran and sunna (sayings and deeds of the Prophet) describe a process of "consultation," which is a more authentic and viable form of democracy. In order to legitimize his controversial reinterpretation of primary sources, he also developed innovative interventions in methodological debates. Not surprisingly, he came down forcefully in favor of interpretation (*ijtihad*) and against the restrictive forms of legal reasoning that were developed in order to limit innovation. He described the Quran as a "multi-faceted" book with literary, theological, philosophical, and historical dimensions. According to Shariati, the problem is that some contemporary Islamic leaders treat history as theological; in other words, the historical practices of groups living at the time of the prophet are mistakenly taken as universal models for all times and places. Instead, Shariati suggests that we should start with the knowledge of God, which can be gained through philosophy, mysticism, or his preferred method of typology, and then proceed to studying the Quran and the life of Muhammad in light of these insights. Although this initially may not sound particularly controversial, the implications are fairly heterodox because they turn the Quran into something like a "living constitution," a set of founding principles that can be interpreted in light of changing circumstances, limited only by a broad consistency with "the spirit of God."[50]

Shariati's democratic and egalitarian Islam was an attempt to create a hybrid tradition, one that embraced the positive heritage of the West without accepting the materialism, individualism, and racism that he felt were also part of its legacy. By recasting democracy as an elaboration of the consultation described in the sunna and equality as a translation of "*al-nas*,"[51] Shariati made the practices and ideals appear less threatening to people who saw the influence of the West as a sign of defeat and a cause of loss and upheaval. At the same time, he provided a language that made it possible for secular reformers to communicate with and mobilize the masses.

Shariati's project was part of the broader anticolonial movement of the 1960s, albeit one that advanced it in a distinctive direction. As a student in Paris, Shariati was exposed to anticolonial ideas and identified the movement to oppose the Shah in Iran as part of this broader project. Most commentators have noted Shariati's interest in the work of Frantz Fanon. According to Hamid Algar, Shariati translated Fanon's writings into Persian and drew on his insights in his speeches and articles.[52] But Iran and Algeria were very different from each other. Algeria was the paradigmatic example of a settler colony, and its experiences were shaped by military conquest, brutal repression, and the proximity and distance between two populations: French and Algerian, colonizer and colonized, exploiter and exploited. Iran, on the other hand, only had foreign troops on its soil for a very short time during World War II. Of course, Europeans had played an important and visible role as economic and military advisers, and European companies held important concessions and monopolies. The railroad and the national bank, for example, were both foreign-owned, and the Iranian government's crushing foreign debt limited its autonomy. In the post–World War II period, American and British influence increased rather than decreased because of the growing significance of oil.

Shariati's writing exhibits concern about foreign economic domination. In "From Where Shall We Begin" he argued that the hysteria around burning books of libertine poetry was a distraction from such real issues as "the exploitations of British Petroleum." And while he could hardly say anything explicit about the foreign-backed coup of August 1953 that organized against Mohammad Mosaddeq and consolidated power in the hands of the Shah, he made it clear that the role of the freethinker was to challenge foreign domination of Iran. In the conclusion to the lecture "From Where Shall We Begin," Shariati insisted that the freethinker must encourage social change by drawing attention "to the existing contradictions from the heart of society and enter them into the consciousness of his society and throw his prophet-like flame of knowledge upon the frigid and cold existence of the masses."[53]

Shariati's most explicit critique of the West is developed in an essay titled "Machinism." According to Shariati, machinism is a social order that is based on private property and regulated by a class of technocratic elites. Machinism achieves a certain degree of efficiency but it also leads to a cycle of overproduction, which in turn generates an ideology of materialism, consumerism, and a state-backed economy that exports these values abroad. In an argument reminiscent of Lenin and Rosa Luxemburg, he also notes that the overproduction of products creates fierce competition to control foreign markets, competition that often expresses itself through military rivalry and imperial domination.[54] The term "machinism" seems to be a metaphor for "modern industrial capitalism," and Shariati's critique is similar to European critiques of modernity, notably the Frankfurt School.[55] He cites Marcuse's concept of "one-dimensional man" with approval and concludes that machinism upsets the balance between the productive and creative dimensions of human existence, thereby paralyzing man and destroying his creativity.[56]

Given the similarities between Shariati's analysis of machinism and other strands of post-Marxist criticism, it is worth asking whether he articulated a distinctively Islamic political theory. Although Islam does not play a prominent role in "Machinism," it was the focus of many of Shariati's lectures and it is a subtext, an unarticulated but implied alternative to machinism. Shariati noted that developing countries had a distinctive experience of machinism. Machinism is a global phenomenon, but it manifested itself in the East in several distinctive ways. First, the benefits of increasing productivity and prosperity were not shared equally among nations. According to Shariati, the economic gap between East and West was vast and was widening. The East experienced the negative side effects of machinism without sharing in the higher standard of living that it produced in the West. The negative side effects include the spread of materialistic, individualistic, shallow values that do not lead to either human improvement or a sense of satisfaction and meaning. Shariati characterized the social order of modernity as a "theatre of the absurd . . . begotten by a hollow order; to exist in order to consume and consume in order to exist." In the East, however, these values and practices have not penetrated society to the same degree that they have in Europe. This means that the West sometimes has to resort to force in order to ensure access to foreign markets. In developing countries, these Western values are not necessarily experienced as organic reflections of popular desires but rather as threatening, alien, and subversive. In Iran, this results in a bifurcation between the masses, who "inherit the (religious) traditions" and the educated elites who inherit a set of Western products, attitudes, and practices. The elites consume these Western products and perform these Western identities, but they do so in a passive fashion. Ironically, westernized elites come to resemble their opposites, the tradition-bound masses, in so far as both follow a set of rigid codes rather than actively creating new meanings.

When "Machinism" is read in the context of Shariati's other lectures, especially "From Where Shall We Begin," the solution is clear. Educated elites—the audience for his lectures at universities and Islamic cultural centers—must recognize the vitality and richness of their Islamic tradition, which he felt provided an alternative to "scientism," "materialism," and "machinism." For Shariati, Islam is based on a vision of human perfectibility and community, one that incorporates worldly flourishing and spiritual idealism. This vision of Islam, however, was not the one that was favored by the *ulama*, who were often deeply implicated in existing structures of domination. Not only did they espouse reactionary attitudes on issues such as gender equality and democracy, but they also defended exploitative patterns of landownership in the countryside. According to Shariati, the dynamic meaning of Islam had to be wrested from traditions that ossified it into a historical relic.

In much the same way as Marx had been unable to say exactly what would emerge from the dialectical tension between bourgeoisie and proletariat, Shariati could not predict exactly how Islamic modernism could reassert control over the machine. He recognized that the machine could not simply be dismantled. He explicitly rejected what he took to be Gandhi's naive antimodernist stance. Yet he also wanted more than simply an Islamic veneer on the existing society. Following Fanon, he insisted that it would be a mistake to make Africa and Asia into another America, but he struggled to elaborate an alternative.[57] It might be unfair to fault him for this omission, since he was lecturing in a police state that tortured opponents and harshly punished public criticism. Given these constraints, many of Shariati's speeches and lectures were allegorical and relied on his audience's familiarity with religious narratives such as the martyrdom of Hosein (Husayn ibn Ali), who Shiites believed was the legitimate successor of the Prophet Muhammad. In Shariati's retelling, Yazid, the person responsible for killing Hosein, stood for the Pahlavi dictatorship. Shariati's students were encouraged to emulate martyrs and other religious figures who struggled against oppression. Rather than describing an alternative political order, he tried to inculcate a spiritually rich, revolutionary subjectivity.

KHOMEINI AND ISLAMIC GOVERNMENT

Ali Shariati died in 1977, two years before the Iranian Revolution, yet he is frequently described as one of the most important influences on the revolution.[58] His work may even have played a role in Khomeini's transition from apolitical scholar to leader of the opposition.[59] Yet his reformist vision was ultimately rejected by the postrevolution regime. Looking at the texts of Imam Ruhollah al-Musavi al-Khomeini (better known as the Ayatollah Khomeini) demonstrates that many of the same concerns of the other theorists in this chapter are evident in his exploration of Islamic government. Khomeini offers a historical analysis of imperialism in Iran along with a solution to alter the present and future.[60] Islamism is often perceived as being a counterrevolutionary movement, a conserving impulse, much in the same way that negritude is viewed as primitivism. However, Islamism is not necessarily conserving of the past as much as it offers an interpretation of the past to serve a revolutionary political mission.[61] Khomeini's essay "Islamic Government" provides another example of how reinterpretation of the past plays an integral element in postcolonial political thought.

Eqbal Ahmad offered the following assessment of the importance of the past in Islamic thought and its revolutionary potential. It is worth quoting at length to serve as an introduction to Khomeini's political theory of national liberation,

as Eqbal Ahmad argues that the Iranian revolution served as the harbinger of
the Islamic political movements to come.

> In the breach, there is a time bomb. When the moral explosion of the
> masses occurs, it will undoubtedly have reference to the past. But its objec-
> tive shall be the future. The past is very present in the postcolonial Muslim
> societies. That it is a fractured past invaded by a new world of free markets,
> shorn of its substance and strength, incapable of assuring the continuity of
> communal life does not make it less forceful. Its power derives from the
> tyranny of contemporary realities and the seeming absence of viable alter-
> natives. For the majority of Muslim peoples, the experienced alternative to
> the past is a limbo of foreign occupation and dispossession, of alienation
> from the land, of life in shantytowns and refugee camps, of migration into
> foreign lands, and, at best, permanent expectancy. Leaning on and
> yearning for the restoration of an emasculated, often idealized past is one
> escape from the limbo; striking out, in protest and anger, for a new revo-
> lutionary order is another. Occasionally, as in Iran, the two responses are
> merged.[62]

One of the most powerful aspects of Khomeini's theory is its unity and clarity.
He claims, "Here is a tradition totally without ambiguity," echoing the starting
lines of the Quran, "This book is not to be doubted."[63] We can take this claim
to be a political strategy more than actuality, since Islamic thought does contain some significant ambiguities. Khomeini's thought begins with the assertion of Islamic faith as the central principle of government, action, history and
justice. But in his discussion of "Islamic Government" it becomes evident that
his approach shares some common elements with other postcolonial strategies
that we have explored. Khomeini offers an explanation for imperial subordination, provides a call to arms, establishes the terms of independence, and lays
out a blueprint for the future. In every sense, this is a postcolonial political
strategy.

Khomeini begins by defining Islam itself in postcolonial terms: "Islam is the
religion of militant individuals who are committed to truth and justice. It is the
religion of those who desire freedom and independence. It is the school of those
who struggle against imperialism."[64] The principle of Islamic government is a
set of ruling institutions that follow the laws, regulations, and morals outlined
by the Quran. Islamic principles are to be followed by the government, which
implements the system of taxation and penalties already outlined in the Quran.
The government's duty is to provide the framework for all believers to lead lives
according to the religion. Khomeini notes, "There is not a single topic in human
life for which Islam has not provided instruction and established a norm."[65] The

responsibility of Islamic government is to enforce these precepts in order to achieve the best possible life for everyone within the country.

Khomeini points out that those who are not believers often view the penal provisions within the Quran as barbaric or harsh. However, he argued these imperatives for daily life "are intended to keep great nations from being destroyed by corruption."[66] In fact, it was the intentional distortion of the teaching of Islam by occupying forces that led to the weakening of the Iranian people.

> But the servants of imperialism have presented Islam in a totally different light. They have created in men's minds a false notion of Islam. The defective version of Islam, which they have presented in the religious teaching institution, is intended to deprive Islam of its vital, revolutionary aspect and to prevent Muslims from arousing themselves in order to gain their freedom, fulfill the ordinances of Islam, and create a government that will assure their happiness and allow them to live lives worthy of human beings.[67]

Circulating alternative interpretations of Islam in Iran provided for the conditions of foreign domination, according to Khomeini. First of all, the plurality of interpretations led to a division within the country between different kinds of believers, and the unity provided by religion was undermined. Second, as the government did not institute the principles of Islam, the population's morals and constitution became naturally weaker, ripe for oppression. "If this mode of conduct had been preserved, and government has retained its Islamic form, there would have been no monarchy and no empire, no usurpation of the lives and property of the people, no oppression and plunder, no encroachment on the public treasury, no vice and abomination."[68] In Khomeini's view, the people derive their strength by following the precepts of Islam; their corruption is the source of their historical subordination. The multiplicity of interpretations also allowed for the corruption of Islamic principles in the law. Khomeini points out that the Belgian Constitution served as the starting point for the Constitutional movement in Iran, "True, they added some of the ordinances of Islam in order to deceive the people, but the basis of the laws that were now thrust upon the people was alien and borrowed."[69] The fusion of the Islamic tradition with European codes led to its distortion.[70]

Revisionist or hybrid Islamic principles led to division within the population, even among professed believers, as well as confusion about the actual rulings of Islam. It was this confusion that precipitated the foreign domination of Iran. "In the past we did not act in concert and unanimity in order to establish proper government and overthrow treacherous and corrupt rulers. Some people were apathetic and reluctant even to discuss the theory of Islamic government, and some went so far as to praise oppressive rulers. It is for this reason that we find ourselves in the present state."[71] Therefore imperialism itself is a symptom of the failure to create an Islamic government.

The utility of this analysis of the past is that it offers both an explanation for the weakness and humiliation of the past while offering a clear path of action in the present. To restore national strength and to repel the imperialist invaders, it is necessary to reassert Islamic government. "In order to assure the unity of the Islamic *umma*, in order to liberate the Islamic homeland from occupation and penetration by the imperialists and their puppet governments, it is imperative that we establish a government."[72]

The other crucial aspect of Khomeini's analysis is that living as a true believer requires living in a state that enforces the same law. There needs to be absolute transparency between laws of the Quran and the state. A state that refuses to implement the principles of Islamic government to govern over an Islamic population is engaged in an act of aggression. This means that such an act of aggression need be met with armed resistance. "It will then be the duty of the Muslims to engage in an armed jihad against that ruling group in order to make the policies ruling society and the norms of government conform to the principles and ordinances of Islam."[73]

Khomeini discusses the duty of all leaders and believers to protect Islam as a "fortress."[74] Islam itself provides clear boundaries, which must then be patrolled: if they are permeated, or questioned, the fortress collapses. An integral element of this fortress is that it provides for unity within the walls, and a clear demarcation between inside and outside. The state that rules this fortress must be within it: otherwise it represents an outside force, which must be repelled at all costs. Imperialism was the penetration of the fortress of Islam, and decolonization must be the reestablishment of the walls, the reassertion of the correct boundaries through religious education, and the development of a state that will rule from the inside of the fortress. Khomeini's political vision invokes this state of military siege and it provides a clear explanation for the past: "It is because we have been lacking in unity, strength, and preparedness that we suffer oppression and are at the mercy of foreign aggressors."[75]

The clarity and elegance of this paradigm cannot be denied. When viewed next to other revolutionary strategies, one is struck by its synthesis of many of the elements in the others.[76] There is a cultural revaluation, an explanation for past oppression, a path toward liberation, the pragmatic necessity for armed struggle is recognized, and there is a ready-made system of order that awaits the newly liberated regime. Does this in some way account for the enduring appeal of Islamism as a postcolonial political movement?

CONCLUSION

It is tempting to ask whether Khomeini's distinctive vision of Islamic government played a decisive role in securing his victory over the secular radicals and
Islamic modernists who made up the anti-Pahlavi coalition. But it is impossible
to answer this question without thoroughly analyzing the array of social forces,
leadership, and political opportunity structure. Furthermore, political ideology
is not separate from these other factors but can be a way of justifying tactics,
incorporating allies, and demonizing opponents. Khomeini's political ideology
shifted in response to political opportunities. As the historian Ervand Abrahamian demonstrates, during Khomeini's exile in Qom, he stressed that Islamic
government would be a source of moral renewal and social order; during the
revolution he adopted increasingly populist language, calling for social justice
for the oppressed; as leader of the Iranian republic, he moderated his rhetoric,
reconfiguring the notion of the people to include the poor as well as the mer-
chant class.

Despite these shifts, Khomeini did articulate a distinctive and influential
view of the relationship between religion and the state. His vision of Islamic
government had no precedent in history; it was especially revolutionary in Iran
where the Shia clergy traditionally were autonomous from the state. Yet it
proved remarkably popular as a mobilizing frame. For the masses it could stand
for legitimate, moral government limited by divine law, an appealing alternative
to unlimited, corrupt despotism. For clerics, it was an opportunity to consolidate their power and use the framework of the state to eliminate cultural trends
that were undermining their influence. Both Shariati and Khomeini advanced
innovative approaches to Islamic sources that created new political theories.
Both saw Islam as a powerful tool for mobilizing people against a brutal, corrupt, foreign backed dictatorship. Shariati's creative reworking of Islamic concepts and stories was extremely popular but it lacked a strong institutional base.
The clerical establishment, on the other hand, despite a long history of tacit
accommodation with the Pahlavi regime, was well situated to take advantage of
the vacuum of power created by the Shah's departure.[77]

The concept of westoxification is crucial in understanding the broad appeal
of political Islam and the multiple visions that it could inspire.[78] Westoxification
was a way of describing the problem so that Islam—not Marxism or liberal
constitutionalism or human rights—was the only possible answer. Islam was
the only cultural formation largely untouched by westoxification. While the
term "*gharbzadegi*" is Persian in origin, the same logic inspired Islamic political
movements in other countries.[79] If this is true, then critics like Bernard Lewis
who have concluded that the secularism, toleration, and rationalism of the
West are simply antithetical to the values of the Muslim world are only partially

wrong.[80] Lewis is correct that the end of colonialism or even the dismantling of some forms of "imperial" domination (disadvantageous oil contracts, military bases, intervention in domestic economic policy, etc.) are unlikely to lead to major shifts in attitudes toward the United States or the West. He is also correct that anger is often expressed through a rejection of cultural symbols rather than opposition to particular policies.

But he is wrong to dismiss the numerous Muslim writers who explicitly place the legacy of colonialism and imperialism at the heart of their analyses. As Al-e Ahmad's book makes clear, "they" do not hate "our" freedoms but rather our hypocrisy—the way Western nations often exercise power to the detriment of the most vulnerable and the way that they exploit other countries' economic resources, in order to further enrich themselves.[81] If westerners' "freedoms" are intertwined with the coercion and exploitation of others, then they are a legitimate object of critique. This argument is made explicitly and forcefully by almost all postcolonial authors, even those like Khomeini who propose an alternative that is not palatable to the left. The relationship between freedom and exclusion has only recently become a prominent theme in political theory, usually through close readings that emphasize its conspicuous absence in canonical works of political theory.[82]

These postcolonial texts also help us think about the very categories of "us" and "them"—how the concepts are constituted politically, undermined, and stabilized. In other words, reading contemporary Islamic political theory is not only a way to understand the history of a particular region, it also illuminates broader political and theoretical issues. First, it reminds us that political Islam incorporates a range of positions. Second, it forces us to rethink the conventional understanding of what constitutes postcolonial theory. In Khomeini's writings there is very little about hybridity, mimesis, or subaltern speech. Yet he is still profoundly concerned with these same issues, albeit using a different idiom and reaching different conclusions. For Khomeini, hybridity and mimesis are symptoms of westoxification, a disease that makes it impossible for "subalterns" to speak with their own voice and instead turns them into ventriloquists' puppets. This type of "essentialist" discourse is usually seen as a relic of the national liberation movements of the 1960s, but it has proven potent and enduring.[83] Finally, these texts challenge us to think more deeply about the relationship between religion and politics. In the canon of Western political philosophy, religion is more often portrayed as the problem that the solution. Following Hobbes, religious conflict is a centrifugal force threatening to tear society apart and politics is the solution. A number of Islamic thinkers, however, suggest the reverse may be true: that politics, in the form of imperial domination, is destructive and religion is a source of unity and resistance.

Self-Determination Reconsidered

Revolutions of Decolonization and Postcolonial Citizenship

To make the revolution, one must first and foremost remold oneself.

—Ho Chi Minh

One doesn't leave one's own self behind as easily as all that.

—Albert Memmi

In *On Revolution*, Hannah Arendt points out the astronomical origin of the word "revolution" and reminds readers that when it first was adopted as a political term, "it was used for a movement of revolving back to some pre-established point and, by implication, of swinging back into a preordained order."[1] It is by taking a longer historical view of the political revolutions of modernity that Arendt, and we, can appreciate the kernel of etymological truth here. Worlds are not so easy to remold after all; tendencies of movement, force, and tension seem to reassert themselves.

John Locke's *Second Treatise of Government* succinctly captures the paradox of revolutions: they are both a break in the present and a return to the past. On the one hand, the ability of a people to overthrow an unjust government is the final arbiter of a government that is based upon the consent of the people. As Locke noted, "The people generally ill treated, and contrary to right, will be ready upon any occasion to ease themselves of a burden that sits heavily upon them."[2] Of course, it may take some time before a population is alienated or aggrieved enough to wage revolution. Locke himself points out that the ability to revolt does not mean instability or rumblings of revolution at every small abuse of power. Instead, a steady stream of abuse and indignity can create the proclivity to revolt and dissolve a government, though history provides many instances where administrative abuse is suffered for inexplicable lengths of time. But Locke's wisdom becomes particularly sharp in dealing with the other aspect of popular revolt:

> This slowness and aversion in the people to quit their old constitutions, has, in the many revolutions which have been seen in this kingdom, in this and former ages, still kept us to, or, after some interval of fruitless attempts, still brought us back again to our legislative of king, lords and commons; and whatever provocations have made the crown be taken from some of our princes heads, they never carried the people so far as to place it in another line.[3]

In other words, the problem isn't that revolutions disrupt order, the issue is that they tend to be incomplete, no matter how radical the temperament that inspires the initial revolt. We need only remind ourselves that Robespierre laid the groundwork for Napoleon, and of Tocqueville's analysis of the vestiges of feudalism that survived into the nineteenth century in his book *The Old Regime and the French Revolution* (1856) to see this as a central issue in both history and political theory.

It is conventional wisdom that revolutionaries are primarily, even myopically, concerned with disrupting power. However, a close examination of some revolutionary theorists of decolonization reveals that some revolutionaries have also been concerned with creating long-lasting political freedom, as opposed to mere regime change. Stated in Locke's terms, they were acutely aware of the dynamic of simply moving a crown from one head to another, and did not want to repeat it. In this chapter, we examine Ho Chi Minh and Frantz Fanon's ideas about popular mobilization—revolution—and the postcolonial citizen. As revolutionaries and as formerly colonized subjects, they inherently distrusted state power. Interestingly, they did not see the nation-state system as hopelessly implicated in the crimes of colonialism, nor was the pragmatism of wanting to reconsolidate power always predominant among their concerns.

In addition to wariness about the state, both Ho and Fanon were French colonial subjects and were very well aware of the dynamics of the French Revolution. Simply stated, they tried to learn its lessons and make sure they were creating a permanent form of decolonization. Their political aim was to achieve a decisive break with the present and to make sure the second tendency of revolutions—to resurrect the past—could not possibly occur. To accomplish this form of complete decolonization, they reasoned, their revolution must create a population that would not submit to subordination again.

Of course, staging a popular mobilization required that the people take up the imperatives of independence. How can you mobilize people to fight for their freedom, and not lose it in the process? Perhaps because of their ambivalence about the colonial state, neither Ho nor Fanon envisioned a state design that would be inherently democratic, thereby institutionally providing a voice for postcolonial subjects. Instead, they favored the notion that reconstructing the people whom the state was to govern would be the only way to create genuine self-determination. They did not see regime change itself as the most meaningful potential development; regime change without a total psychological shift on the part of the governed would have little impact. Ho's and Fanon's revolutions aimed to change the people, not merely the government.

After all, the most effective methods of colonial administration in the French and British empires involved the active participation in government by members of the subordinated population by employing indigenous administrators or declaring colonial subjects "full citizens." The French and British both understood that participation in governmental administration or even achieving the status of citizen was not tantamount to self-determination. It did not matter who sat in the administrative seat if those underneath them still saw the government as arbitrary and outside of their control.

Current events suggest that Ho's and Fanon's concerns about the continued subordination of a population in a formally sovereign nation were prescient. Reading the newspapers in the early twenty-first century, one can see the strain of dictatorships that has arisen in many former colonies around the globe, as will be discussed in chapter 4, "Colonialism and the State of Exception." We could say that these are indications of a thwarted or incomplete popular revolution, and to some extent we would be right. Clearly the sense that a government must be or even can be held accountable to its population has not become standard in postcolonial regimes. (And, indeed, is a tenuous achievement in all others.) This current phenomenon makes it all the more remarkable that some revolutionary leaders were abundantly clear about the potential pitfalls of revolutions of independence. While the historical record suggests many continuities between colonial and postcolonial regimes, examining revolutionary political theories of decolonization can help remind us of the other aspirations that were in play.

DECOLONIZATION, REVOLUTION, AND SELF-DETERMINATION

In this chapter, we examine the core dynamic in Ho Chi Minh's and Frantz Fanon's plans for decolonization: establishing a new regime that would enable popular sovereignty by enabling a complete shift in behavior, expectations, and beliefs on the part of the population. These theories of decolonization offer a particularly interesting way to reconsider our ideas about self-determination, as they offer starkly different terms than those predominant in contemporary democratic theory. These theories, paradoxically to our ears, emphasize the capacities and dispositions of citizens rather than the structure of institutions.

It is vaguely embarrassing to talk about revolution as offering invaluable tools for political theory. Perhaps because many of us have come to be cautious about taking democratic idealism very seriously, somehow those who are interested in revolution have come to seem distinct from those who study democracy. "Democratic" most frequently appears in theoretical and analytic literature as a normative principle. Procedures, institutions, deliberation, and units of measurement are evaluated as either more or less democratic, and provide for more or less self-determination. Jeffrey Isaac has noted the evolution of democratic theory in the years following the world wars of the twentieth century into a field largely concerned with normative principles and empirical measurement.[4] Furthermore, a great deal of attention has been paid to the institutions and practices which either directly or indirectly support democracy through creating norms, behaviors, and social connections, and distributing public opinion. And while this literature certainly makes a strong contribution to understanding how regimes that call themselves democracies function and create stability, it seems the central ideal of liberation through collective self-determination has been pushed to the periphery in current discussions of democracy and even democratization. Creating human freedom through politics is certainly more easily discussed than achieved. However, another dimension can be added to our current debates about democracy and democratic citizenship by carefully examining twentieth-century theorists of revolution.

They provide a more nuanced view of the relationship between collective struggle and self-determination; oftentimes we think about people as providing the foundation for a democracy, not how the populace's mobilization is necessary beyond that founding moment. Recently, scholars in democratic theory have engaged this problem, thinking about how "the people" have served as the foundation for democratic regimes in revolutionary moments, but also trying to extend consideration of "the people" as an open ended process, or as an aspect of political imagination that must be carefully constructed.[5] Ho and Fanon help us to consider the dynamics of self-determination beyond the founding moment, and outside of regimes such as the French and American ones that are most frequently taken as paradigmatic for providing models of democratic citizenship.

The people—the masses—have been an object of fascination and fear; the power of the collective is the Pandora's box of modern politics. One interpretation of modern revolution is that it is a manifestation of popular fury into the world that changes the trajectory of history and government. Many revolutionary theorists have tried to inspire and describe the potentially momentous force of popular involvement sweeping away structures of law, ideas, institutions, and governing groups. This is not to say that revolutions are not longer processes than they might appear, and many historians and social scientists have debated whether these violent uprisings are the result or catalyst of much longer periods of social, cultural, and institutional shifts.[6] Nonetheless, revolutions are seen as evidence that humans can indeed change their environments: they are instances of political regeneration provided by the people who demand that their government serve them, rather than the reverse.

But just as the people are the source of power in some views of revolution, another common account of revolution is how political authority comes to reestablish rule over the people. This most frequently happens as a revolutionary leader consolidates and then starts to use (or abuse) his or her power in representing (or in the name of) "the people" or the logic of history. But revolutionary ideology itself can also play a role in disempowering the people through its claim to newness. This promise of newness can be ossifying, delivering an unshakable platform from a particular moment, or it can create a dynamic of eternal revolution. On the one hand, it would seem that completing the promise of revolution would mean fulfilling the vision of independence that drove it from the start. On the other hand, what is a revolution if it is not a willingness to question and discard already established wisdom? Robespierre famously asked some Dantonists, "What you want is a revolution without a revolution?" when they were horrified by the unexpected twists and detours of the French revolution.[7] Building a regime and mobilizing a population around a revolutionary vision can lead to endless purging according to original doctrine, a negation of any institutionalization or stability, or the crystallization of a revolutionary mystique around a particular figure as an unquestioned agent of "the new order," to identify a few historical models that we have seen. The claim to newness can feed an impulse to recreate the future from a particular moment, rather than necessarily opening up the space for new dreams to be dreamed. In other words, the *ideal* of revolution itself may end up precluding popular sovereignty: an idea that is supposed to serve the masses ends up doing exactly the opposite, and the masses become enslaved to the regime of newness.

What should be evident is that these two aspects of revolutionary politics, the force of the people and the adherence to an ideology, do not sit comfortably with one another. Many of us learned in the lessons of modern revolutions have become guarded precisely because this second group of dynamics has been so evident. But more generally, we have historicized revolutionary politics into cycles in order to encompass both elements in our understanding. First, the people assert power, then ultimately their power is institutionalized.

Revolutionary agents are often dismissed as unthinking and unaware, sacrificial lambs on the altar of historical trajectories. Democratic idealists will be replaced by ruling pragmatists. Ho and Fanon, however, do not fit into this conceptual model: both sought to develop ways to institutionalize the values and principles of revolutionary struggle into a lasting regime that created the space for true self-determination on the part of their citizens. Coming out of the context of colonialism, they were not going to accept any watered-down substitutes for what they saw as genuine self-determination.

This is not to say that they were successful in their endeavors. Of course, we must take measure of the institutional, behavioral, and economic legacies of colonialism to understand the structure of postcolonial regimes. But even setting aside these concerns for this chapter, we can examine these theories to see the promise of self-determination in revolution, but also to see how the project to decolonize—to remake a population—can all too easily become thwarted.

One distinction Hannah Arendt makes in *On Revolution* can help to illuminate the difficult relationship between self-determination and revolution. She distinguishes between "liberation" as a desire to live free from oppression and "freedom" as the capacity for self-rule and engagement in politics. Although she chastises others for forgetting the distinction, she admits, "It is frequently very difficult to say where the mere desire for liberation, to be free from oppression, ends and the desire for freedom as the political way of life begins."[8] We could say that Arendt's acute understanding of the problem of freedom has made her misjudge the facility of the "mere" desire and ability to achieve liberation.

Even though she carefully distinguishes between liberation and freedom, she suggests that in the American case, the struggle for liberation did, even if inadvertently, show the path toward freedom for those who participated. Arendt observes, "For the acts and deeds which liberation demanded from them threw them into public business, where, intentionally or more often unexpectedly, they began to constitute that space of appearances where freedom can unfold its charms and become a visible, tangible reality."[9] Somehow then, the struggle itself, the struggle for liberation, creates the ability to achieve freedom. Arendt's understanding is emblematic of many of our vague notions about the relationship between democracy and revolution. If one is able to resist, then the ability to rule cannot be far away. Whether this resistance is the guarantee of "popular sovereignty" within representative government or the expression of collective will, the power of popular revolt and the ability to establish self-determination are linked. What Arendt offers this discussion is a caution to not confuse liberation and freedom, along with the insight that revolutionary struggles offer a chance to ruminate on the connections between the two practices.

While this may initially seem like categorical parsing, surveying the works of Ho Chi Minh and Frantz Fanon reveals that this distinction was very much on their mind. Liberation from colonial administration was one goal, but their work shows that they were already trying to lay the foundation for political freedom in the struggle itself. Furthermore, these works help demonstrate how acutely aware these two thinkers were that the struggle for liberation did not automatically lay the groundwork for the practice of freedom; they were not blindly idealistic, but instead they understood the difficulties of creating post-colonial citizenship.

There is an interesting contrast between Arendt's analysis of revolution and these theorists of revolution. Arendt's analysis is that revolution as an act of freedom has become occluded by the historiography of revolution: revolutionary actors play roles rather than writing their own script. In her explanation of how revolutionary progress becomes thwarted, Arendt observes: "The trouble has always been the same: those who went to the school of revolution learned and knew beforehand the course a revolution must take. It was the course of events, not the men of the Revolution, which they imitated."[10] Arendt argues that the view of revolution as a given, preordained historical progression defeats the impulse for human action as Hegelian and Marxist history becomes prevalent. While her point is well taken, the thinkers discussed here suggest that she is incorrect in claiming this perspective is universal.

HO CHI MINH, THE PEOPLE, AND REVOLUTIONARY MORALITY

Ho Chi Minh arrived in France in 1911 as a twenty-one-year-old man and reported two big surprises: the first was that French people as a whole were much more civilized, pleasant, and accommodating than those he had encountered in Annam; the second was that not all French people were wealthy, as were those he had encountered in Annam.[11] He asked, "Why don't the French civilize their own people instead of trying to civilize us?" revealing a still engrained sense of Western cultural superiority, as well as the inclination to question it.[12] While in Marseilles in 1911 he applied for admission to the *École Coloniale*, the central academy in Paris that trained future colonial administrators. It is interesting to ponder how different twentieth-century Vietnamese history might have been if he had attended. Instead, he set out on a journey to many different countries, spending significant time in the United States and England before settling in Paris in 1917 and adopting the name Nguyen Ai Quoc, meaning "The Patriot."

As already mentioned in Chapter 1, after settling Paris, Ho wrote a proposal titled "Demands of the Annamite People" that outlined demands for self-determination in this region of Indochina and presented it to the Versailles Peace Conference in 1919, where it was ignored. He then became one of the founding members of the French Communist Party, deciding to seek international solidarity in other venues. Nonetheless, he also put together an expatriate network in Paris; a small dynamic group that formed the Association of Annamite Patriots, and also the Intercolonial Union, a group of leftists seeking to end colonial rule more generally. The Intercolonial Union had its own journal, *Le Paria*, in which Ho (then Quoc) was a frequent contributor. The second volume contains a satirical piece that he wrote, titled "Zoology," in which he describes how different "animals" are trained to administer European laws around the world. "If you take the largest and strongest member of the herd and fasten a bright substance to its neck, a gold coin or a cross, it becomes completely docile . . . This weird and wonderful animal goes by the name of *colonis indigeniae*, but is referred to according to region as Annamae, Madagascan, Algerian, Indian . . ."[13] The biting humor also displays a keen sense of awareness of the malleability of people in the interest of power. How can you keep those who have power from being corrupted by it? How can you keep the powerless from currying, to their own detriment, the favor of the powerful?

Having received a superior colonial education back in Annam, Ho was well aware of Rousseau's struggle with this dilemma, and the trajectories of French revolutionary history.[14] Evidence suggests he was able to incorporate elements of the particular adaptations of Confucianism in his native region to develop a unique synthetic response to this problem. In his political philosophy, one can see elements of Leninist approaches to revolutionary mobilization, Rousseau's visions of citizenship, and Mencius.[15] By combining these three traditions, Ho sought to cultivate the citizens of Vietnam as superior men, those who act according to the good of society rather than self. However, to do so, they needed to maintain adherence to revolutionary mentality, a state of permanent revolution. One of the central contributions of Mencius is the notion that leaders serve in the name of the people and that they must be strictly bound by the people's interests.

Alexander Woodside has argued that the structure of the Vietnamese revolution can be traced back to the area's particular veneration of Mencius.[16] Examining regional variations in the influence of *The Four Books*, he points out that in 1394, the official version of the text that was circulated in China was censored, excluding elements of the chapter titled "The Mencius."

> The forbidden chapters were the ones in which Mencius had argued that the people were the most important element in any polity, and rulers the least important element; and the ones in which Mencius had condoned the regicide of kings who misbehaved, on the grounds that rulers who lost the hearts and minds of their people had become "mere fellows" and were no longer kings.[17]

The Neo-Confucianist tradition believed that every ruler was appointed with a mandate from heaven (*t'ien ming*). As long as rulers cultivated virtue and ruled in the interest of their people, they continued to have this mandate and could make decisions without being challenged. But, in an interesting twist, Mencius endorsed the phrase "common people speak for heaven."[18] So while the mandate of heaven can be viewed as a way of trying to limit the abuse of power on the part of rulers, it also contains a seed of democratic sentiment, which Ho exploited brilliantly. Rulers are there according to the "mandate of heaven," but the condition of the people is the ultimate judge of whether he is following that mandate. One can see how omitting this last qualification would fundamentally change the interpretation of this tradition.

In the area that would ultimately become Vietnam, Woodside points out that the complete *Four Books* circulated, and was part of the routine examination for civil servants starting in the fifteenth century. These examinations were taken by as much as one-quarter of the population, therefore their content was well disseminated. The Tay Son rebellion, a series of uprisings that ended both the Le and Trinh dynasties, began in 1771 and lasted until 1802. The leaders of this movement engaged in wealth redistribution, winning the support of the peasants to end dynastic rule. The rebels cited Mencius and his theories about the relationship between the leader and the population as the justification for revolt. The Tay Son rebellion was adopted as a popular revolutionary model in the region for the next hundred and fifty years, and was invoked by twentieth-century Vietnamese generals.[19]

Woodside argues that Mencius provided the theoretical justification for what became a long tradition of revolution in Vietnam. However it is also interesting to think about the importance that Mencius places upon the people as the source of ultimate virtue. One passage remarks, "There is a common saying among the people: 'The empire, the state, and the family': the foundation of the empire lies within the state; the foundation of the state lies within the family; the foundation of the family lies with the person."[20] Ho's colonial subject, "the weird and wonderful animal," is the root of the corrupt colonial state and the distortions of the French empire. Change must occur in every person, otherwise it cannot be maintained in the nation. A state or leader that does not foster virtue in citizens will soon be corrupt and therefore lacks the mandate of heaven.

The assertion that there must be resonance between public and private virtue in "The Mencius" appears as deeply compatible with Rousseau's search for freedom through the general will (see below). Elements from both traditions are combined in Ho's writings. Like Rousseau, who was very concerned with the cultivation of appearance and a sharp awareness of the politics of display, Ho Chi Minh looked to the nation to provide a space where reality can be perceived and citizens can be recognized in public.

Patriotism is like valuable objects. Sometimes they are exhibited in a glass or a crystal vase and are thus clearly visible. But at other times they may be discreetly hidden in a trunk or a suitcase. Our duty is to bring all these hidden valuables into full view. That is, every effort must be made in explanation, propaganda, organization and leadership so that patriotism of all may find expression in work benefiting the country and the Resistance.[21]

Tellingly, it is the task of the party—and ultimately the state—to provide an opportunity for people to display, exhibit, to make evident their inner qualities. Brilliantly drawing upon Confucian traditions and fusing them with Rousseau's democratic theory, Ho developed a political theory of revolution and citizenship that answered to Vietnam's colonial history. Ho sees different regimes as either corrupt or virtuous; whether the inner goodness of a person is able to appear depends upon the regime they live under. Ho is able to say that his people were always capable of virtue, it was only because of the corrupt colonial rulers that the country was in disarray and colonial subjects took the misshapen appearance of beasts. Following Mencius, citizens have the right—even the duty—to replace a corrupt authority with a virtuous one.

Even emerging from the often brutal context of colonization, Ho had seemingly boundless faith in the virtue of people. He saw the role of the revolutionary and the citizen as the cultivation of this personal virtue: everyone from the lowliest peasant to the ruler of the nation must try to become a superior man in order that the revolution can be achieved.[22] In this sense, self-determination is created by self-cultivation: it must be a complete process that is pursued with diligence and complete sincerity. It is the role of everyone to cultivate what Ho called "revolutionary morality." For leaders this means "uniting with the masses in one body, trusting them and paying close attention to their opinion."[23] For everyone, revolutionary morality must be continually invoked even after the initial struggle is complete: "People with revolutionary virtues remain simple, modest and ready to face more hardships, even when meeting with favorable conditions and winning success."[24]

In August 1945, two weeks after Japan surrendered to the Allied Powers and Vietnamese emperor Bao Dai abdicated, Ho Chi Minh formed a provisional government of Vietnam and made himself president. He was careful to say that the work of making a free country had only just begun. In order to be successful in this long-term project, he adopted Mao's emphasis upon criticism and self-criticism as absolutely central to the achievement of liberation and self-rule.

When making criticism and self-criticism, we must sincerely expose our shortcomings. If we make mistakes but don't want to expose them, that is like a patient who refuses to tell his disease to the doctor. When we do a lot of work it is difficult for us to avoid making mistakes. So we use the method of criticism and self-criticism to help one another in correcting our errors, and to be determined to correct them in order to make progress together.[25]

Ho exemplified this behavior and he encouraged party and military officers to always model revolutionary values. He gave speeches at various junctures of the struggle for Vietnamese autonomy and to different audiences. He invariably identified mistakes that were made in the recent past and offered ways of correcting them.

Criticism and self-criticism are principles and practices that can walk the razor's edge between the two aspects of revolution and democracy. On the one hand, these practices rely on an idea of rationality, public deliberation, and progress made through collective engagement and common purpose. It means that those in the regime question themselves and encourage others to question them in order to achieve higher standards and a greater good. On the other hand, criticism and self-criticism can also lead to purges, as those who are identified as embodying anything less than revolutionary morality are destroyed in the name of the revolution, as in the Cultural Revolution in China. Ho took great pains to avoid this latter dynamic, offering asylum to his political and military enemies. One of his first declarations after becoming president was to offer to make the former emperor Bao Dai a "supreme advisor" to his provisional government.[26] Nonetheless, his followers were more prone to be consumed by anger and give in to the need for revenge. There are accounts of wealthier merchants who had assisted early anti-colonial efforts, then being shot and treated brutally as land reform swept through the countryside.

Confucianism combined with nationalism is certainly a vibrant pairing. The measure of self-cultivation and virtue is how completely subservient one is to the interests of the nation. To create national unity even within the militia where frequently militarization leads to hierarchy, Ho argued that officers must see themselves as part of the militia, not above the recruits. "Only when officers are close to soldiers like the limbs of the same body, can the soldiers love the officers like their kith and kin."[27] Ho was able to develop his avid following because he was known as an extremely moral man. Legends from when he traveled the countryside and stayed with families, cooking for them, caring for his children, made his leadership unquestioned during his lifetime. "On many occasions, Ho denounced the 'mandarins of the revolution' and when villagers offered him a quilted blanket—quite a luxury at the time—he refused, making do (for the time being) as they did by covering himself with tree bark for the night."[28]

Ho taught in a school for a time and introduced his students to the ideas of Voltaire, Montesquieu, and Rousseau. The principle of the general will in

Rousseau's *Social Contract* (1762) seems to have deeply influenced his view of democratic rule. Rather than lack of virtue more generally, Ho identified individualism as the main impediment to progress. Everyone must relinquish the desire for interests that may run counter to the collective (general will). In the case of the leaders, the biggest temptation would be to use their new powers for their own ends.

> Without the people, we shall have no strength; without the government no guidance. Therefore, the government and the people must form a monolithic whole. We have now founded the Democratic Republic of Viet Nam. But without happiness and freedom for the people, independence would be meaningless . . . But we must make a correct start. We must bear in mind that all government organs, from the central to the village level, are the people's servants, that is to say that they must work in the public interest, not oppress the people as government organs did under the French and Japanese rule.[29]

Ho made it clear that his government would serve the people, and anyone who sought to promote individual interests would be cast out of his government.

But what this means in turn is that the people themselves had to serve their government as well. In a description of self-determination akin to the idea that one can be "forced to be free," Ho described democracy as follows:

> Don't misunderstand democracy. When no decision is yet taken, we are free to discuss. But when a decision is taken, we should not discuss any longer. Any discussion then could be only discussion on the ways and means to carry out the decision quickly and not to propose that it should not be carried out. We must prohibit any such act of unruly freedom.[30]

Here we start to see how the discipline of collective mobilization can undermine the "unruly freedom" of democratic practice. While Ho wanted unity above all, and even after the establishment of an independent Vietnamese state, he continued to seek unity of the entire country as a way of completing the process of the revolution and ridding the territory of outside influence.

Ho Chi Minh's revolutionary philosophy underscores the form of nationalism that would come to haunt Frantz Fanon: how can a new regime use the people to achieve legitimacy and yet not speak in their name and wield them as a ploy for legitimization? Ho worried about eventual corruption of both public officials and private citizens, concerned that the unity of struggle would give way to profiteering or individualism. He scolded party members who "wrongly think that now that the colonialists and feudalists have been got rid of in the

North, the revolution has been successfully completed. That is why they let individualism develop within themselves, demand enjoyment and rest, and want to pick their own work."[31] During his lifetime he strove to be an example of the leader who wields power only for the sake of others, but his statements routinely addressed the lack of morality that appeared among his followers, and, even worse, among those who previously had led the revolutionary struggle. As soon as they gained authority and some success in their struggle, "[T]hey grow arrogant and luxurious, indulge in embezzlement, waste and unconscious bureaucracy, thus becoming *guilty in the eyes of the revolution*."[32]

Ho's paradigm of self-determination is then a fascinating blend of the Maoist impulse to total revolution and the process of self-criticism and the ideals of Mencius. In order to maintain a truly revolutionary morality, it must be aimed toward making sure that the government serves the people and provides a space for them to become virtuous themselves. His answer to the question of what comes after the revolution was to assert that the revolution will never end. Only by having permanent revolution could Ho claim that his nationalism was democratic. The content of this revolutionary morality incorporates elements of Confucian philosophy, whereby the morality of the leader determines whether or not the people should be devoted to him. Yet it also displays elements of Rousseau's vision of rule by the general will: when all of us are equally driven to live by and refine revolutionary morality, there will be no discord; everyone will have perfect harmony between their internal beliefs and impulses and the regime at large.

This convergence of self and state is one of the classic solutions to the search for freedom. The problem is that the permanent revolution needed to maintain it is untenable. Furthermore, any mechanistic solution to the problem of how to legitimize government and balance individual and collective needs quickly becomes oppressive.

The genius of Confucian thought was the insistence that the relationship between a leader and the people was evolving and subject to change. This is the dynamic that is absent in Ho Chi Minh's revolutionary morality. The ideals of Mencius provided a potential outlet for democratic citizenship, but Ho ceased to emphasize them as he began to bow to the need to consolidate power. The Chinese, Japanese, and French all had armies in his territory during the time he tried to establish national sovereignty. Biographers report that he became resigned to the need to first establish a Vietnamese nation, and then work to make sure the cultivation of virtue was predominant.[33] It is important to remember, however, that Ho had the ability to organize and win followers to his cause by the invocation of these ideals of humility and virtue for more than twenty years. If a government's rule is by the mandate of heaven, and if the people speak for heaven, then this concept provides some promise for postcolonial democratic citizenship in a way that the permanent revolution does not. Furthermore, Ho's link between self-cultivation and self-determination is a more strident vision of what many democratic theorists have observed in other contexts. Ho's problem, as with many revolutionaries before him, was that he could not establish his mandate without sacrificing his virtue.

FANON: REVOLUTION, REALITY AND CITIZEN FORMATION

One of the central tensions within democratic thought is whether self-determination is better upheld by citizenship as valiant individualism or by citizenship as devotion to the collective good. It is not surprising to find a similar split between Ho and Fanon, even as they both seek the origins of freedom in the experience of revolution itself. We might think that the phase of collective mobilization would emphasize common good and subordination to the collective above all. This tendency is clearly evident in Ho's theory that the transformation of the population into a unified body and the defeat of individualism is central to securing freedom. On the other hand, Frantz Fanon saw individual—not collective—transformation, in the midst of struggle as the key to becoming a citizen as opposed to subject, or rather a master as opposed to slave. His individualist orientation may be one of the reasons why he is more palatable to contemporary audiences than Ho. Both Ho and Fanon saw how the injustices of colonial rule were written onto the psyches of its subjects, and they defined revolution as the overcoming of this impression. But their solutions are remarkably distinct, and in some ways, we can look to Fanon's theory a correction to some of the more overzealous aspects of Ho's revolutionary virtue.

Fanon was born in Martinique (like Aimé Césaire, who was Fanon's teacher for a short time), but then educated in Paris to be a psychiatrist. Like the founders of the negritude movement, it was his experience in Paris that heightened his awareness of how colonization created permanently disenfranchised populations whose common position in relation to the French state unified them across national boundaries. He worked in Algiers as a psychiatrist, and clinical experience led him to develop analyses of the relationship between identity constitution and colonial politics that he later presented in *Black Skin, White Masks*.[34] His work on identity has captured the attention of many scholars, even if it has also been interpreted in such various and highly idiosyncratic ways that Henry Louis Gates has called Fanon "a Rorschach blot with legs."[35] The fascination with Fanon's theory of identity needs to be matched with more attention to his ideas about historical context, so a more complete picture of Fanon as a theorist of identity *in the context of political struggle* can emerge. Too frequently political struggle and identity reformation are taken as synonymous.

Fanon was interested in how the revolution can create the conditions for liberating the colonized subject. But this is not exactly a form of sacrificial violence; the slave is not born out of the ashes of the master as a phoenix comes back to life. Instead, Fanon sees violence as providing a rupture with past psychology because it provides for a physical release of the internalized violence of colonialism, thereby creating a new trajectory of history and personality. Physical action and release lay the groundwork for psychic change, but in a broader sense Fanon is pointing to the interconnection between identity and history. Since the world conditions who we are, the real question of revolution is how this dynamic can be reversed: How can we change the world? This will only be possible when we have a new vision of who we are, and what the world can be.

Fanon's book *The Wretched of the Earth* (1961) and his essay "Algeria Unveiled" (1959) illustrate the many contours of his theory in which revolution, identity, and gender play significant and intertwined roles. Fanon remarked upon the particular historical moment of revolutions of decolonization: "Decolonization never goes unnoticed . . . for it focuses on and fundamentally alters being, and transforms the spectators crushed to a nonessential state into privileged actors. . . ."[36] In fact, rather than defining decolonization in some formal administrative terms, Fanon sees decolonization as this restructuring of subjects of history into agents of history. While the transformation happens through a collective engagement in the world, Fanon's work continually emphasizes that this transformation is individual. "The people" do not rise in revolution; rather, the collective "subjects" that have been represented by colonial rule as an indistinguishable mass become individuated through their struggle. Under colonial rule, "the people" were not given any substantive realization or even seen as real: instead they were "relegated to the realm of imagination" as "the natives," "the uncivilized," "the population" that must be administered.[37] So revolutions of decolonization burst the illusion of this imaginary "people" that can be terrorized, subdued, or civilized, and out of this fog emerges "a kind of class of individually liberated slaves."[38]

Because of his relatively unique stance on the matter, most commentators have focused on Fanon's theory that violence serves as the agent of this change from collective subjects of history to individual agents of it.[39] Therefore we will not dwell on this topic here. What has been less noted, however, is Fanon's concern that this transformation from the imaginary "people" to the individually liberated slave is a tenuous accomplishment, no matter the means by which it is pursued. Joan Cocks notes that Fanon concludes *The Wretched of the Earth* by describing the mental patients who are haunted and fractured by their participation in the crimes of colonialism and the violence used to resist it. By pointing out the similar disfigurements in both groups, Fanon seems to undercut his own endorsement of violence earlier in the text. Cocks notes that the slave/native/colonized "can win freedom from the master/slave relation with these weapons but not freedom from the reverberations of his own acts."[40] This is one way that the revolution itself may undercut its own aims, as many nonviolent activists would agree.

In his discussion of the new nationalistic government that comes after the colonial state has been defeated, Fanon laments the fact that, "Paradoxically, the national government's attitude toward the rural masses is reminiscent in some ways of the colonial power."[41] He points out that the ossification of the rural tribal structure was one way the colonial regime could more easily achieve administrative control over unfamiliar territory, so there may be some truth to the sense that "The nation may well have a rational, even progressive head, but its huge body remains retarded, rebellious and recalcitrant."[42] In this case, the legacy of colonialism could be to blame for the new nation's ills.

However, he sees how the mobilization of the mass in revolution can also serve to perpetuate ills not directly linked to the legacy of colonialism. Fanon's work is haunted by the possibility that collective politics, at its worst, will come back to dominate the decolonized regime. Here is where Fanon can contribute to our understanding of achieving self-determination from a very different perspective. Fanon points to a dynamic within the revolutionary movement itself that gains importance in the text of *The Wretched of the Earth* as he moves from his analysis of the psychological and social effects of colonialism, to the struggle for independence, into the problems of instantiating self-rule. The collective movement of revolution, which was necessary to decolonize, comes to hinder the progression of individual freedom later:

> This spectacular voluntarism which was to lead the colonized people in a single move to absolute sovereignty, the certainty one has that all the pieces of the nation could be gathered up in one fell swoop and from the same shared perspective, and the strength grounded in this hope, have proved in the light of experience to be a very great weakness. As long as he imagined he could switch straight from a colonized subject to sovereign citizen of an independent nation, as long as he believed in the mirage sustained by his unmediated physical strength, the colonized achieved no real progress along the road to knowledge.[43]

The revolutionary mobilization is dependent upon two things, imagination and direct antagonism. Both of these dynamics can end up going horribly awry. The imagination of victory, or complete empowerment and solidarity, can even create the fantasy that it would be possible to return to an idyllic pre-colonial past. Given enough strength of mind, perhaps the colonized could decide that colonialism itself was an elaborate historical hoax, or a collective nightmare.

Such thoughts, while seemingly empowering, can just be delusory. Second, such a revolt is driven as a response: it is the antithesis to colonialism. This unity, struggle, and pride cannot be maintained after colonial rule, and in being so focused upon the crimes of the colonist, it forecloses growth toward true sovereignty, which is to set one's own actions into play and not be governed by reaction. Rather than grand ideas of freedom and sovereignty, Fanon points out that the person who picks up arms is driven by the image of replacing the colonizer with himself. Once the initial battle is won, there is no counterpoint from which to define oneself: "It would be perverse to count on the enemy who always manages to commit as many crimes as possible and can be relied upon to widen 'the rift' thus driving the population as a whole to revolt."[44]

Furthermore, the revolutionary struggle produced a new kind of imaginative reality in which fantasies of complete empowerment replaced the colonial fantasies of complete control. It is the illusions that accompany revolution that most concern Fanon. One of the more interesting aspects of *The Wretched of the Earth* is his insistence that the path from subordination to sovereignty is an awakening to a more complex reality, away from fantasies and simplified representations of reality. "On their arduous path to rationality the people must also learn to give up their simplistic perception of the oppressor. The species is splitting open before their eyes." In the aftermath of the collective and unified surge against the colonist oppressor the myth of "the group" must be replaced by the individual who has been "reintroduced into the world."[45] During the time of colonization, the colonized found release in magic, ritual dance and a devotion to an invisible reality. The revolution, with its dreams of glory, power, and nation has not necessarily placed its adherents back into the world.

After the collective struggle gives birth to the new nation, it is the role of the nationalist leader to make sure the nation is truly democratic by empowering the masses. "To politicize the masses is to make the nation in its totality a reality for every citizen."[46] But this form of nationalism, Fanon points out, must in some way eradicate the individual that emerged from revolutionary violence. "Since individual experience is national, since it is a link in the national chain, it ceases to be individual, narrow and limited in scope, and can lead to the truth of the nation and the world."[47] We need others to recreate a world in which reality can appear. But by joining together, we may lose the very sense of the real that we strive for. Fanon points out that individuals need to be part of a collective, but that the collective can also threaten our grip on reality.

At other points in his text, Fanon is confused by the need to have a nation, and the leader that must accompany it. Does having any leader destroy the individual's chance of liberation? "Leader comes from the English verb 'to lead,' meaning 'to drive' in French. The driver of the people no longer exists today. People are no longer a herd and do not need to be driven."[48] Nonetheless, he acknowledges that "the people" still can be displayed and driven as a herd in order to demonstrate the leader's popularity and strength.

> It is not by mobilizing dozens or hundreds or thousands of men and women three or four times a year that you politically educate the masses. These meetings, these spectacular rallies, are similar to the old preindependence tactics whereby you displayed your strength to prove to yourself and to others that you had the people on your side. The political education of the masses is meant to make adults out of them, not to make them infantile.[49]

How can the nation, or a leader, politically educate the masses so that they are awake to "reality" while ensuring that they do not become captive to another mass delusion?

Here we are back to the central question of democratic citizenship: what are the conditions necessary for citizens to rule themselves? Fanon describes how a sense of individuation and collectivity need to balance one another out, and observes that the role of the leader is to make sure that all citizens are "introduced" to reality. At the same time, Fanon shows how revolutionary struggle tends to create fantasies of omnipotence and make the individual more susceptible to following a leader who speaks for "the group." Furthermore, colonialism has created a distortion of individual and collective perception, fully detailed in Fanon's other works. He has elaborated for us how the experiences of both colonization *and* revolution made the task of sovereignty ever more difficult to achieve.

Fanon's revolutionary theory points to the ambiguous status of the human body, as it is both material and social. The "tense muscles" of the slave that have the violence of colonialism embedded in them are a material manifestation of colonial history. The essence of colonialism is that physical acquiescence was all that could be demanded, because the mind could never be controlled entirely. For this reason colonialism created a division between the truth of colonial oppression in the body and the resistance to it in the mind. Fanon notes the large-scale effects of such fracturing: "The truth is that colonization, in its very essence, already appeared to be a great purveyor of psychiatric hospitals."[50] The liberation that must occur is not just of the body, but also "from our minds."

One can start to see how central this idea is to Fanon by looking also at his description of women's mental liberation in "Algeria Unveiled." Fanon's work suggests that individual liberation from history can happen in a number of different fashions. The gender dynamics in *Black Skin, White Masks* (1952) are troubling, though there is no doubt that this work has generally contributed to feminist theories of identity construction. Power and sexuality are never separated, and Fanon unleashes his analysis of interracial sexual relationships, equating colonization with emasculation. At times, his analysis has the uncomfortable suggestion that women and their bodies can and should be taken as the marker of freedom or subordination.[51] Because of his awareness of the female body and sexuality as contested colonial terrain, it should not be surprising that his book *A Dying Colonialism* (1959) explores the structure of the family in detail and begins with a metaphor of colonial Algeria as a veiled woman. He wrote this text after the uprising against the French had been in progress for six years, and given that the revolution had begun, the first essay, "Algeria Unveiled," presents his description of the process of decolonization on both a personal and national level. The essay repeatedly focuses upon the Algerian woman's body, first as a target of colonization and then as an agent of violence and revolution.[52]

Fanon pointed out that the occupying powers from Europe focused on the veiled woman to justify the logic of colonization. The veil itself is seen as evidence of the barbarism of the local inhabitants. In an argument worth reflecting upon in the context of world politics today, Fanon mimicked the argument of the occupying powers: in the name of liberating veiled women, occupying forces needed to proceed with abandon. But Fanon argues that because women and the family played such an integral role in the maintenance of Algerian society, this targeting was smart tactics: "If we want to destroy the structure of Algerian society, its capacity for resistance, we must first of all conquer the women: we must go and find them behind the veil where they hide themselves and in the houses where the men keep them out of sight."[53] Hence, every time a woman dropped her veil, the colonial power welcomed it as a sign of its successful campaign to weaken or even eradicate the culture of Algeria.

But the veil also acts as a provocation. Fanon delves deeper into the drama of subordination and desire, arguing that the European male wants to unmask the mystery of Algeria, to place himself at the privileged site of viewing what is hidden in the country. "This woman who sees without being seen frustrates the colonizer. There is no reciprocity. She does not yield herself, does not give herself, does not offer herself."[54]

The politics of colonization are played out in full with the actual and imagined conquests of the veiled woman.

Initially, resistance to colonization is expressed by holding on to the veil and burrowing more deeply into culturally specific practices. This resistance only infuriates the colonizer, who wants to penetrate the country in every regard. Fanon points out that there is no seduction; instead the violence of colonization is evident through the conquest of the veiled woman.

The history of the French conquest in Algeria, including the overrunning of villages by troops, the confiscation of property and the raping of women,

the pillaging of the country, has contributed to the birth and crystallization of the same dynamic image. At the level of the psychological strata of
the occupier, the evocation of this freedom given to the sadism of the conqueror, to his eroticism, creates faults, fertile gaps through which both
dreamlike forms of behavior and, on certain occasions, criminal acts can
emerge. Thus the rape of the Algerian woman in the dream of a European
is always preceded by a rending of the veil. We here witness a double
deflowering. Likewise, the woman's conduct is never one of consent or
acceptance, but of abject humility.[55]

Though this metaphor and analysis of colonization is by now relatively familiar,
Fanon's description contains an important subtlety. This interplay of resistance
and violence is played out according to script. The Algerian woman appears as
the unconquerable, and the aggressor violates her. Each is responding to images
that the one character has of the other, and in responding to these caricatures,
each figure becomes a caricature of him- or herself. What happens around the
veil, then, is where the struggle for domination occurs: the entire colonial
process is crystallized. But while violence is one part of this process, the other
is the distancing of oneself, the adaptation of a role that is being played out in a
long-standing drama.

Fanon says that with the development of the resistance movement, "The attitude of the Algerian woman, or of native society in general, with regard to the
veil was to undergo important modifications."[56] The veil ceased being a sign of
resistance within the familiar script and was transformed into a revolutionary
element, deployed with different, and disarming effect. Culture was activated as
a weapon of aggression. Algerian women were slowly included in the armed
struggle in the city of Algiers since police repression of the male population
made their tactical disruptions more difficult to achieve. Militant women could
"pass" as Europeans, or camouflage themselves as Europeanized locals who
supported French rule. They would not arouse suspicion as they planted bombs
or transported them over military checkpoints. Fanon describes how deploying
an inauthentic persona in public paradoxically led to the development of a new
person. To play the role of European or sympathizer, a woman needed to overcome her fear of the colonizer; to achieve this required she relinquish her narrative of the occupying power. She also had to understand that the role of
traditional female, the woman to be unveiled and "liberated," was also a charac-
terization that was developed through colonization, not actually her authentic
self as assumed in the posture of resistance. "She must consider the image of the
occupier lodged somewhere in her mind and in her body, remodel it, initiate
the essential work of eroding it, make it inessential, remove something of the
shame that it attached to it, devalidate it."[57]

Entering the violent struggle allows the woman to recognize the positions of colonizer and colonized as roles to be deployed and changed, rather than a given reality that must be resisted. This realization allows her to begin to write her own script. "What we have here is not the bringing to light of a character known and frequented a thousand times in imagination or in stories. It is an authentic birth in a pure state, without preliminary instruction. There is no character to imitate. On the contrary, there is an intense dramatization, a continuity between the woman and the revolutionary."[58] The break in the cycle of identification allows the Algerian to see that the future can be different from the past. The characters of colonizer and colonized were doomed to recreate the same interactions over and over: after all, their interactions and raison d'être were limited to one another: there was only one story to tell and no resolution possible. Progress stopped with the overtaking of the national plot by these two figures. "Initially subjective, the breaches made in colonialism are the result of the victory of the colonized over their old fear and over the atmosphere of despair distilled day after day by a colonialism that has incrusted itself with the *prospect of enduring forever*."[59]

Fanon hails "a new dialectic of body and world" that emerges from the tactics of armed struggle.[60] The veiled woman no longer connects to her world through image; instead, she uses image—whether of assimilation or traditionalism by donning the veil—to make herself a more effective instrument of revolution. Initially the veil played a key role in the process of colonization and resistance: its centrality displayed that the power structure was intact, the character sketches performed, and the future held at bay. The revolution gives birth to a new woman whose body is in a dialectical relationship with the world: she is an actor whose power is in writing her own script and her own future. The veil symbolizes the past, and while the veil is still present, a new relationship to it has emerged. The past becomes a weapon, rather than a fixed identity.

While "Algeria Unveiled" details the transformation of the Algerian woman into a revolutionary in close detail, and with a great attention to the personal difficulties in this sort of political mobilization, *The Wretched of the Earth* is a call to arms for Algeria's male inhabitants.[61] While Fanon's careful description of the female militant is focused on the moment of mobilization and the transformation that it produces, *The Wretched of the Earth* draws much grander brushstrokes, placing the transformation through liberatory violence and the reassertion of national consciousness in a larger context. Both texts ultimately talk about self-determination and liberation in the context of being able to write one's story from a position of understanding the world as it exists.

There are three important elements in Fanon's theory. First, one does not take the world as unchanging, and a person does not have to merely choose between the roles that have been made available. Second, one's actions and choices cannot be driven by a sense of unreality or delusion and still be truly revolutionary. Third, self-determination is a combination of these two other elements: to be able to see the world as it exists and to be strategic in the knowledge that each of us *chooses* how to respond to it. At the individual level, self-determination then is a balance between ascertaining the world as it exists, and not letting the present crush alternative futures. And herein lies another key distinction between Ho and Fanon: Ho evaluates revolutionary morality based upon a transcendental ideal, while Fanon sees revolutionary self-fashioning requires that one become responsive to the ever shifting environment. Thus, as Ho started to accommodate the pragmatic necessities of consolidating rule, his theory of revolutionary values became both more ruthlessly applied yet less significant as a check upon his political power.

Taking stock of Ho and Fanon's theories of self-determination and decolonization, it becomes clear that they are talking about something much more difficult, personal, and vital than some sort of formal transfer of power. In fact, these ideas are reminiscent of the debates about what democracy really meant in earlier ages, before it came to be equated with the electoral process. Think about these ideas in juxtaposition with the formal processes of decolonization established by the United Nations. In 1961, the U.N. General Assembly established a Special Committee on Decolonization (also known as the U.N. Special Committee of the 24 on Decolonization), and every year the Committee dutifully issues reports stating the progress made toward self-determination in the world. In 2009, the committee still had sixteen countries on its list of territories that had not been "decolonized," and the Secretary General urged all speed in finishing the process.[62] But, taking these richer ideas about self-determination into account, it is clear the problem is much more widespread and deeply rooted than is commonly recognized—and far from complete.

4

Colonialism and the State of Exception

The site of the massacre was the Hola concentration camp, which was located in a remote and desolate area of Kenya. The year was 1959, the seventh year of a State of Emergency that legalized the brutal measures the British government needed to crush the anticolonial insurgency movement known as the Mau Mau. The camp was divided into two sections. There was an "open camp" for formers members of the Mau Mau movement who were willing to cooperate with British officials but still too dangerous to return home. The "closed camp" contained about five hundred of the most hard-core prisoners who had endured years of detention, torture, hunger, and brutality without confessing that they had taken the notorious oath promising to defend their land and freedom. The British press and the House of Commons had begun to show some interest in the fate of the massive numbers of Kenyan detainees, and a motion to authorize an independent inquiry into the conditions in the camps had recently failed by a vote of 288–232. The local British officials decided that they had to dismantle the camps quickly, but first they had to break the last of the detainees, even if this meant systematically employing torture.

On March 3, 1959, Hola's camp commandant, G. M. Sullivan, decided to implement the Cowan Plan, which was a systematic application of method of "dilution" that had been used haphazardly throughout the Emergency. "Dilution" was a process whereby hard-core inmates were broken up into small groups, surrounded by British officials and African guards, and beaten until they agreed to comply with all commands. The most important command was that they confess and repudiate their oaths of allegiance to the land and freedom movement. Many prisoners had participated in rituals that sacralized a vow of secrecy, so this order amounted to an order to beat them to death. And that is exactly what happened. According to one survivor of the Hola massacre, the guards selected around one hundred detainees and brought them to a work site, where they were ordered to dig an irrigation trench.[1] Hundreds of armed African guards had been called in to execute the plan. When the detainees refused to begin work, claiming they couldn't possibly complete the task in the time allotted, Sullivan blew a whistle and the guards began beating them with clubs, sticks, and shovels. After a second whistle, the officers counted six dead bodies. Sullivan blew a whistle again and the massacre continued until there were ten dead and dozens more severely injured.

The camp officials tried to cover up the massacre, claiming that the ten men died after accidentally drinking tainted water, but overwhelming evidence contradicted this account. An investigation ensued, and the senior resident magistrate W. H. Goudie concluded, "In each case death was found to have been caused by shock and hemorrhage *due to multiple bruising caused by violence.*"[2] Despite the undeniable evidence of excessive force, Goudie found that no criminal wrongdoing had occurred. He concluded that it was impossible to decide which blows were legitimate attempts to force detainees to work and which were excessively punitive. In any case, the actions were carried out under the directive of the Cowan Plan and the judge felt that it was not the responsibility of the judiciary to evaluate questions of colonial policy.

Although the massacre at the Hola Camp attained some notoriety in the British press, it was by no means a unique instance of violence against Mau Mau detainees. In her book *Imperial Reckoning: The Untold Story of Britain's Gulag in Kenya*, Caroline Elkins documents widespread patterns of rape, torture, and murder. She estimates that 1.5 million Kikuyu were detained during the State of Emergency (1952–59), either in concentration camps or in villages that were surrounded by trenches and barbed wire to cut off any contact between Mau Mau guerrillas and their supporters. British officials put the number of Kikuyu dead at 11,000, but Elkins uses demographic data to support other estimates that place the number of casualties closer to 100,000.[3] The term "State of Emergency" refers to a specific period in the history of colonial Kenya, but it can also help illuminate the debates about the broader theoretical concept "state of exception."

Ironically, the State of Emergency that was implemented in order to secure British rule may have accelerated decolonization. Although the Emergency achieved the goal of crushing the Mau Mau, it also made colonial government more costly, both economically and politically. Moreover, it undermined the popular myths that European control over Africa brought legality, civilization, and economic development to indigenous peoples. From one perspective, some might see this episode in colonial history as evidence that it is ultimately impossible to defeat a popular movement for national liberation. But this optimistic assessment overlooks the long-term political consequences of the State of

Emergency. The State of Emergency was an intensification of existing modes of colonial governance that destroyed the remnants of indigenous sources of authority and order and replaced them with unmitigated coercion.[4] This chapter focuses on the work of two African intellectuals, Ngugi wa Thiong'o and Achille Mbembe. Both have suggested that the State of Emergency reveals the inner logic of "colonial rationality." Furthermore, they both draw attention to the way that this logic continues to structure postcolonial states and undermine popular government. Their work advances current debates in political theory by deepening our understanding of the political effects of the state of exception. Their approach to the concept of the state of exception, with its attentiveness to the lawlessness at the heart of legality itself, illuminates the problem of founding a new state out of the violent vestiges of the old order.

THE STATE OF EXCEPTION

In the past decade there has been renewed interest in the related concepts of martial law, emergency powers, and the state of exception. The state of exception exists when crises are resolved by granting prerogative to the military or the executive and curtailing the rights of citizens and their representatives.[5] In the field of political theory, this interest has focused on the controversial work of Carl Schmitt and Giorgio Agamben. Agamben published a timely book titled *State of Exception* that concluded that the state of exception (or martial law) is a space devoid of law. He argued that it was not the logical consequence of the state's right to self-defense, nor was it a straightforward attempt to reestablish the juridical order by violating the letter of the law.[6] For Agamben, martial law and other exceptional measures reveal the Janus face of sovereignty: the power to declare the state of exception is the same power that invests individuals as worthy of rights.

Until recently, most of the scholarly research on the state of exception had focused on the paradigmatic case of Weimar Germany and the influential writing of Carl Schmitt.[7] The age of empire, however, forced an earlier generation of political and legal theorists to confront the conceptual difficulties that emerge when the law provides for its own suspension.[8] In the nineteenth century, the frequent and bloody use of martial law to quell uprisings in the colonies prompted extended public and scholarly debates about the nature and limits of the law.[9] Surprisingly few contemporary political theorists have considered the significance of emergency measures in consolidating colonial rule and structuring postcolonial governance.[10]

Two notable exceptions are Achille Mbembe and Ngugi wa Thiong'o. Ngugi is a novelist and critic who lived through the State of Emergency as a youth in rural Kenya. Two of his best known novels, *A Grain of Wheat* and *Weep Not, Child*, are extended reflections on the moral and political ramifications of the Emergency.[11] His treatment of the topic, however, differs from the existing theoretical literature. Most of the debates about the state of exception—for example, the famous dispute between William Carlyle and John Stuart Mill about martial law in Jamaica—take the legitimacy of colonialism for granted.[12] The subject of disagreement is confined to the necessity, effectiveness, and negative consequences of extralegal measures. Ngugi approaches the topic from the opposite perspective and forces the reader to ask what the emergency tells us about the legitimacy of colonialism itself. The most interesting aspect of his work, however, is the penetrating and complex analysis of the colonial approach to law and exception. Ngugi's literary depiction of postcolonial Kenya is similar to Mbembe's theoretical concept of *commandement*, the distinctive form of government in colonial and postcolonial regimes. Drawing on the work of Mbembe and Ngugi, this chapter tries to understand the way that the colonial polity's distinctive approach to law and exception contributed to the authoritarian character of many postcolonial African states.[13]

NGUGI'S EMERGENCY STORIES

Ngugi enriches our theoretical understanding of the state of exception by depicting the social and political consequences of the State of Emergency that was declared in colonial Kenya from 1952 to 1959 Ngugi came of age during the State of Emergency, and his writing is particularly attentive to the micropolitical effects of the tactics employed during the Emergency (torture, screening, arbitrary arrest and incarceration for extended periods, forced labor, and mass confinement in villages surrounded by barbed wire). In his novels, he captures the way that these tactics undermined the capacity for resistance and weakened alternative (i.e., noncolonial) sources of order.

Ngugi's analysis of the state of exception is also distinctive because of his concern with the legitimacy of the *state* rather than the legitimacy of the *exception*. He has no interest in asking whether exceptional measures are appropriate means of safeguarding the sovereignty of the state, since this question is posed from the perspective of the colonizer. Instead, he looks at the issue from the opposite perspective and asks how the Emergency undermines a politics of resistance and weakens alternative, noncolonial sources of order. Not only is Ngugi's anticolonial perspective distinctive, but his style is original too. His critique of colonial legality is developed in a series of literary works that describe the political and psychological consequences of the Emergency.

Weep Not, Child is Ngugi's first published novel.[14] It is set in the late 1940s through the 1950s and traces the story of a family of landless peasants during the Emergency. The novel explores the way that violence and repression destroy the fabric of the community. The story is told from the point of view of the youngest son, Njoroge, the only member of the family who has the opportunity to go to school. The British colonial government is depicted through the figure of Mr. Howlands, the white farmer who owns land taken from Njoroge's father, Ngotho, and Jacobo, the loyalist Kikuyu chief.

The conflict over the ownership of land is a source of anguish that motivates the characters in the novel. Ngotho feels an intense connection to his ancestral land and works diligently for Mr. Howland in order to protect his *shamba*, the land that he feels is part of himself. Mr. Howlands initially sees Ngotho as a dedicated and grateful employee; but when the Kenyan nationalist movement calls a strike to protest terrible labor conditions, Mr. Howlands warns his employees that anyone who participates will be fired. This strike is the event that sets off a chain of violence that tears apart the ties between fathers and sons, husbands and wives, as well as the more precarious bonds that link whites and blacks in the system of forced colonial labor.[15] The first act of violence is domestic. Ngotho slaps his wife when she begs him not to take part in the strike and risk losing his job. This scene of domestic conflict draws attention to the way that the looming Emergency undermined the traditional sources of order within the Kikuyu community and even within the family itself.

After Jacobo, the loyalist chief, addresses a crowd of workers in order to convince them not to strike, Ngotho rises from the audience to confront him. The audience surges forward and then the police attack the crowd, shooting and beating the unarmed workers, including Ngotho. Although Ngotho survives, he is fired from his job and his family is forced to leave their huts, which are located on land owned by Jacobo. Under the pressure of poverty and dislocation, Ngotho's family falls apart. One son goes to join the Mau Mau fighters in the forest and another goes to Nairobi to find work. After Ngotho is arrested in connection with a Mau Mau attack on Jacobo's home, he is brutally tortured and dies from his injuries. Despite Njoroge's academic success at Siriana, a prestigious missionary-run preparatory school, he is not immune to the reach of the Emergency and is detained and tortured. The novel ends on a pessimistic note. Njoroge is forced to leave school to support his mother because his brothers are in prison awaiting execution.

What does this novel tell us about the Emergency? The most prominent theme is the way that the Emergency undermined the unity of the Kikuyu people. In order for the white minority to maintain economic and political control over the vast African population, they needed allies, which meant that there had to be some segment of the African population that benefited from white rule. In order to effectively implement a regime of coercion, the British government had to simultaneously organize consent. At first the colonial state relied on cultural assimilation carried out by institutions such as the church and the school system. These institutions were supposed to breed a new generation of English-speaking subjects who were deeply committed to the colonial order. This technique of cultural assimilation, however, proved to be more complicated than expected. Although many Kenyans converted to Christianity, the influence of European missionaries was permanently weakened during the circumcision controversy of the 1920s. The Protestant missionaries opposed the practice of female circumcision, which was the most important life-cycle ritual in traditional Kikuyu culture. When the missionaries decided to forbid their converts from participating in this rite of passage, masses of African Christians left the European-dominated institutions to establish their own independent churches and schools. This issue inspired the first large-scale political mobilization. In an effort to stamp out the practice of female circumcision, the missionaries pressured local native councils to enact a ban. Opponents of the ban formed the Kikuyu Central Association (KCA), which was committed to resisting the "civilizing mission" of the colonial state.[16] Much to the surprise of the British government, many of the Africans who were educated in the missionary schools and churches became the leaders of this nascent movement for self-government, which meant that the colonial government had to seek new allies.

In *Weep Not, Child*, Ngugi depicts a system of local government organized around "chiefs" whose authority comes from the colonial state rather than the local community. In the precolonial period, the Kikuyu did not have a system of chiefs, but instead relied on a more informal process of consultation. In Kenya, as in many parts of Africa, the chieftaincy was a colonial institution set up to facilitate colonial administration.[17] The British established a system known as indirect rule, which relied on chiefs who were supposed to administer customary law. As Mahmood Mamdani has shown in *Citizen and Subject*, this customary law was invented by the colonizer and had several important benefits for the colonial state. First, indirect rule was a matter of expediency because the colonial bureaucracies typically had only a handful of experienced white officials to govern extremely vast territories, and so they needed to delegate administrative tasks. Second, the system created a group of Africans whose personal power was dependent upon colonial authority. Third, it used a nascent theory of multiculturalism to rationalize the treatment of Africans as second-class citizens. The colonial administration characterized customary law as a concession to the indigenous people's desire to be governed by their own traditions and practices. But it also provided a rationale for a dual system of justice that treated whites as citizens and Africans as subjects. The concept of "customary law" reinforced Africans' exclusion from equal treatment under the law because it provided none of the legal protections guaranteed to white settlers but all of the obligations. Even where "customary law" was employed, the colonial administrators still had the jurisdiction to overturn the decisions of native courts or to enforce compliance with national rules. According to Mamdani, customary law, as invented by the colonizer, was never concerned with the problem of limiting state power, only enforcing it.[18] In a similar vein, Martin Chanock argues that the invention of customary law provided a screen that obfuscated the far-reaching institutional changes brought about by colonialism.[19]

The customary law created as an instrument of indirect rule incorporated elements of traditional practices, but these were distorted by the vastly changed power dynamics of colonialism. For example, in the precolonial polity, when a village elder adjudicated a dispute, he did so with the knowledge that his authority depended on widespread legitimacy. This informal accountability provided a check on abuse and despotism. Under the new system of indirect rule, however, the "chief" was backed by the coercive power of the colonial state and had little need to build consensus or respect shared norms. Mamdani describes this system as "decentralized despotism."[20] This is exactly what Ngugi depicts in his novels. In *Weep Not, Child*, Chief Jacobo is responsible for carrying out Mr. Howlands's orders and ensuring the compliance of other villagers. In return for his support of the regime, Jacobo had amassed a significant amount of land, which was the main source of both wealth and prestige in Kikuyu society.[21] Since land was extremely scarce, he used his lands to ensure that any resistance was crushed. When Ngotho challenged Jacobo, he and his family had to leave their huts, which were built on Jacobo's land. Ngotho could not appeal his exile by turning to public opinion because Jacobo's authority came from Mr. Howlands.

The political structure of indirect rule also contributed to the economic transformation of Kenya, a process that accelerated during the Emergency.[22] The new chiefs were involved in the distribution of communal lands. In the colonial period, the Kikuyu were confined to reservations that did not contain enough agricultural land to feed the population, therefore decisions about how to allocate this land had enormous consequences. Those without land had to go to work on white farms and accept any wages to survive. During the Emergency, the land of Mau Mau detainees was frequently given to Loyalists and Home Guards. This process of concentration contributed to the transformation of Kenya from subsistence peasant agriculture to more commercial agriculture. The Emergency helped create a class of black landowners and landless laborers. This process, which had already begun under colonialism, intensified during the Emergency because over one million people were relocated and forced into fortified villages or camps. Ngugi paints a picture of the Emergency as a radicalization of practices that had their roots in the structure of the "normal" colonial state.

Weep Not, Child articulates a critique of colonial legality and the system of indirect rule. It indicts both the white and black faces of the colonial state. The most explicit statement of this critique comes in a scene where Njoroge's family is gathered in his mother's hut and they hear the news that Jomo Kenyatta, the political leader of the nationalist movement, has been convicted of supporting the Mau Mau. Njoroge's mother laments:

> The white man makes a law or a rule. Through that rule or law or what you may call it, he takes away the land and then imposes many laws on the people concerning that land and many other things, all without people agreeing first as in the old days of the tribe. Now a man rises and opposes that law which made right the taking away of the land. Now that man is taken by the same people who made the laws against which that man was fighting. He is tried under those alien rules. Now tell me who is that man who can win even if the angels of God were his lawyers. . . .[23]

This statement is an indictment of the Emergency, which made it a capital crime to take an oath of solidarity, to possess a weapon, to criticize the government or to give material aid to the fighters in the forest. It is a critique of the farce of a trial that was the basis of Jomo Kenyatta's imprisonment.[24] But, more importantly, it is an astute observation that the Emergency is not a temporary aberration but instead reflects the true nature of colonial legality. As we will see below, Ngugi develops this argument in his theoretical writings, including *The Trial of Dedan Kimathi* and his prison memoir *Detained*.[25]

The Trial of Dedan Kimathi (1976, coauthored with Micere Githae Mugo) is probably the most openly didactic of Ngugi's literary works. It is a play that aims to teach the Kenyan people about the history of colonialism, resistance, and the violent repression of that history at the hands of the British.[26] It is not a psychological exploration of resistance and betrayal but rather a Brechtian staging of events and actions that expose the absurdity of the legalism used to justify the violent defense of British colonial rule. As in Bertolt Brecht's epic theater, Ngugi and Micere's script uses generic labels such as "woman," "boy," and "girl" to describe some of the characters. These labels turn the characters into representative figures and draw attention to the structural rather than individual causes of their actions. Although Dedan Kimathi is an historical figure who was executed for his role in the Mau Mau struggle, the play is not a dramatization of the actual trial but rather a highly stylized attack on the British ideology of the rule of law and its role in mystifying the basis of British authority.

The play begins with a set of mimed scenes depicting African history: a black king with a white slave trader; a slave auction; a ruthless black plantation overseer whipping slaves. The final scene in this prelude links together the past and present: it is a depiction of the "screening" process used during the Emergency that consisted of a hooded collaborator identifying fellow villagers as supporters of the Mau Mau. This vivid reminder of the rule of law during the Emergency, which was based on anonymous denunciation and detention without charge or conviction, set the stage for the action of the trial.

The courtroom drama opens with a scene that casually exposes the bases of colonial society: the color line and the monopoly on violence. In the court room, whites and blacks sit on opposite sides talking among themselves. When a black clerk orders the spectators to be quiet, it is not entirely clear whether he is only addressing the blacks. A white settler shouts "how dare you" and the other whites pull their guns.[27] The settler is outraged because a black official has unwittingly challenged the rigid hierarchy of colonial society. It is also significant that a number of spectators immediately pull their weapons, because the offense for which Dedan Kimathi is being tried is possession of a firearm, a capital offense for blacks under the Emergency Laws.

The scene is staged in a way that draws attention to the absurdity of the ritual legalism of the trial. For example, Kimathi does not initially respond when the judge asks for his plea, so the judge threatens to put him in prison for contempt of court. This threat of a prison sentence for contempt, however, is ridiculous, since Kimathi's execution is a foregone conclusion and a dead man cannot be punished for contempt. Again the judge asks, "Guilty or not guilty."[28] In his response, Kimathi puts the colonial state on trial. He does this by challenging the question itself. He asks, "By what right dare you, a colonial judge, sit in judgment over me?" What follows is a debate over the legitimacy of the court itself. In response, the judge takes a patronizing tone, suggesting, "Perhaps you don't understand. Maybe your long stay in the Forest has . . . I mean . . . we are here to deal fairly with you, to see that justice is done."

During his courtroom appearance, Kimathi makes an economic, democratic, and cultural argument against the legitimacy of the colonial courts. He does not take the position that the Emergency Laws are a violation the rule of law because he assumes that, far from being exceptional, they reflect the core logic of the colonial order. Instead, he tries to expose the way in which the violence of the Emergency, which the settlers perceive as an aberration and blame on the Mau Mau, is a necessary product of the violence of colonialism. His first argument against the legitimacy of the trial is based on the undemocratic character of the laws. He insists, "I will not plead to a law in which we had no part in the making,"[29] to which the judge responds, "Law is law. The role of law is the basis of every civilized community." The judge defends what legal theorists call a realist view of law: the law is what those in charge say it is, and its legitimacy does not depend on any preexisting moral principle. Its legitimacy is based on a tautology: the law is legitimate because it creates law and order, which is necessary for civilization. Kimathi challenges this view and insists that law is not the same as force because law is based on consent. The colonial rule of law is an oxymoron because colonialism is a political order based on force, not consent. Furthermore, it is premised on unequal rather than equal treatment of two groups of people, natives and settlers.[30]

Kimathi also exposes the economic basis of the colonial legal order. Whereas the judge insists that there is a single universal law, Kimathi responds that the ostensible universality of the law simply disguises the fact that in reality there are two kinds of laws, one for the poor and hungry and another for the man of property.[31] The judge counters, "I am not talking about the laws of Nyandarua jungle." In response, Kimathi deftly reverses the terms of the binary that equates settlers with civilization and Africans with barbarity. He asks, "The jungle of colonialism? Or exploitation? For it is there that you'll find creatures of prey feeding on the blood and bodies of those who toil." Kimathi elaborates on the ways by which the law has been used to enforce compulsory labor, a form of slavery. Native Kenyans were forced into wage labor by the British state, which charged taxes equivalent to two month's wages and imprisoned anyone unable to pay. The judge responds, "There's no liberty without law and order," to which Kimathi replies, "There is no law and order without liberty." In this concise exchange, the play summarizes a long and complex debate about the nature of law. Kimathi's democratic-socialist critique of the "rule of law" has been developed in more detail in works such as Franz Neumann's *The Rule of Law* and E. P Thompson's *Whigs and Hunters: The Origin of the Black Act.* The play captures the essence of this argument about the class character of the law while also foregrounding the distinctive colonial dimension of the issue.

The play makes it clear that the coercive side of the law is necessary when individuals and groups have the courage to resist the hegemonic forms of order established through religion, greed, need, and habitual deference. The real, inner trial of Dedan Kimathi is not the drama that unfolds in the courtroom in front of the colonial judge. Instead, Kimathi's trial takes place after he is returned to his cell in the form of three temptations that appear to him in prison during a break in the courtroom drama. The first temptation comes from a settler named Shaw Henderson who encourages Kimathi to confess and collaborate in exchange for his life. To underscore the point about the illusory nature of legal objectivity and neutrality in the colonial state, Henderson is played by the same actor as the judge, and Kimathi draws attention to this, stating "you cannot deceive me, even in your many disguises."[32] Henderson illustrates another face of colonialism. This time he does not make any pretense of legality or neutrality. He explains that his motive for sparing Kimathi's life is purely prudential. He admits, "Look, between the two of us, we don't need to pretend. Nations live by self-interest. You challenged our interests: we had to defend them. It is to our mutual interest and for your own good that we end this ugly war."[33] But Kimathi does not share Henderson's assessment of his own interest. Kimathi's primary interest is communal regeneration, not his own survival. He is interested in a collective rather than an individualistic sense, and therefore concludes that his interest lies in inspiring others to continue the fight against slavery and exploitation.

The second and third delegations are important because they draw attention to the temptations offered by collaboration with the neocolonial state rather than the colonial order. This time, Dedan Kimathi is asked to give up armed resistance and collaborate with the powers behind the colonial state rather than with the state itself. The temptation is greater because now exploitation has a black face. The second delegation is made up of a multiracial group of businessmen who try to entice Kimathi with the lure of material wealth. The white banker emphasizes the opportunities for black elites to profit in the coming postcolonial polity, while the black business man nods his head in silent agreement. The third delegation is made up of three blacks; an African businessman, a politician, and a priest. They also urge Kimathi to confess, describing the earthly and spiritual benefits of collaboration. Ngugi and Micere make it clear that they see a connection between collaborating with colonialism and collaborating with Kenyatta's neocolonial regime.

The *Trial of Dedan Kimathi* makes the connection between colonial and postcolonial (il)legality explicit. This is a motif that extends through Ngugi's work. He depicts the Kenyan State of Emergency not as an exception but rather as the truth of the colonial order—an order and a law based on coercion and not consent. Nevertheless, the Emergency had distinctive characteristics that he exposes in detail. The intensification of violence undermined communal solidarity by starkly opposing individual self-interest and communal good. It tore apart the existing social order and left a polity made up of opportunists, survivors, and resisters—a very fragile basis for the postcolonial order. From Ngugi's perspective, this was by no means an unintended consequence of the Emergency. The British realized that decolonization was inevitable, therefore the Emergency was not really an attempt to prevent Kenyan independence. It was a struggle to plant the roots of the neocolonial order. It did so by destroying its most resolute adversaries, undermining the sources of unity, and ensuring that collaborators would have privileged access to the economic bases of power.

RULE AND EXCEPTION IN THE POSTCOLONIAL POLITY

The demystification of "law and order" is an underappreciated theme that runs throughout Ngugi's novels and plays. His most pointed analysis of the politics of law and exception, however, is found in *Detained* (1981), his prison memoir. The memoir does not describe his experience as a youth during the Emergency but rather his imprisonment by the postcolonial Kenyan government.[34] The connection between the colonial and postcolonial legal system is a central theme in *Detained*. The first scene of the book highlights this connection. A prison warder (warden) asks, "professor . . . why are you not in bed . . . What are you doing?" Ngugi answers, "I am writing to Jomo Kenyatta in his capacity as an ex-detainee."[35] The warder replies that the cases are different because Kenyatta's was a "colonial affair." But Ngugi insists that his own imprisonment is a neocolonial affair and ruefully concludes that Kenyatta learned how to jail Kenyans from the British.

The central argument in *Detained* is the claim that there is a causal link between the colonial culture of fear and the repressive tactics of the independent Kenyan state. In order to make this argument, Ngugi has to refute the view that the Emergency was an exceptional period with little in common with either the pre-Emergency colonial state or the postcolonial government. He provides evidence that the brutal measures employed during the Emergency were not exceptional but rather intensifications of existing practices. Ngugi challenges the view that the Mau Mau uprising and the counterinsurgency strategies of the British were an aberration in an otherwise successful civilizing mission. He argues that the legal order was always guaranteed by the extralegal violence because that was the only way to achieve compliance with an unjust social order.

In *Detained*, Ngugi provides several examples of what he calls the "culture of legalized brutality" in the period before the Emergency. In March 1907, Colonel Ewart Grogan and four associates flogged several Kenyans for carrying a rickshaw incorrectly. Even though the victims had to be hospitalized, the culprits were given a sentence of a week and they were allowed to serve this sentence at home while entertaining guests.[36] In 1919 two British peers beat a Kenyan to death and burned his body. They were found guilty of "a simple hurt" and fined 2,000 shillings. One subsequently became an official charged with dispensing justice to the "natives." Ngugi lists a number of similar examples and concludes:

> Thus all these eruptions of brutality between the introduction of colonial culture in 1895 and its flowering with blood in the 1950s were not aberrations of an otherwise humane Christian culture. No. They were its very essence, its law, its logic, and the Kenyan settler with his sjambok, his dog, his horse, his rickshaw, his sword, his bullet, was the true embodiment of British imperialism.[37]

According to Ngugi, the postindependence ruling class had been socialized in this understanding of law as a means of domination rather than a limit on the power of government. Moreover, they also inherited a set of detention laws, rules, and practices that reinforced this view.[38] Ngugi cites the Native Courts Regulations of 1897, which provided for the preventative detention of any Kenyan likely to commit an offense as well as anyone critical of the government. Any Kenyan deemed to be dangerous to the colonial order could be arrested without trial. The Vagrancy Regulations of 1898 made it possible to detain Africans who were moving about without employment or means of subsistence. The Native Pass Regulations gave the colonial governor the power to control the movement of Kenyans, and the Preservation of Order by Night Regulations of 1901 set up the legal framework for declaring curfews.[39] Detention was widely used not only to prevent any type of political resistance but also to create a large mass of people who could legally be exploited for slave labor. Nor were these restrictions a peculiarity of the British government in Kenya. The Natal Code of Native Law of 1891 (South Africa) was even more draconian, providing that colonial administrators had "absolute power" to supply labor for public works and to move any tribe or portion thereof to any part of the colony.[40]

Many of these provisions were incorporated in the postindependence legal system. Although the notorious Emergency Powers Order of 1939, which provided the legal basis for the State of Emergency in the 1950s, lapsed, some of its key components were incorporated into the Preservation of Public Security Act (1967). According to Ngugi, the repudiation of "emergency" was semantic, not substantive. Given the strong negative associations with the term "emergency," the new Kenyan government chose to justify these provisions in terms of "public security." Nevertheless, many of the illiberal and antidemocratic measures implemented during the Emergency—including detention without trial, executive discretion, and the absence of civil and political liberties—were enshrined in law. Thus for Ngugi, the legacy of the colonial legal system was an authoritarian mode of governance that was adopted with little modification by the postcolonial African elites.

In *Detained* Ngugi also considers the political logic of extralegal detention. He makes two interesting points. First, he reflects on the ritualistic aspects of extralegal detention. Although detainees are hidden from view in unidentified prisons with little access to the legal system, there is nevertheless a visible theatrics of power. The audience for this political theater is the populace, which must be taught to fear the state. As an example, Ngugi notes that he was arrested at his home during the middle of the night. The police arrived in two Land Rovers, one of which had a flashing red and blue light on its roof, as if publicizing the arrest to the community. He was chained and guarded by policemen with machine guns. The armed members of the special services who searched his home were backed up by additional police with long-range rifles. This theatrical show of force was hardly necessary to arrest an intellectual who had no history of violence and would have willingly responded to a summons to appear at the police station. The ritual of fear continued at the gates of the prison: the entire surrounding area was put under curfew so that no one would be able to identify the arriving prisoners. Yet, far from disguising the repressive actions, a rigid curfew at midday actually drew attention to the arrival of new political prisoners. According to Ngugi, the goal is to inculcate a culture of silence and fear that makes the people feel weak and powerless before the state.[41] The world of the detainee is hidden in order to augment inscrutability, but his disappearance is also publicized in order to increase general insecurity. The detainee is hidden insofar as his relatives do not know where he is incarcerated and he himself does not know the nature of his crime or the length of his sentence. At the same time, the goal is to make sure that the population recognizes its own vulnerability. Through inscrutability and dramatic violence, the state comes to seem like a "malevolent, supernatural force."[42]

Ngugi also points out that the symbolic use of detention and torture is a way of exercising power economically. Intellectual and cultural figures are threatening to the government when they have a connection to a mass movement, and it is the mobilization of the people, not the ideas of intellectuals, that the government fears. But it is difficult to arrest an entire community, so the government identifies a few individuals, labels them power-hungry or attention-seeking agitators and punishes them. Ngugi explains,

> Ideally the authorities would like to put the whole community of struggling millions behind barbed-wire, as the British colonial authorities once tried to do with Kenyan people. But this would mean incarcerating labour, the true source of national wealth: what would then be left to loot?[43]

Although Ngugi does not use the language of law and exception, this remark explains why something like the State of Emergency was an exception, albeit one that revealed the logic of the law itself. During normal times, institutions can foster consent and violence that can be used symbolically to ensure compliance; when hegemony breaks down, then the "exceptional" side of law and order—the use of force rather than fear—is necessary.

COMMANDEMENT IN THE POSTCOLONY

Ngugi's autobiographical and literary works deepen our understanding of the challenges involved in founding a new polity out of the rubble of the colonial state; Achille Mbembe addresses this same issue but writes in a different genre. Mbembe is a contemporary historian and political theorist. Born in Cameroon and educated at the Sorbonne, he is the author of several books on colonial and postcolonial Africa. His influential study *On the Postcolony* (2001) defies disciplinary norms by employing a poetic style that combines history, literary analysis, empirical political science, philosophy, and psychoanalysis.[44] Mbembe argues that the political science literature on Africa is based on reductionist assumptions. Furthermore, the dominant concepts such as democracy and civil society emerge out of European historical experience and hide more than they illuminate. According to Mbembe, the more theoretically oriented discipline of postcolonial studies, however, is not much better because it focuses too much on discourse and representation and fails to interrogate the relationship between cultural practices and their material or economic dimensions. *On the Postcolony* provides an alternative mode of analysis that exposes the continuity between specific practices of colonial rationality and their spectral reappearance in postcolonial Africa.

According to Mbembe, colonial sovereignty rested on a specific imaginary of the state, which he calls *commandement*. The main feature of *commandement* (French for 'commandment', 'command', 'authority') was a distinctive combination of law and lawlessness. The essential lawlessness of colonial rule was rooted in the act of founding itself: violent conquest. This meant that colonial rule based its legitimacy on force rather than on consent, mutual benefit, or tradition. It also maintained its authority through a system of coercion supplemented by arbitrary rule.

The story of the foundation of the colonial polity through conquest bears little resemblance to the liberal myth of the social contract.[45] According to social contract theory, rational individuals voluntarily recognize the need to cede some of their natural liberty in order to create a sovereign authority capable of protecting their rights or their interests. Of course, Hobbes recognized that polities were often founded through conquest ("sovereignty by acquisition") rather than social contract ("sovereignty by institution"), yet he still insisted that they were based on consent because the conquered chose submission over death.[46] In the *Leviathan*, Hobbes makes it clear that the social contract is not supposed to be read as conjectural history but rather as a thought experiment that explains why it is rational to submit to existing political authority. But the rhetoric of equality, consent, and mutual benefit in social contract theory ("sovereignty by institution") serves to mystify the enduring inequalities that are introduced through conquest ("sovereignty by acquisition"). Conquest is the process whereby the colonial power uses its military superiority to conquer a weaker society and exploit the native people and resources for its own benefit. It defines its own practices, economic organization, religion, and system of government as "civilization." It calls the culture and practices of the conquered society "barbarous." From the point of view of "civilization," barbarians will benefit from adopting the values and way of life of the conqueror, but due to their irrationality and incapacity, they will not choose it. The underlying premise is the logic of *commandement*: the assumption that the native peoples are not capable of consent and therefore must be compelled.

Even after the end of armed resistance to conquest, the colonial polity was still structured on the model of warfare rather than consent and civil society. Native peoples were frequently governed by martial law or an equally draconian native code, while European colonists were granted representative institutions and civil liberties.[47] Mbembe concludes that in both theory and practice, the *commandement* was the exact opposite of the liberal model of deliberative democracy.[48] In the colonial state, there was no room for debate or discussion, no system of checks and balances, and no institutions designed to limit the government's power over the native people.[49]

Despite its authoritarian character, the colonial project was frequently justified as a civilizing mission that brought the rule of law to peoples governed by brutal despots. How is this possible? Part of the answer has to do with the dual nature of the concept of *Recht*, a German term that is translated as right, justice, or law. Right can refer both to the sovereign's right to command and the individual's right to protection from the power of the state. According to social contract theory, these two dimensions are related.[50] The right of sovereignty is a consequence of the individual's natural right to freedom. Mbembe notes that the opposite is true in the colonial context; the supreme right of the colonial state—its monopoly on violence—is simultaneously the supreme denial of right.[51] Law was defined as the practices necessary to maintain an order controlled by and for the European colonists. This law was both the means and the end of colonialism.

The *régime d'exception* was rationalized as a way to bring about discipline and obedience, which were considered necessary preconditions for the rule of law.[52] According to the logic of colonialism, the rule of law had to be suspended in order to bring about the type of social order that made law possible. This argument is a radicalization of the position held by John Stuart Mill, who insisted that representative institutions were only possible when a people achieved a degree of civilization, namely economic development and complex social organization. In order to achieve this level of economic and social development, a people must become accustomed to obedience and discipline, which usually required a period of despotic government. According to Mill, despotism could foster democracy and force could facilitate freedom. But Mill himself did not go so far as to conclude that a *régime d'exception* could bring about the rule of law. In fact, he insisted on just the opposite view.[53] Mill argued passionately and unsuccessfully that a colonial government that failed to adhere to the rule of law would not build civilization abroad and would undermine law at home. Despotism might be necessary to advance civilization, but it must be must be somehow limited by law in order to ensure that it does not become tyrannical, selfish, and arbitrary because such a government would not advance the capacities and interests of the subject people.

Despite (or perhaps because of) Mill's career as a bureaucrat in the British East India Company, he misunderstood the logic of colonial government. He believed that colonialism could be founded on the rule of law and he failed to recognize that the colonial state was inevitably based on *commandement*. According to Mbembe, one of the defining characteristics of *commandement* was "the lack of distinction between ruling and civilizing."[54] Since obedience was taken to advance civilization, obedience became both an end and means. Performing rituals of obedience became part of the theatrics of colonial power, and any reluctance to play the assigned role was met with severe punishment. From the perspective of the colonizers, this punishment, no matter how disproportionate and brutal, advanced civilization and therefore could not really be contrary to law or morality. The colonists' demand for ritualistic obedience also had material benefits, and the underlying motive for colonialism—as a way to provide resources for the metropole (the parent state of the colony) and create privileged economic opportunities for the European population—was still economic. In order to reap these benefits, the colonists had to compel the native population to either extract natural resources from mines or grow cash crops on plantations for export. In the colonial imaginary, however, this system of forced labor was not figured as exploitation because labor was a means to inculcate the virtues of self-restraint, perseverance, and productivity.

In *On the Postcolony*, Mbembe identifies *commandement* as the distinctive practice of colonial sovereignty. Yet he also recognizes that there are a number of similarities between colonial and feudal sovereignty. Mbembe notes, "One characteristic of *commandement* in the colonies was the confusion between the public and the private; the agents of the *commandement* could, at any moment, usurp the law and, in the name of the state, exercise it for purely private ends."[55] The most extreme examples are found in the slave societies of the Caribbean; as in feudalism, these slave societies also granted juridical power to patriarchs and elided the lines between personal service and legal obligation. In fact, the early phases of colonialism were often organized on feudal principles. From the Spanish *encomienda* labor system to the British East India Company, European sovereigns regularly granted private individuals or companies the right to raise taxes and armies, fight wars, compel labor, and settle disputes in the colonies.

Is *commandement* simply another way of describing the patriarchal government of the ancien régime? Not really. There are also a number of differences between the ancien régime and the colonial polity. Although both are based on a strong distinction between ruler and subject, in most colonial polities this was marked by racial and cultural difference. And, unlike feudal society, colonial society lacked a shared language, religion, and history, so there were no shared norms to help limit the despotic exercise of power. Even in places where the indigenous people gradually adopted the colonizers' language or religion, the colonizers were deeply attached to a social order based on their own superiority (and the economic benefits attached to a caste society) and the racial distinctions proved very stable. Two other important differences between the old regime and the colonial polity have to do with the capacity of the state and the complexity of the economy. Feudal lords may have exercised juridical power over their subjects, but they could not necessarily count on a very strong state to help them exercise domination. By the zenith of colonialism in the late nineteenth century, however, European powers wielded very sophisticated state apparatuses that ensured control over their empire. Furthermore, colonial relations of reproduction were also embedded in a global capitalist economy.

According to Mbembe, *commandement* was a "*régime d'exception*," in other words, a polity that was not governed by the common law. The term *régime d'exception*, however, does not imply that the despotic character of colonial government was the exception rather than the rule. Perhaps a better term would be the English concept of martial law, which captures the way that the departure from the common law or civil code could itself become codified. The colonial *régime d'exception* diverged from liberal norms in at least two different ways. First, as indicated above, colonialism was often structured by royal charters that created private governments with elaborate privileges and immunities. King Leopold II's privately owned Congo Free State is the most notorious example.[56] Second, even in colonies that were directly governed by European states there was no sense that a single law applied equally to all people residing in the same territory. Most colonies had a differential system of law distinguishing the rights and duties required of Europeans and natives. In some cases different legal status attached directly to persons (citizens versus subjects). In other cases, the law classified natives as members of national, tribal, or religious groups and disputes between members of the same group were governed by customary law. Of course, disputes between settlers and natives were still decided by colonial courts composed exclusively of settlers. Some colonies relied on territorial distinctions, providing for democratic government in European areas and martial law in native areas.[57] These territorial distinctions were often reinforced by a system of pass controls and legal segregation to ensure that natives could not live in European areas.

The concept of *commandement* is not simply a reformulation of familiar criticisms of colonialism. Mbembe is concerned with the way in which *commandement*, with its distinctive political logic and supporting practices, came to structure the postcolonial polity. Mbembe challenges the conventional wisdom that the postcolonial potentate (the figure that political scientists often call the patrimonial leader) is the atavistic resurgence of precolonial tribal authority. He emphasizes the underlying continuity between the colonial and postcolonial forms of government. He identifies "the étatisation of society, the socialization of state power, and the privatization of public prerogatives" as the three key dimensions of "postcolonial African authoritarianisms."[58] Each of these hybrid formations has roots in the fundamental confusion between public and private that was characteristic of the structure of colonial governance. Similarly, many postcolonial regimes have also used force against their own citizens, violated individuals' civil rights, and adopted repressive "emergency measures." In other words, they have jealously protected their patrimony, government by *commandement*.

CONCLUSION

In some ways, the world of *commandement* is a familiar one. The news regularly reports stories of postcolonial regimes that are torn apart by violence, ruled despotically, or crippled by corruption. A critic might argue that the analysis presented in this chapter amounts to a sophisticated articulation of the conventional wisdom: colonialism was bad but independence, in many cases, has been worse. We believe that this objection is misguided. It rests on a misleading picture of colonialism as relatively benign, and this depiction must still be challenged. However, the goal of this book is not primarily to assess either colonial or postcolonial regimes in terms of good and bad but rather to illuminate the connection between them so that we can recognize colonialism as a productive rather than simply a repressive exercise of power.[59] Ngugi's literary works show that the people who were trying to rebuild Kenya were themselves formed by their experiences during the Emergency. He dramatizes the psychological and micropolitical transformations wrought by the Emergency and their consequences for the postcolonial state.

It is this connection that is usually overlooked when the politics of postcolonial states are discussed in the mass media. For example, from 2000 to 2008 there was extensive media coverage of Zimbabwe, which focused on land occupations and featured vivid accounts of assaults against white farmers. While the stories condemned the violence and the violation of property rights, there was little reflection on the injustice of existing land ownership patterns. After thirty years of voluntary sales and government-sponsored land redistribution, the small white minority (less than one percent of the population) still owned 50 percent of all arable farm land in Zimbabwe.[60] The violence of colonialism and the injustice of the system that it created are repressed in these depictions of postcolonial pathology. The authors discussed in this chapter remind us of the need to link the stories of colonialism and postcolonialism back together.

The goal of this chapter, however, is not simply to draw attention to the brutality of colonialism but rather to theorize the relationship between law and exception in light of this history. The state of exception was not really an exception because it created the conditions that made rule possible. This position differs markedly from the liberal view of the state of exception, which has typically focused on the legitimacy of the *exception* without questioning the legitimacy of the underlying rule.

John Stuart Mill's critique of martial law is emblematic of the liberal position. His views on law and exception were developed in response to events that took place in Jamaica in 1865. After a small riot that resulted in several deaths, Edward John Eyre, the governor general, declared martial law and thousands of black Jamaicans were killed, arrested, or beaten by British soldiers. Even after the unrest was over, martial law was not abolished for several weeks and during that period, William Gordon, a mulatto member of parliament and critic of Eyre, was executed. Eyre's defenders argued that martial law was necessary to maintain order in a colony where poor blacks vastly outnumbered privileged whites. Mill, on the other hand, insisted that the rule of law must apply equally to black and white, colonizer and colonized. According to Mill, once the security of the state had been ensured, there was no reason to abrogate rights or create a zone devoid of law. Public opinion polarized into two camps: the majority supported the conservative/realist view that colonialism required brutal measures to supplement normal forms of discipline, and the minority supported the liberal view that colonialism could be beneficial but must adhere to moral and legal norms in order to fulfill this promise.[61] Ngugi articulated a third alternative, one that was largely absent from the parliamentary debates about martial law in Jamaica. He argued that the need for "exceptional" measures was symptomatic of the basic injustice in the distribution of land, power, and freedom that was endemic to the structure of the colonial state.

Ngugi and Mbeme provide thoughtful diagnostics, but what cure, if any, do they point toward? It is tempting to conclude something like the following: despite its pretenses, the colonial state was never liberal, which made it very difficult to create a liberal postcolonial state. The solution, then, is more liberalism. From this perspective, too much postcolonial critique could even be harmful if the effect is to undermine confidence in universal values such as the rule of law and rights. This "Millian" conclusion is tempting but ultimately misguided because it rests on a flawed assumption about the relationship between law and exception.

Legal scholars have differed about the theoretical and political significance of the state of exception. For some scholars, the state of exception is a legitimate part of positive law because it is based on necessity, which is itself a fundamental source of law. Similar to the individual's claim of self-defense in criminal law, the polity has a right to self-defense when its sovereignty is threatened; according to this position, exercising this right might involve a technical violation of existing statutes but does so in the name of upholding the juridical order. The alternative approach, which was explored most thoroughly by Carl Schmitt in his books *Political Theology* and *Dictatorship*, emphasizes that declaring the state of exception is the prerogative of the sovereign and is therefore essentially extrajuridical. For Schmitt, the state of exception is a violation of law that expresses the more fundamental logic of politics itself. Following Derrida, Giorgio Agamben calls this force-of-law.[62] The state of exception is disturbing because it reveals the force-of-law, the remainder that becomes visible when the application of the norm, and even the norm itself, are suspended.[63]

At this point it should be clear why many postcolonial theorists are deeply skeptical of the liberal call for more vigorous enforcement of the rule of law as a means of combating cruelties and excesses carried out under emergency powers. They see the emergency powers as symptomatic, a reminder of the force that usually masquerades as law. From this perspective, putting the mask on more securely accomplishes very little. The only solution is to try to confront and dismantle the power that is expressed in both the law and the exception. This argument is reminiscent of Marx's famous critique of rights in *On the Jewish Question*. For Ngugi, the force that is revealed during the Emergency and endures in the postcolonial state is not an intrinsic characteristic of sovereignty but rather a consequence of economic inequality and domination.[64] The solution is more radical resistance rather than stricter adherence to law.

This is a powerful argument, but there is also another approach, one that works within the law in order to reconfigure the relationship between law and justice. This is the approach pursued in post-apartheid South Africa where the foundational narrative was based on reconciliation rather than retribution, the future rather than the past. Yet the new polity still had to deal with the legacies of brutal repression, disenfranchisement, and economic exploitation. The South African Constitution is considered a ground-breaking document because of its inclusion of social as well as civil and political rights. The founding document specified that the government has the responsibility to ensure that the basic needs of all citizens (food, housing, health care, water) are met. In the *Grootboom* decision (2000), the Constitutional Court of South Africa made it clear that the government cannot simply ignore these responsibilities.[65] In a sense, these constitutional provisions bring the problem of economic inequality inside the law rather than externalizing it. It remains to be seen how much this can shift the relationship between law, power, and privilege.

Grounds of Resistance

Land as Revolutionary Foundation

They want to take our land so that our feet have nothing to stand on.
—Subcomandante Insurgente Marcos

The sudden rise in food prices in 2007 and 2008 created new interest in farmland in countries and investors around the world. Shortages of food, and the potential for worse to come, combined with the rapid development of biofuels, means that leasing land may be one of the more successful investment strategies of the future. Countries that have a shortage of arable land are interested in providing food security for their inhabitants and have started leasing what appears as abundant, and available, territory in Africa. Some commentators have called this the second land grab in Africa, a reprise of the 1884 Berlin Conference (also known as the Congo or West Africa Conference) that divided African territory among European powers. It is such a significant trend that the United Nations Food and Agricultural Organization (FOA) sponsored a report on the growing instances of land lease deals on the African continent that found that more than one million acres of African land have been leased by different countries and private organizations between 2005 and 2009.[1] Jacques Diouf, the director-general of the FOA, warned that this trend runs the risk of "creating a neo-colonial pact for the provision of non-value added raw materials in the producing countries."[2]

Adding to the perception that this is a revival of colonial extraction, the stated rationale behind the deals is reminiscent of the "empty lands" hypothesis that blessed the "doctrine of discovery" that was used to legally justify the taking of lands during the Age of Discovery. The head of Daewoo, a South

Korean conglomerate, explained to the *Financial Times* upon the announcement that his company had acquired the right to use 44 percent of Madagascar's arable farmland to produce corn and palm oil entirely for export, that this land was "totally undeveloped" and "had been left untouched."[3] In fact the secrecy surrounding it, the displacement of population and farmers (Daewoo appears to have been misinformed about the emptiness of the land in question), and the outrageously poor terms of the land deal seem to have played a central role in galvanizing popular support for the coup d'état that occurred in March 2009.[4] The new president's first announcement was a cancelation of the Daewoo deal: "Madagascar's land is neither for sale nor for rent."[5] While this failed deal was the largest proposed land acquisition in terms of area, the general trend continues apace, and it demonstrates that the land and its bounty is emerging as one of the central political issues of the twenty-first century.

Land does not seem to find its way into political theory very frequently. Or rather, it makes brief appearances before being transformed into a metaphor for the nation and no longer appears as land—the dirt beneath our feet. Most famously, in John Locke's *Second Treatise of Government*, land is transformed into private property through labor and becomes a commodity that can be bought or sold. Sovereignty is dependent upon and bounded by territory, but the relationship is actually tautological; territory is land already transformed into territory by the assertion of sovereignty. Henri Lefebvre's production of space supersedes a conception of land per se. And Raymond Williams's "country" exists as a cultural construction that is opposed to the city, and, as he emphasizes most emphatically, is not to be mistaken for the land itself.[6] Every political order depends upon a relationship to inhabitable space; there must be ground beneath our feet. So it is certainly one of the most fundamental aspects of political order to define and transform that dirt underneath our feet into city, property, territory, nation, landscape, farm, or even "wilderness," to name but a few of the options.

This chapter is about the dirt beneath our feet and how it has played a central role in colonialism, decolonization, postcolonial politics, and resistance to globalization. Controlling land was a basic goal and mechanism of colonialism; this is apparent in the term itself, which derives from the Latin word *colere* meaning to cultivate, inhabit, guard. Reflecting upon these examples in the first paragraph, we can start to see that one of the most momentous aspects of colonialism was its application of categories for sorting land all over the globe. As Carl Schmitt writes in *The* Nomos *of the Earth*, "No sooner had the contours of the earth emerged as a real globe—not just sensed as myth, but apprehensible as fact and measurable as space—then there arose a wholly new and hitherto unimaginable problem; the spatial ordering of the earth."[7] Though in recent years colonization has often been viewed through the lens of racial, sexual, and nationalist politics, the history of colonization can also be read as the hegemonic application of conceptions of property, territory and sovereignty. European powers made maps, drew boundaries, decided which spaces were "empty" and which were already occupied, introduced different forms of agriculture, and even imposed cultural conceptions of how views and landscapes should be perceived.[8] Since colonization transformed land through various military, legal, representational, and political means, it follows that one aspect of *de*colonization is about challenging these categories and transformations.

In this chapter, we examine two theorists for whom land plays a central role in imagining a postcolonial world and in developing the means for asserting self-determination. Both Amílcar Cabral and Subcomandante Marcos (also known as Subcomandante Insurgente Marcos), the black-masked leader of the Zapatista Army of National Liberation (EZLN) in Mexico, rejected the idea that land is a commodity that can legitimately be sold to the highest bidder irrespective of the needs of the population. They advance an argument that is both normative and political. They claim that the system of land tenure must be designed in order to support the resident population and not primarily to extract surplus for the benefit of others. This also entails an argument in favor of self-determination and decentralization, since a community must decide collectively how to ensure this goal is met. Land reform is a method of repudiating one of the most central elements of colonial administration, but it is often stymied because of conflicting interests and ideas about property rights, efficiency, productivity, community, and history.

Postcolonial theorists have invoked the land in different ways. Land tenure systems such as communal property play a key role in sustaining cultural practices and identity. A number of contemporary indigenous theorists have also argued that the land is imbued with intrinsic value and should not be seen simply as a commodity to be exploited. For example, the native (First Nations) Canadian John Borrows explained, "Our loyalties, allegiance, and affection are related to the land. The water, wind, sun, and stars are part of the federation."[9] This formulation is striking because it suggests a relationship with the land that is very different from ownership. Instead of a purely instrumental relationship, it evokes an attitude of respect and responsibility. This metaphysical approach to the land may to some degree be an invented tradition, but if so, it is no different from any other founding narrative. It is an important and intriguing approach, though it is outside the scope of this chapter. Instead, we focus on postcolonial writers who have developed a materialist critique of economic exploitation in agrarian societies, a critique that highlights the importance of these theories for addressing persistent economic inequalities.

It is important to remember that the special relationship between indigenous groups and their land has not always been a ground of resistance to colonialism; more frequently it has been one of the instruments of colonialism that provided the means for legal expropriation of territory. Arguing that natives had a "different" relationship to the land was the basis of the concept of aboriginal title, best known as the device making it possible for governments to take land from indigenous groups. Aboriginal title was a right that could only be extinguished, not transferred; it asserted that inhabiting the land was not the same as owning it.[10] Therefore, it was possible for conquering powers to claim exclusive rights to extinguish aboriginal title.[11] In this way, the "special relationship" between population and territory has been used to disempower and displace tribes around the globe. One could argue that continuing to base claims upon this special relationship is particularly risky.

Yet there seem to be some rewards for focusing upon the land as a site of political identity and meaning. Interestingly, the land provides the basis for an economic critique of colonialism and globalization outside of class-based Marxian analysis. The land is a link to a history of habitation that precedes colonization, and is an integral aspect of the structure of self-determination. These two facts mean that the land can provide a postcolonial foundational claim of the sort described in Chapter 1, "Postcolonial Political Theory and the Problem of Foundations." Here, we explore these arguments about the land in depth and argue that they have particular strength in dealing with the economic legacies of colonialism and globalization.

LAND AND EUROPEAN POLITICAL THEORY

Reviewing recent literature about colonialism and political thought, one finds fascinating accounts of how the seizure of territory and the claims of conquest were sorted out according to the legal and political categories of the time. James Tully has explored how John Locke's writings were deeply invested in encompassing the experience of colonialism in the Carolina territories and elsewhere.[12] Richard Tuck, in *The Rights of War and Peace*, also established the lineage of empire from More's *Utopia* through the work of Grotius and then Locke, explaining how classical liberal political thought accommodated and explained the realities of colonialism.

One of the most striking aspects of much of modern European political thought is that it displays a decidedly abstract conception of the conditions of founding, as exemplified by the state of nature. This tradition continues all the way to John Rawls's original position, a position that could never possibly exist in actual space. The grounds of the liberal social contract seem never to have hit any dirt at all. We should not continue to replicate this dynamic, and in fact, thinking about land as the grounds of a polity may yield different insights into the relationship between territory and political order.

Political theorists, however, are trained to think in terms of abstraction and have little vocabulary to understand land. This is the case for a number of different reasons, the most obvious being that political theorists are simply not geographers; we think primarily about concepts and their way of ordering the physical world, not the reverse, the way the physical world orders our concepts. But the primary reason for our dearth of vocabulary is that neither the structure of classical liberal political theory nor the categories of the Marxist tradition are conducive to ideas about land.

Modern European political thought tracks the gradual decline of feudal property with its overlapping rights, responsibilities, and restrictions toward a simplified paradigm: the abstract space of the social contract. The space in which sovereignty can be established falls into three different categories: uninhabited territory or *terra nullis*, land held in common, or private property. Clearly, the practices of modern liberal democratic states favor private property above the other two options. Less well considered is the fact both processes of colonization and processes of decolonization involved a struggle over the appropriate designation of and relationship between the three categories of land. However, James Tully has led the way by developing an analysis of territory as the central element of colonization in "The Struggles of Indigenous Peoples for and of Freedom."

> The essence of internal colonization, therefore, is not the appropriation of labour (as in slavery), for this has been peripheral, or depopulation (genocide), for indigenous populations have increased threefold in this century, or even the appropriation of self-government (usurpation), for at different times indigenous peoples have been permitted to govern themselves within the colonial system (as in the early treaty system and perhaps again today). Rather the ground of the relation is the appropriation of the land, resources, and jurisdiction of the indigenous peoples, not only for the sake of resettlement and exploitation (which is also true in external colonization), but for the territorial foundations of the dominant society itself.[13]

Tully has developed his work by looking at internal colonialism, but his argument is equally true of external colonization. In both cases, the appropriation of the land, its jurisdiction and its productive capacities are central. One version may attempt to extinguish previous claims more absolutely, but in both cases the land is no longer controlled by its previous occupants.

In her work on the Settler Contract, Carole Pateman has written that expansion was frequently justified based upon the principle of *terra nullius* or empty territory.[14] The justification for conquest was, and still is, explained by the principle that the territory was uninhabited, or, more accurately, unused. Claims of indigenous groups to their status as first nations are designed to repudiate the assumptions of vacancy. Asserting previous occupancy is a way of countering the justificatory claims of European political thought.

In the Americas, the European settlers acknowledged that the land was not really vacant, but it appeared underutilized from the perspective of European ideas about productivity and efficiency. As Carole Pateman points out, *terra nullius* could be understood as the absence of private property or the absence of sovereignty, but the former was particularly influential in the Americas. Drawing on the ideas of Grotius and Locke, settlers emphasized "the right of husbandry"; they argued that indigenous lands were empty insofar as they were not intensively cultivated to maximize agricultural productivity. There has been an extensive secondary literature on Locke's writings on colonialism so this argument is now quite familiar. Private property is created and justified through labor, therefore legitimate title to land results from the labor of improving the land through cultivation. According to Locke's theory, common property that is used for hunting and gathering belongs to no one and may legitimately be appropriated by "the industrious and the rational," in other words, the colonists in the New World. The problem with this principle is that it would have revolutionary implications if applied to the large estates of Europe. As Roger Williams (the Puritan leader who founded the colony of Rhode Island) pointed out, "Noble men in England possessed great Parkes, and the King, great Forrests in England onely for their game." According to Locke, the right to appropriate common property only applied to places that were still in the state of nature. Lands left in common by compact are jointly owned and not *terra nullius*. Thus the doctrine of *terra nullius* becomes tautological; it purports to justify colonialism but actually relies on an under-theorized assertion of European sovereignty or, more precisely, on its absence. This is one reason why many theorists see the claims of indigenous politics creating an irresolvable tension for the liberal political model, but this is not our primary concern here.[15] Instead, we are interested in another aspect of Locke's theory, his claim that initially, private property (the appropriation of the bounty of the earth and the land itself) was limited to that which fulfilled basic human needs. It is this idea that was abandoned by Locke but reasserted by the theorists of decolonization.

Duncan Ivison, Paul Patton, and Will Sanders ask in the introduction to their *Political Theory and the Rights of Indigenous Peoples*, "[W]hat resources exist in political theory for thinking differently about these relations and about the possibility of 'decolonising' relations between indigenous and non-indigenous peoples?"[16] The recognition of the rights of indigenous groups may well provide for more security, stability, and prosperity for these groups in the future. But decolonizing the relationship would also entail moving beyond the established terms of classical liberal political thought. For instance, recognizing rights to land is an improvement over denying them, but rights are still taken as the central aspect of the debate. It is impossible to pretend that colonialism never happened, and to discard all appeal to rights would be a foolhardy political statement.

However, political theorists can learn by examining movements that have specifically repudiated both the practices of colonialism and the categories of classical liberalism. This chapter presents two thinkers, Amílcar Cabral and Subcomandante Marcos, who take the land as a measure of self-determination, emphasizing the proper relationship between a population and the land it inhabits. These theorists offer a way of thinking about the land that differs from the framework of rights and property.

They also offer a corrective to the Marxist tradition, which views the intersection of economics and political change through class mobilization. Because Marxism so deeply inflects political theories of revolution, revolutions of decolonization continue to baffle many leftist political theorists. The political and economic structures of colonial extraction thwarted the class formation that often accompanied the development of market production, therefore revolutions of decolonizations could not, and did not, follow the Marxist script. In his introduction to *Revolution and the Making of the Modern World*, Göran Therborn sorts through the incongruities of revolutionary theory and anticolonial history. "Anti-colonial armed struggles for liberation may often refer to themselves as revolutions. But set against a foreign enemy and fighting for national independence, they are very different, in their alignments and their consequences, from the European kind of revolutions."[17] The fact that they do not follow identifiable trends leads this theorist to conclude that perhaps they weren't as momentous as European revolutions.

> By way of conclusion, it is fair to say that revolution made European modernity. Revolution set the course of the Americas, though the significance of revolution to modernity in Latin America is, at least, ambiguous. But it did not make modern Asia and modern Africa. Revolution turns out to be a surprisingly Eurocentric concept.[18]

This conclusion reflects more the biases of our paradigms than the importance of anticolonial revolutions. Leftists look for class-based revolutions, and, more generally, we associate revolutions with a particular form of modernity and progress. In the dominant conceptual paradigms provided by class analysis, revolutions move us away from the land, not toward it. But this is based on the assumption that all history proceeds according to the path set by European history.

Postcolonial Marxist theorists like José Mariátegui, however, insisted that this was not the case. Mariátegui argued that the land tenure system imposed by the Spanish conquistadores was a form of feudalism that undermined economic development and halted historical progress. This view of colonialism was a departure from Marx's notorious analysis of the British in India. Marx argued that the British raj would foster economic development because it broke up the political structures of "oriental despotism" and introduced technological innovations. Drawing on a detailed analysis of his native Peru, Mariátegui reached the opposite conclusion. He condemned colonialism from a purely economic perspective: it had failed to create a productive economy. To emphasize the basic feudal structure of colonialism, he naturally looked at land distribution policies, agrarian labor, and agrarian yield. What he found was that smaller, communal units of production that were held in common by Indians were seized and liquidated into much larger tracts of property. These large landowners then held the majority of political influence, and, like feudal lords in Western Europe, were invariably backward-looking. "The love of adventure, the drive to create, and the organizing ability that characterize the authentic capitalist are almost unknown in Peru."[19]

Mariátegui traces all of the dysfunctions of Peru back to the distribution of land. "The land tenure system determines the political and administrative system of the nation. The agrarian problem, which the republic has not been able to solve, dominates all problems. Democratic and liberal institutions cannot flourish or operate in a semi-feudal economy."[20] This is a fundamentally Marxist argument: base determines superstructure. Because the land is not productive, it does not produce a surplus of wealth, and a monopoly on power remains in the hands of very few individuals. A modern state cannot be grafted onto feudal roots; the attempt to modernize the educational system is one example that Mariátegui develops in order to show how resistant neo-colonial structures of power are to reform.

Marx notoriously found rural environments and peasants on the whole idiotic and counterrevolutionary. In response to this dismissal, postcolonial theorists attempt to reconfigure Marxist orientations toward revolution, production, and indigenousness. In the work of Amílcar Cabral you see a sober accounting of the effects of colonization that is based in a view of colonization as a seizure of space and land, not only the tools of self-definition but the means of production. Because his critique of colonization is framed by the impact upon the productive capacities of the land, his approach toward dismantling the effects of colonization is similarly geared toward restructuring land use and production capacity. In doing so, Cabral provides a linkage between colonial critique and postcolonial power. By focusing on the economic substance of colonial history, he develops plans for the economic substance of his country's liberation.

What emerges is the possibility for the land to provide a materialist basis for revolutionary struggle outside of the Marxist paradigms of class struggle, which, after all, had been complicated by the realities of colonization. It would be overly simplistic to say, as Fanon claimed, "You are rich because you are white, you are white because you are rich."[21] If this were true, then the economic and racial aspects of colonization could be collapsed into the same problem. But class struggle could not be outlined on purely racial grounds and provide a link to the Marxist revolutionary tradition because there were native groups who also profited from the economic structures of colonization. What hindsight reveals is that frequently revolutions of decolonization simply shifted more formal power to this group of indigenous elites, and that the same dynamic of economic exploitation remained. A revolution of decolonization that would create equality would require this group to commit "suicide" as a class, as Cabral noted. The clear problem is how to have a revolution of decolonization that fundamentally restructures the economic system put into place by colonization. Nationalist movements would keep indigenous elites in power. To enact a revolution of decolonization that would change the economic structure of the former colony would require an entirely different strategy, one rooted in the land.

Land struggles are central for understanding the structure of postcolonial politics as well as antiglobalization politics in Mexico. For instance, recently Mahmood Mamdani has argued that westerners do not understand the support that President Robert Mugabe has in Zimbabwe. From our perspective he is a corrupt dictator. But he also oversaw the largest redistribution of land in southern Africa since Zimbabwe's (formerly Rhodesia's) independence, and he is credited with finally dismantling the economic structure of colonialism.[22] To develop a better understanding of how important the land is for the politics of decolonization and postcolonialism, then, we must look to the leaders who articulated these ideas.

CABRAL: LAND, STRUGGLE, AND INDEPENDENCE

The difference between the strategies for reconstructing the past into a revolutionary present based upon cultural models such as negritude, and the strategies for its reconstruction based upon revolutionary struggle and economics, is captured by a proverb quoted by Amílcar Cabral: "When your hut is burning, it is no use beating the tom-tom." This is not to say that Cabral was not concerned with the culture that colonialism had wrought, but rather that he believed action to change the environment was the only way to provide a definitive break with the patterns of colonialism and subordination.

Amílcar Cabral and Frantz Fanon have been grouped together as postcolonial thinkers because of their common endorsement of revolutionary violence.[23] Fanon believed violence allows the previously colonized person to begin to be an agent instead of object or victim in her history. Cabral endorsed the use of violence, not as a cleansing sacrifice or shift in identity, but as a way of interrupting the progression of history in a given space. There are significant differences between Cabral and Fanon that suggest that it is not so much their position on violence that should characterize their thought as it is their conception of political action. Fanon believed revolution meant restructuring the subjectivity of the colonized population. Like many other postcolonial thinkers, he wanted a revolution to create individual and collective liberation, not merely a regime change. Cabral can be considered as either more or less ambitious in his goal: he believed in revolution in order to free the land and its inhabitants from external control. Rather than focusing on the restructuring of subjectivity, he wanted objective, external means to provide the opportunity to reshape the economy and politics of the colonized region. The influence of Marxism makes him more concerned with historical structures as they constrain and inspire human action.

Therefore, he did not place as much importance in revolutionary subjectivity as he did in a larger historical progression of production and politics that would bring change. Ultimately, it isn't the means of struggle that is central to Cabral's revolutionary theory, but rather the mode of analysis that outlines the necessity for struggle and defines its goals. Cabral's theory of territory or land provides the logic for revolution and the means to measure a revolution's success. His foundational narrative is that a people and its territory must support one another; this insight is the source of political unity, the inspiration for revolt, and the central principle of self-determination.

Amílcar Cabral, a mulatto who was one of the more privileged subjects of the Portuguese colonial system, was born in Guinea and then moved with his family to Cape Verde for his childhood. He received his education first from his parents (his father was a schoolteacher) and then at various Catholic schools in Cape Verde, where he suffered through an eight-year-long drought that killed thousands of Cape Verdeans, exposing the fragility of the island country's economic system. In 1945 Cabral obtained a scholarship to study agricultural science in Lisbon, and there he became involved in student antifascist organizations and studied Marxian thought, though he deliberately chose not to affiliate himself with any socialist party. Following the abrupt death of his father toward the end of his advanced studies in Lisbon, he returned to Guinea and took up a position in the Portuguese agriculture and forestry services. His job provided the foundation for his later revolutionary activity: he spent fifteen years surveying and studying the land, geography, and agricultural production of Guinea, Cape Verde, and Angola. In the most specific sense, he knew his territory, the actual ground under his feet, and territory was the guiding principle of his theoretical system of culture, history, and revolution.

In "The Weapon of Theory," his most often-cited speech (given before the first Tricontinental Conference of the Peoples of Asia, Africa and Latin America in Havana in 1966), Cabral offers a theory of historical development that is clearly influenced by Marxian thought, but takes the relationship between a land and population as the most significant element of historical progression, rather than the history of class struggle. He points out that seeing history as class struggle has the effect of erasing the history of the colonized country because, before imperialism, there had been no fully developed class structure. His experience surveying the territories of Guinea, Cape Verde, and Angola also led him to the observation that there were large sections of the population that had had little or even no exposure to either the colonizers or their culture: instead, the chiefs of these indigenous populations kept their traditional social, cultural, and political structure intact and served as the link between the natives and the imperial powers. As class structure had not been significantly introduced into these populations, Cabral points out, the Marxian version of history would mean that all of these groups would be existing "outside history, or that they have no history."[24] Furthermore, Cabral asserts, Marx's theory of history proposes that the incorporation of African countries into imperialism is what brings them into the course of history.

Finding Marxian assertions untenable, Cabral offers his own theory of history, based upon the land and different modes of production. He claims that history has three different stages: the first is characterized by a low level of productive forces, whereby "man's mastery over nature" is tenuous and primary activities include hunting, fishing, and foraging. The second is an increase in man's productive capacities over the land: an agrarian society. Here the development of classes occurs, as does privatization of property and the development of the state. The last phase is an advance of these productive capacities that allows the renunciation of private property, elimination of the classes and the return of the social and political structure to horizontal development.[25]

Clearly these phases are influenced by Marx's vision of history, but the theory allows Cabral to make an important adjustment to the predominant theories of imperialism and history. Colonialism does not advance the progression of history by introducing class structures into Africa. Instead, Cabral points out, colonialism actually brought historical development to a halt. By removing the surplus value, supplanting the development of an indigenous state, and preventing the development of private property owned by the indigenous class structure, colonization thwarted the natural progression of history through the agrarian phase. Cabral declares that the essential characteristic of imperialist domination is a "denial of the historical process of the dominated people, by means of violent usurpation of the freedom of the process of development of the national productive forces."[26] Cabral uses his idea of history to reframe the imperialist past and recapture the history of people that is denied by the Portuguese and by communist theories. If imperialism stops history in the colonies, the national struggle must be aimed at starting it again: "The national liberation of a people is the regaining of the historical personality of that people, it is their return to history through the destruction of the imperialist domination to which they were subjected." Because the process of history was ground to a halt through the violent intervention of the imperialist power, national liberation requires a similar kind of intervention. "The important thing is to decide what forms of violence have to be used by the national liberation forces, in order not only to answer the violence of imperialism but also to ensure, through the struggle, the final victory of their cause, that is true national independence."[27]

One of the merits of Cabral's theory of history and liberation is that it includes an analysis of neocolonialism: here the comparatively late struggle for independence from the Portuguese empire enabled him to see that political independence did not necessarily achieve economic self-determination. For Cabral, the measure of true national liberation is to be found in control over the land. Are the processes of production and sustenance being governed by the interests of the people, and for their exclusive benefit? As part of Cabral's revolutionary strategy, he encouraged party members to sabotage all cash crop ventures, especially the production of groundnuts, which he saw had particularly disastrous environmental and sustainability issues for the regions where it was practiced. He encouraged the redevelopment of small-scale production, geared toward meeting the needs of the population inhabiting the producing territory.[28]

Cabral's reliance upon the land, and his revision of Marxist history, most likely originate from his pessimistic assessment of the potential for revolutionary agency in the two classes in Guinea. First of all, his extensive experience with the populations in the Portuguese colonies led him to doubt the revolutionary potential of those who had not been affected much by colonization and still existed within more traditional tribal contexts. Largely untouched by colonial rule, how would they perceive the need to struggle against it for a more promising future? This left the petit bourgeoisie, who were the primary native inhabitants who benefited from colonization and hence had little predisposition to end colonial rule. Cabral admits that the revolution relies upon this group to "be capable of committing suicide as a class," to renounce their current identifications and class position in favor of another.[29] By shifting his founding narrative to the land, he was able to suggest a unity of territory since there was not a unified experience of colonialism that could create common ground.

This curious revolutionary strategy also resonates in his description of struggle. Cabral's vision of struggle is distinct: it does not exclusively apply to organized resistance or violence, but instead he roots it in natural processes. He points out that struggle is not necessarily a revolutionary condition; instead it is the natural condition of people, of all objects on the earth. The laws of motion, gravity, and entropy are examples of forces that human beings must struggle with every day. Furthermore, nature is filled with examples of forces that counterbalance one another: rocks may slide into a river and change the direction of the flow; eventually the current of the river will wear away the rock in turn. Struggle is not necessarily generated from consciousness, but rather as a response to another force that has been exerted. The struggle for national liberation in the context of Cape Verde and Guinea was to overcome the force of the Portuguese upon their land: it was a counterforce.

> In our specific case, the struggle is the following: the Portuguese colonialists have taken our land, as foreigners and occupiers, and have exerted a force on our society, on our people. The force has operated so that they should take our destiny into their hands, has operated so that they should halt our history for us to remain tied to the history of Portugal, as if we were a wagon on their train.[30]

The forces of imperialism overcame the inhabitants of the land and soon set up their own trajectory of history. Overcoming this trajectory required the exertion of force by the inhabitants of the territory. Just as more energy is required to break up a trajectory of motion than is required to continue along its path, so national liberation needed to exercise violence to overcome the force that stopped the history of Cape Verde and Guinea and replaced it with the history of Portugal.

Through struggle, the land would be freed to sustain those who live upon it. This struggle is not a revolutionary break as much as it is a restoration. Cabral had already defined different stages of history as marked by an evolving relationship between a territory and its inhabitants. Colonialism was a force that interrupted this natural relationship. Independence must use force to reestablish this history, a history in which inhabitants and territory are mutually sustaining. Because colonization stopped indigenous history, colonialism in effect existed outside of the territory's sequence of time. This conceptualization allows Cabral to establish two important aspects of his foundational narrative, it provides an explanation for and natural cessation of the colonial era, and it can help explain why the people will unify in struggle.

Interestingly, the revolution doesn't change history; it restarts it, linking the future to the precolonial past. By redefining historical progression according to the increasing sustainability of the land, thereby making the land a measure of economic and political progression, Cabral can argue that the era of colonialism stands outside of indigenous history. The immediate past no longer serves as the prelude to the present; instead, the true past, present, and future of Guinea will be marked by a unity between people and their territory.

Cabral's theories of history, economics, and struggle based upon the land exhibit an elegant harmony. He is able to wrestle the demon of past subordination while finding the basis of unity for all people, whether still existing in tribes or part of the petit bourgeois. All of these groups, even though they have not shared the same experience of colonization, live in the same place and can support themselves there as long as they take their territory and its production back for their own use. Just as importantly, the measure of the land's productivity and the dictum that it needs to support the indigenous population provides a clear goal to be achieved after independence. Are the economic activities in a given area supporting its inhabitants? This is a measure of independence that can still be used to critique current forms of economic production and resource extraction. The critique shows resilience, and has reappeared in movements that seek to resist contemporary economic developments. For instance, in southern Mexico it became one of the primary elements in a platform for political change by the Zapatistas.

GROUNDS OF STRUGGLE: THE ZAPATISTA PHILOSOPHY AND MOVEMENT

Since the late 1980s there has been a growth in fourth world activism and indigenous land claims influenced by the era of identity politics. This is one reason why indigenous claims to the land are frequently interpreted as claims of identity. The convergence with identity politics is not only in the eyes of observers however. Indigenous politics and the focus upon identity is also due to the International Labor Organization Convention 169 (ILO 169), which is derived from the United Nations' provisions against genocide and which reaffirms the right of indigenous groups to exist. This provision has become one of the strongest tools indigenous movements have in asserting their interests against different national governments. In Mexico, this provision was incorporated into the Mexican Constitution as Article 27, which was a commitment to land redistribution. On January 1, 1994, when the Zapatista Army of National Liberation (Ejército Zapatista de Liberación Nacional, EZLN) declared war against the state of Mexico, one of the Zapatistas' primary points was that the terms of North American Free Trade Agreement (NAFTA) required that the Mexican government relinquish its stated commitment to land redistribution in order to assure favorable conditions for international investment. (The date of the Zapatistas' declaration was not coincidental: implementation of NAFTA began on January 1, 1994.) Interestingly, the San Andreas Peace Accord of 1996 between the EZLN and the Mexican government incorporated both of these precedents and joined land and identity, stating that land would be allocated to indigenous groups as the "materialist base of reproduction of a people."[31] In Mexico, the Zapatista movement has combined an indigenous emphasis upon identity, a radical democratic critique of the Mexican state, and a repudiation of global economic production in favor of local sustainability that emphasizes land as a key dimension of economic and political self-determination.

Thus, while indigenous politics are often understood in terms of identity politics, in the case of Mexico, it is accompanied by an insistence upon land as the necessary precondition for identity formation and survival. In this way, claims of identity become economic ones as well; there is not the conceptual division between claims of recognition and claims of redistribution that has often been discussed in American political thought.[32]

The Zapatistas' land claims became a way to synthesize their demands for identity recognition, economic sustenance and political self-determination, making them contemporary inheritors of the trends evident in Amílcar Cabral's struggle against Portuguese colonialism. Courtney Jung has also noted the resonance between indigenous antiglobalization in Mexico and earlier revolutions of decolonization. "The term internal colonialism, which has been used to describe the structural relationship between modern states and their indigenous population, seems to capture the logic that links the political exclusions of the colonial era to those of post-colonialism."[33]

There are many fascinating aspects to the Zapatista movement, so it is not surprising that the movement has garnered an unusual amount of scholarly attention. For instance, Courtney Jung's *The Moral Force of Indigenous Politics* and Neil Harvey's *The Chiapas Rebellion* have explored what the movement offers to the realm of democratic and liberal theory. Jung and Harvey are astute in their focus upon the Zapatistas and democratic theory, as the movement is distinct from previous models of social mobilization. Though the accounts of the organization of the movement vary, and one suspects they are embellished by the leaders, the outline of its development is roughly as follows.

Activists from Mexico City versed in Leninist, Maoist, and Guevarist tactics had been going to rural Chiapas since the 1970s. These leaders were part of the National Liberation Forces (Fuerzas de Liberación Nacional, FLN), an organization founded in 1968 after the Mexican government's brutal repression of the student uprisings. Because it was one of the poorest regions of Mexico, FLN leaders went to Chiapas in order to organize the peasantry, thinking this could be a natural base for their national, socialist revolution. At one point, three of these activists abandoned their allegiance to the *Foco* theory of revolution[34] and stopped presenting themselves as leaders for the peasants to follow. They instead began a practice of studying indigenous traditions and beliefs. By the start of the 1980s, veterans of the FLN and indigenous groups in Chiapas unified with Catholics inspired by liberation theology and formed a group called Slop (Tzeltal for "root"), providing external evidence of the group's early organizational efforts. In these meetings, party leaders from the EZLN would present themselves as servants of the population and gave the people the power to decide the program of the party. Starting in 1988, the movement gained tremendous support throughout the region and grew rapidly.[35] One marker of how thoroughly the leaders abandoned the *Foco* theory of revolution that features militant men as its centerpiece is the fact that a woman, Major Ana Maria, led the invasion on January 1, 1994.[36]

The Mexican government responded with a campaign of repression and terror. Local activists who could be identified were often assassinated by the militias that local ranchers would hire in defense of their interests or by state agents. The circumstances drove innovation, and the leaders saw that they would have to abandon the long Mexican tradition of caudillo ('chief') movements, political rebellions organized around one central figure such as Emiliano Zapata (1879–1919). The long organization period and the tactical repudiation of a figurehead explains the persona of Subcomandante Marcos.

Marcos calls himself a "subcommander" to indicate that he serves the population, he does not lead them. He wears a ski mask in order to emphasize that he himself is not important, and that any person in the organization can wear the mask and speak on behalf of the people. This repudiation of the charismatic caudillo identity has naturally only added to his appeal, precisely because he states that he is against it. Marcos's tactics are extremely theatrical and intended to generate media attention to exert pressure on the Mexican government, since the EZLN lacks the resources to actually threaten the Mexican state militarily. Popular support for the movement around the country and the world has pressured the Mexican government into negotiations.

Walter Mignolo has observed that territory and space are central to understanding the structure of indigenous politics.

From the Amerindian perspective, territoriality consisted of emptying the center rather than emptying the space. The memory that might have survived among Amerindians of territoriality as a way of governing, defining social relationships, and organizing populations had to negotiate the new reality of complex bureaucracies, of having their space emptied or negated, and of figuring out the new and disguised sources of power.[37]

This observation applies to both the colonized population and the indigenous population. Previous residents remain in place, while a new framework of definition and control descends upon them. Just as Carl Schmitt describes, a new framework of controlling space accompanies the conquest of it. Therefore, decolonization requires the assertion of alternative conceptualizations of that space, something one can see in the writings associated with the Zapatista movement.

One of the more prominent themes in the writing of Marcos is his attention to landscapes of inequality. For instance, in a piece written in 1992 and then publicly released at the end of January 1994, Marcos takes readers on a tour of Chiapas. He imagines showing an outsider the territory from a new perspective, and in the process, shaming the Mexican government into seeing how they have developed the region. He "walks" a fictional guest through the streets of San Cristóbal de las Casas, the largest city in the region, and up into the mountains. He takes his visitor to a school serving the local children in a village: "No, don't go closer, don't look in, don't look at the four groups of children riddled with tapeworms and lice, half-naked . . ." In a passage reminiscent of Fanon's famous juxtaposition of the colonial town and the Arab town, Marcos contrasts the indigenous school with the nicer buildings down the coast: "Do you see them? Modern buildings, nice homes, paved roads . . . Is it a university? Worker's housing? No, look at the sign next to the cannons closely and read: 'General Army Barracks of the 31st Military Zone.'"[38] In this essay, he points out how much of his landscape is taken as given, but he tries to inspire visitors to see it differently: "Without leaving your uncertainty behind, drive on . . ." We must become uncertain in order to see the landscape of Chiapas anew.

The Mexican government did engage in land reform in Chiapas as promised after the Mexican revolution of 1910. It is crucial to remember how central the promise of land was in recruiting popular support for the revolution. Clearly, the Zapatistas are inspired by the words of Emiliano Zapata, whose original manifesto focuses upon the land.

> We must continue to struggle and not rest until the land is our own, the property of the people, of our grandfathers, taken from us by those who crush the land with their stone step, beneath the shadow of those who have gone before us, who command us: that with the strength of our heart and our hand held high, we raise, to be seen by all, that beautiful banner of dignity and freedom of we who work the land; that we must continue to struggle until we defeat those who have crowned themselves, those who have helped take the land from others . . .[39]

Remarkably, the same basic points are repeated in the EZLN platforms; it seems the land and its products are the unfinished business of the revolution.

As in other postcolonial situations, land distribution was a primary platform of the revolutionary party. "In rural Mexico the most important instrument for creating a new institutional framework, generating legitimacy, and establishing political clientele, was agrarian reform, through which land was distributed to peasants in the form of communal land grants (*ejidos*)."[40] While many believe that land reform did not happen in Chiapas, it did. One analyst has even concluded that the way land reform was carried out determined the local population's perceptions of the state, and hence indirectly laid the groundwork for the Zapatista mobilization during the 1980s and 1990s.[41] In rural Chiapas, collectively owned spaces for subsistence farming existed side by side with rancheros, creating increasing tension as the local population grew and more shared land was needed in order to support them. Within the *ejidos*, the state had written regulations, but in practice the communities made all of their own decisions about distribution and production. Though the *ejidos* were granted by the state, the ultimate result was large numbers of people who had essentially no contact with the state and hence developed no affiliation with it. In respecting the rights of communal property, the land redistribution program ultimately undermined the state's importance in Chiapas. This is not to say that the local population prospered; to the contrary, the landholdings stayed constant while the population grew, hence the standard of living steadily dropped.

The slow decline of subsistence and the neglect of the state changed with the passage of NAFTA. As Patricia Huntington observed, "Salinas (and Zedillo after him) hammered the final nail in the coffin of indigenous life in Chiapas; the North American Free Trade Agreement and the 'gutting of Article 27' effectively mean that larger corporations can buy up all landholdings, thus eliminating the only counterpoise the peasants ever had against a long history of colonial expropriation of their land, their culture, and their independence."[42] The population could no longer grind out an impoverished existence at the edge of the culture and economy of the state: they had to act.

You can see the results of this trajectory in the rhetoric of the Zapatistas. They juxtapose themselves as belonging to the territory, while the state is an artificial entity with no relationship to the land. They, not the Mexican government, have guardianship over the territory. Their habitation of the land is of course the center of this claim, but so also is the mismanagement of the land by the state.

Chiapas loses blood through many veins: through oil and gas ducts, electric lines, railways; through bank accounts, trucks, vans, boats and planes; through clandestine paths, gaps, and forest trails. This land continues to pay tribute to the imperialists; petroleum, electricity, cattle, honey, coffee, banana, honey, corn, cacao, tobacco, sugar, soy, melon, sorghum, mamey, mango, tamarind, avocado, and Chiapaneco blood all flow as a result of the thousand teeth sunk into the throat of the Mexican Southeast.... Since the beginning, the fee that capitalism imposes on the southeastern part of this country makes Chiapas ooze blood and mud.[43]

The land is anthropomorphized, making the people and the land indistinguishable in their rhetorical position.

In some ways, this can be understood as a reimagination of the national territory, a focus upon the land as constitutive of the nation allows the EZLN to question the sovereignty of the state by detaching the state from its territory. They also focus upon civil society in Mexico, arguing that the notion of popular sovereignty in the Mexican constitution means that the population, not the state, is truly sovereign. "The problem of power is not a question of who rules, but of who exercises power."[44] Marcos distinguishes between those who administer the government and those who must wield power. EZLN leaders have done multiple tours through the country placing proposals before the people and listening to their response. While they say that they fight for popular sovereignty, they also claim their right to power in the state based upon their territory. Because they and the land are one, they assert their privilege to represent their territory based upon their understanding of its dynamics. The Mexican government does not understand the land, and therefore makes poor decisions. In an interview Marcos commented upon NAFTA:

Yes, as I have said, NAFTA is a death sentence for the indigenous people. NAFTA sets up competition among farmers, but how can our campesinos—who are mostly illiterate—compete with the U.S. and Canadian farmers? And look at this rocky land we have here. How can we compete with the land in California, or in Canada?[45]

This method of legitimization helps explain why the Zapatistas sign declarations by registering their location. There is a series of (EZLN) Declarations from the Lacandon Jungle, others are "From the mountains of the Mexican Southeast."

The emphasis upon the connection between themselves and their territory is also tactical. Marcos has claimed that because they and the land are inseparable, the Mexican government cannot eradicate the movement without destroying the territory. Marcos claims, "The EZLN and the civil population are so intermixed that it is difficult to draw a line marking the interests or territory of one or the other. In order to eliminate the Zapatista Army, this territory itself must be wiped from the face of the planet."[46]

Marcos also fuses these more economic and political aspects of the platform with myths from the Zapatista region to distinguish them from Mexican national history and to ground the legitimacy of the struggle for self-determination in a separate history and a prior claim on the territory. Foundational claims become wrapped in separate cultural and historical trajectories and a unique relationship to the land, as in this fable:

> The dispossessed fight and dream for humanity.
>
> This is the true history. And if it does not appear in primary school textbooks, that is because history is still being written by those above, even though it is made by those below.
>
> But even though it's not part of the original curricula, the story of the birth of the world and the map that explains where it is, is still held in the scars of the mother *ceiba*.
>
> The eldest of the elders of the communities entrusted the secret to the Zapatistas. In the mountain, they spoke with them and told them where the note was left by the first gods, those who gave birth to the world, so memory would not be lost.
>
> Ever since, because they were born without faces, without names, and without individual pasts, the Zapatistas have been students of the story taught by the land.[47]

Because national history has replaced local history, national citizenship has tried to erase indigenous identity, and indigenous people are thought of as extinct, they are born without faces, names, or an individual past. Marcos argues that they have been literally written outside of the present, and simultaneously robbed of their past. Since they cannot find themselves in the present or past as it is written anymore, Marcos turns to the land as the connection between past, present, and future. The land holds the connection to unearthing the past, and hence making claims in the present and the future. Marcos acknowledges that this may look like a politics of nostalgia when he says, "Although it looks like we are defending the past, in reality, in *La Realidad*, we have agreed to defend tomorrow."[48]

The essential problem of the land, introduced by processes of colonization and continuing today under processes of integration into a global capitalist framework, is the disjuncture between those who inhabit a given space and the political, legal and economic systems that define, control and appropriate that space from other locations. Taken together, Cabral's and Marcos's theories offer alternative ways of thinking about sovereignty and self-determination outside of the liberal legal framework. Do the people who inhabit a space have the ability to determine its use in order to fulfill their basic needs and achieve sustainability within that space? Claims to the land provide a way of combining economic and political claims. This is particularly valuable since liberal, legalistic frameworks evaluate political rights as separate from economic status, and Marxist critiques of economic subordination place too little emphasis upon the importance of political sovereignty. This model of grounding resistance synthesizes elements of both traditions and offers a new model for evaluating self-determination in the twenty-first century. It also helps us think about the normative issues at stake in initiatives such as the land sales discussed at the beginning of the chapter. Is it wrong for foreign conglomerates to purchase or lease large swaths of land, mechanize production, and export food when the surrounding population is hungry or malnourished? If these deals are structured according to existing laws, then liberal democratic theory has little to offer and these theories of decolonization may find new audiences, and fresh relevance.

The Philosophy of Liberation

There has been a lively debate in Latin American studies about the term post-colonialism.[1] This debate was sparked by J. Jorge Klor de Alva's controversial essay "Colonialism and Post Colonialism as (Latin) American Mirage."[2] Klor de Alva argued that the experience of most Latin American nations differed fundamentally from the countries that became independent in the second half of the twentieth century. According to Klor de Alva, "it is misguided to present the pre-independence *non-native* sectors as colonized, it is inconsistent to explain the wars of independence as anti-colonial struggles, and it is misleading to characterize the Americas, following the civil wars of separation, as postcolonial." He points out that the people who fought the wars for independence from Spain were culturally European creoles or mestizos who constructed nations based on European identities, languages, religion and institutions. The popular term "Latin America" marked the connection to Europe and reinforced the marginalization of the indigenous population, which had been decimated in the process of colonization.[3] Even the identity of *mestizaje* was not based on a hybrid of European and indigenous cultures but was rather a starkly assimilationist project.[4] Finally, Klor de Alva emphasized that the temporal distance between the nineteenth century and the twentieth century means the two phases of national independence have little in common. If Klor de Alva is correct, then most countries in Latin America have little in common with the new nations of Africa and Asia. Patricia D'Allemand has echoed these concerns, pointing out that the temptation to read Latin American history through the lenses of postcolonial theory risks dehistoricizing particular traits, diluting discourses, and silencing local debates.[5]

Other scholars, however, have forcefully argued that theories of postcolonialism help illuminate the history of Latin America by developing critical perspectives on modernity, power, and identity.[6] They also point out that some of the most influential postcolonial critics have come from the Americas, especially the Caribbean.[7] These include canonical figures such as C. L. R. James, Frantz Fanon, and Aimé Césaire. Perhaps these thinkers developed critical approaches to European ideologies of freedom, equality, and universalism in part because their experience of racial exclusion rendered these categories suspect. But critiques of colonialism and its legitimating ideas also emerged in Spanish-speaking, creole intellectual circles. Roberto Fernández Retamar, José Mariátegui, César Vallejo, Leopoldo Zea, Enrique Dussel, and Paolo Freire have all written about dynamics of power and powerlessness between nations and within them.

According to Walter Mignolo, postcolonial perspectives are of central importance not only to Latin American studies but also to the broader project of understanding Western modernity.[8] Postcolonialism challenges the discursive authority of the center by exposing its violent effects and listening to voices that provide alternative perspectives. Latin America, of course, was the site of some of the bloodiest chapters of colonial history.[9] Unlike Klor de Alva, Mignolo defines colonialism as a broad term that encompasses the settler colonialism of the sixteenth to eighteenth centuries (North and South America, Australia, etc.) as well as the economic, military, and political domination of Africa and parts of Asia in the nineteenth century. From this perspective, postcolonialism can describe the situation of newly independent states, but it can also describe the longer, more complicated process of dismantling the cultural practices, ideologies, and inequalities created through colonialism and imperialism. In order to distinguish between these two different dimensions, Mignolo uses the terms "postcolonial situation" and "postcolonial ratio." The latter has been the focus of Latin American theorists in the twentieth century.

These debates present the opportunity to consider where, when, and why theories of decolonization are relevant. The lines of colonial history tend to blur the more closely one examines them. For example, as we mentioned in Chapter 2, Iran was never formally colonized, yet local leaders decried outside political and cultural forces that they felt had eroded their sovereignty and traditions. Although Latin America was transformed by independence movements in the nineteenth century, today it is a center of activism against neocolonialism. We don't want to be overly expansive in our use of the terms colonization and decolonization. Any term, whether it be "oppression," "sovereignty," or "power" loses its vitality and critical utility if it is applied without discretion. Yet we believe that colonization created the modern world and its ideological, political and economic legacies still influence international and domestic power arrangements. In a world of unequal resources, colonial critique and ideals of postcolonial power still resonate.

The two theorists presented in this chapter, José Carlos Mariátegui and Enrique Dussel, draw attention to two legacies of colonialism: the persistence of global economic inequalities and the dynamics of internal colonialism. The term "internal colonialism" comes from Lenin and Gramsci, who used the concept to describe the unevenness of national economic development.[10] Today it is often invoked as a way of describing the situation of indigenous peoples in settler colonies. In many ways, colonial critique is more difficult but just as important after the period of formal colonization has ended. Frantz Fanon was concerned that liberatory struggles would falter absent the Manichean simplicity of colonized against colonizer. When the origins and instruments of the system of inequality become less obvious, it is much more difficult to orient oneself and one's actions. The project of challenging unequal power structures is no less pressing, however, even as the terms and grounds have become occluded. The difficulty of critique is compounded when the dominant terms of political life separate political and economic injustice. Marx was one of the first to denounce this segregation as ideological in "On the Jewish Question" (1843). To think about economic issues as ethical ones is a now growing, but still oppositional, viewpoint. The combination of political, economic, and ethical critique is one of the most important contributions made by the two theorists in this chapter.

In Latin America, there is a long tradition of postcolonial critique that emphasizes that political independence does not necessarily lead to economic independence. Nor is foreign economic control the only challenge to self-rule. Once the binary opposition between colonizer and colonized ceased to organize the political landscape, there were other sources of inequality that emerge to take its place. In Latin American studies, postcolonial critique highlights the way that race, color, and ethnicity continue to be sources of power and inequality. It challenges the universality of European ideas and institutions and explores indigenous culture as a source of ethical and political insight. Finally, it draws attention to the economic patterns such as the quasi-feudal agricultural system that are contemporary legacies of colonial institutions.

This chapter focuses on two thinkers who explored these issues in depth: José Mariátegui and Enrique Dussel. They were selected because they are creative and influential representatives of two important intellectual currents: Marxism and philosophy of liberation.[11] Marxism has provided a language for articulating critiques of economic inequality and a powerful theory of social change. Yet, as many scholars have noted, using Marxist categories to illuminate the experience of the colonial world has been problematic for a number of reasons, notably the absence of race/culture as a category of analysis and a Eurocentric account of historical development.[12] Much of postcolonial political theory attempts to modify Marxist analysis to illuminate a world in which there are multiple axes of power and a global division of labor that complicates the division between proletariat and bourgeoisie and restructures capital. As we saw in the last chapter, some postcolonial theorists have turned to the "the land" as a way of modifying the concept of mode of production to include diverse modes of production (communal agriculture, natural resources, crafts, and manufacturing) linked together by proximity and interdependence. This approach makes it possible to identify "the people" as equivalent to "workers" and insist that the people benefit from the value they create, rather than allowing it to be expropriated by powerful countries or multinational corporations. This chapter explores another way of rewriting the Marxist narrative, one that involves rethinking the agent of social change. The industrial proletariat was not large or unified in Latin America, yet economic exploitation was still an important concern; this meant that political theorists had to look for sources of critique and other social forces that could advance the project of liberation.

LATIN AMERICAN MARXISM

Marxism has had a significant impact on Latin America, both in political theory and practice.[13] One of the most important figures was José Mariátegui (1894–1930), a Peruvian activist, theorist, and writer.[14] He was born in Moquegua, Peru. His father abandoned his family during Mariátegui's youth, creating economic difficulties that were further exacerbated by a serious injury to his left leg that left him in poor health for much of his life. He entered the newspaper trade as an errand boy, ultimately taking on the position of a writer. In 1916 he began working for a leftist newspaper, *El Tiempo*, before establishing his own newspaper, *La Razón*, two years later. *La Razón* published many articles on university reform and in defense of the young labor movement in Peru, drawing attention from Peruvian officials who urged Mariátegui to cease publication of his paper in exchange for an opportunity to travel abroad.

Mariátegui traveled throughout Europe and settled in Italy for two years, long enough to get married and gain exposure to Italian trade union activism and experience the dangers of nascent fascism firsthand. He returned to Peru in 1923, committed to political action and began forming connections with populist movements. In 1924, Mariátegui nearly died from a tumor in his left leg. The only possible treatment was its amputation. For the rest of his life he relied upon others to carry him and provide for his physical mobility. This episode seemed to only catalyze his intellectual energies, however, as he founded a new journal, *Amautu*, in 1926 to advance discussions of socialism and culture in Latin America, and two years later founded what would become the Communist Party of Peru. Also in 1928 he published *Seven Interpretive Essays in*

Peruvian Reality, his best-known theoretical work.[15] In addition to developing a materialist analysis of the exploitation of indigenous people in Peru, he wrote widely on education, art, literature, and religion.[16]

Mariátegui is remembered as one of the founding fathers of Latin American Marxism, but his analysis of neocolonialism and dependence departed from the orthodoxy of his day. Mariátegui used the method of historical materialism, but he challenged the assumption that all societies follow the same stages of economic development. This model did not describe the situation of former colonies and the new global system of which they were a part.

Mariátegui's analysis of the economics of underdevelopment was very similar to the approach that would come to be known as dependency theory. Mariátegui emphasized that all countries were not following through the same stages of capitalist development and explained that there were both political and economic reasons for this outcome. He argued that peripheral nations like Peru were part of a global system, and advanced capitalist countries had the resources to structure these relations of exchange to their advantage.[17] In order to obtain industrial products and technology, Peru had to export natural resources (agricultural products, guano, nitrates, rubber), but these extractive industries reinforced feudal social relations, which in turn further weakened the possibility of internal capitalist development. Mariátegui emphasized the political and cultural logic of this process. For Mariátegui, neocolonialism was not simply a matter of foreign-owned companies exploiting Peru. Neocolonialism reinforced domestic institutions that were themselves products of Spanish colonialism. These institutions, particularly the feudal land tenure system, underpinned Peru's location within the global system.

Mariátegui engaged in the debate raging both inside and outside of Marxist circles about whether colonialism and imperialism brought economic growth and civilization to the territories they conquered. In *Seven Interpretive Essays on Peruvian Reality*, Mariátegui challenged the view that the Spanish conquest ushered in an era of greater productivity in Peru.[18] He argued that demographic evidence proved that the preconquest Incan empire was more economically productive than Peru under Spanish rule because it had been able to support a population of ten million compared to only one million after three centuries of Spanish rule.[19] He juxtaposed the high level of economic and social organization under the Incas with the dispersed, impoverished condition of the indigenous people under the neocolonial regime.[20] Mariátegui's critique of colonialism and neocolonialism was not based on ethical arguments but rather on economic ones. Given that postconquest Peru was less productive, it could not be considered more progressive than indigenous Incan "despotism." He concluded that "colonization stands condemned not from any abstract, theoretical, or moral standpoint of justice, but from the practical, concrete, and material standpoint of utility."[21]

Mariátegui also challenged the contention that the *criollo* estates and haciendas were more productive than the independent indigenous communities. He presented statistics that documented slightly higher yields from large estates compared to Indian peasant communities but noted that when you take into account that the Indians almost invariably had the least fertile land, the difference was negligible.[22] The goal was not simply to demystify the pretenses of colonial productivity and efficiency but also to challenge the assumption that there was only one path to economic development. By disrupting the narrative of historical progress, Mariátegui opens up the possibility of a direct route to Peruvian socialism, one that is not advanced by urban industrial workers and does not need to pass through capitalism. He noted that indigenous communities, despite their traditional farming methods, were actually less adverse to innovations than the feudal landlords, who feared that any change might jeopardize their total control over their workforce. Mariátegui claimed, "when a 'community' (*ayllu*) is connected by railway to commerce and central transportation, it spontaneously changes into a cooperative."[23] He noted examples of Indian communities that functioned as producer, consumer, and credit cooperatives, and suggested that these new forms of organization were logical extensions of indigenous practices like the *mingas* (gatherings where the entire community would help one member with digging irrigation ditches or building a house). According to Mariátegui, the strong solidarity-minded ethos of the *ayllu* precariously survived both the brutal Spanish conquest and the individualistic ideology of the postindependence polity: "When expropriation and redistribution seem about to liquidate the 'community,' indigenous socialism always finds a way to reject, resist, or evade this incursion."[24] Mariátegui repeatedly drew attention to the fact the Peruvian peasants, unlike the peasants in France whom Marx notoriously described as a "sack of potatoes" (i.e., isolated and individualistic), had strong collective traditions that could be the basis of a new socialist mode of production.

One of the enduring interpretive controversies is whether Mariátegui's approach to the indigenous question was a form of romantic essentialism or an innovative introduction of cultural analysis into Marxist theory. At first it might seem puzzling to suggest that Mariátegui was a cultural essentialist, given that he challenged the racial theories of his contemporaries in Peru. He continually dismissed those commentators who believed that Peru's problems came from the presence of "an inferior race."[25] The originality of Mariátegui's approach is the way he links materialist and cultural analysis. The Indians are a potentially revolutionary group because they are an exploited class with a concrete stake in change (e.g., they produce a surplus that is appropriated by others) and a set of communal traditions that can facilitate collective action. These same traditions contain the seeds of a viable alternative to the capitalist/feudal hybrid economy that traps Peru in a position of economic dependence.

This also suggests an answer to the criticism that this is simply an exotic version of the utopian socialist nostalgia for a return to an idealized pre-capitalist past. But Mariátegui's point is that Latin America differs from Europe and therefore familiar markers of progress/stagnation may not apply. Mariátegui follows Marx in assuming that bourgeois capitalism did represent an advance over European feudalism in so far as it increased overall social utility, even if it also brought about endemic crises that would ultimately lead to its own collapse. This made European capitalism inevitable and therefore any alternatives inspired by earlier modes of production could only be nostalgic. In Peru, however, the Spanish conquest and the capitalist-feudal hybrid economy that emerged were regressive from the standpoint of social utility since they did not increase productivity. Therefore, elements of pre-Incan communalism could be progressive forces. Mariátegui did not advocate a return to the social, political, and economic organization of the Incan empire. Such a return would be both impossible and unattractive, given the authoritarian character of Incan society. Nevertheless, Mariátegui implied that a modern hybrid that incorporated elements of indigenous agrarian communism should not simply be dismissed as backward. Given that feudal and communal agriculture are equally productive, the choice between them is not a matter of economic inevitability but could be determined by the outcome of political struggle.

The problem is that this political struggle faces enormous challenges. In *Seven Interpretive Essays in Peruvian Reality*, Mariátegui concludes that an indigenous revolution is neither inevitable nor impossible.[26] The question that haunts Mariátegui's text is how this potential mobilization is going to be brought about, given that hundreds of years of Spanish and feudal domination had weakened the position of the Indians. His answer appears in a footnote where he writes,

> The soul of the Indian is not raised by the white man's civilization or alphabet but by the myth, the idea, of the Socialist revolution. The hope of the Indian is absolutely revolutionary. That same myth, that same idea, are the decisive agents in the awakening of other ancient peoples or races in ruin: the Hindus, the Chinese, et cetera.[27]

The language of myth reflects the influence of Sorel.[28] Mariátegui continually insisted that Marx and Sorel, Marxism and revolutionary syndicalism were not antithetical, irreconcilable paths. For Mariátegui, material conditions provided the opportunity and myth provided the motive and inspiration required for revolution. This mythic aspect, however, was not simply an empty slogan, but rather a component of Mariátegui's more detailed political analysis of the revolutionary process.

For Mariátegui, the myth of socialism is something both inside and outside of history. It cannot be explained in terms of historical logic, but it is necessary to achieve historical progress. But what exactly is myth? Mariátegui gives several examples in the text. He notes that the myths of the liberal revolution were "liberty, democracy and peace."[29] He also observes how the most enduring myth—God—has been "corroded and dissolved" by the disenchanting effects of "reason and science." Yet reason and science themselves have not proved to be alternative sources of myth and meaning because they are premised on a denial of humans' creativity and metaphysical aspirations. He criticizes reason and science for the way they demystify human existence without providing alternative sources of meaning. He explains "[Man] does not live productively without a metaphysical conception of life. Without myth, man's existence has no historical meaning. History is made by people possessed and enlightened by a higher belief and a superhuman hope."[30]

In "Man and Myth," Mariátegui's debt to Sorel is quite explicit. He calls Georges Sorel (1847–1922) "one of the greatest representatives of twentieth-century French thought" and cites *Reflections on Violence* at some length.[31] Although it is beyond the scope of this chapter to examine thoroughly the similarities and differences between their respective understandings of myth, it is worth noting how Mariátegui's discussion differs markedly from the protofascist theory often associated with Sorel.[32] Mariátegui understands myth as an empty signifier rather than a universal principle or telos. This provocative insight emerges in his discussion of a poem by Henri Frank titled *The Dance Behind the Ark*. We quote the passage at length in order to avoid the confusion that might emerge from summarizing Mariátegui's summary of the poem:

> Henri Frank speaks to us of his profound "will to create." As an Israelite, he first tries to illuminate his soul with faith in the god of Israel. This attempt is in vain. The words of his fathers' god sound foreign to our era. The poet does not understand them. He declares himself deaf to their meaning. As a modern man, the word from Sinai cannot captivate him . . . The voice of the modern proposes its false and precarious myth: reason. But Henri Frank cannot accept it . . . "Reason without God is a room without a lamp." . . . The poet leaves in search of God. He has need to satisfy his thirst for the infinite, for eternity. But this pilgrimage is fruitless . . . Man carries his truth within himself. "If the ark is empty where you hoped to find the law, nothing is real but your dance."[33]

Mariátegui notes that philosophers have elaborated this same point about the illusory nature of foundations and the fact that meaning is created not discovered.[34] But he also recognizes that "humanity resists following a truth that it does not believe absolute and supreme." He identifies the paradox that universal ideals are contingent, historical, and unstable yet still absolutely necessary as a source of meaning and inspiration for action. He insists, "It is futile to recommend the superiority of faith, of myth, of action. One must propose a faith, a myth, an action."[35]

Mariátegui believed that social revolution was the most viable myth, because it was the one that addressed urgent problems and proposed viable alternatives. Socialism was a myth rooted in material reality and therefore uniquely able to identify plausible solutions to economic problems. Other political movements drew on potent religious myths, but Mariátegui felt that these movements would not result in real liberation; for example, in a nuanced essay on Gandhi, he noted, "The spinning wheel is powerless to resolve the social question of any people."[36] In other words, a myth that romanticizes a regressive socio-economic vision will ultimately prove untenable (see Conclusion).

Fascism too made use of the power of myth, but it mobilized metaphysical longings in service of a reactionary and therefore ultimately unstable ideal. Since the dominant fascist myths harked back to medieval corporatism and paternalism, the resulting social order would prove unable to solve modern problems. For Mariátegui, Marxism was both method and myth but not science. It was a method because it focused attention on the materialist explanations of history and a myth that could inspire a meaningful challenge to the dominant mode of oppression. Moreover, these two dimensions were intrinsically linked. A myth that was not rooted in material reality would prove unstable and a philosophy unwilling or incapable of inspiring the quasi-religious fervors of the people would remain inert.

Mariátegui implies that myth is necessary because it animates political action. Although he does not use the language of rational choice theory, his concept of myth is a way of solving the collective action problem. From the standpoint of rationality, each individual would wait for others to engage in revolutionary action hoping to share in the benefits without taking the risks and making the sacrifices. But the mythic dimension of political activity makes this calculation seem irrelevant. Political participation is not simply an instrument to achieve a goal but rather a source of intrinsic meaning. By working toward something noble and historic, each individual gains a sense of meaning and solidarity that ennobles the suffering of everyday life. Mariátegui recognizes that this is essentially the politicization of religious faith.

Although this account of myth is convincing, it also explains the character and appeal of other political movements such as fascism. Mariátegui has a harder time explaining why the myth of social revolution is more viable than its rivals. If, as he puts it, the ark is empty, then it is unclear why social revolution is superior to other myths such as democracy, the free market, or even the triumph of the master race. Mariátegui suggests that socialism is better suited to solving contemporary problems than its backward-looking rivals (e.g., Catholicism, fascism), but he does not seem to consider the possibility that nationalism and the free market could also function as myths, and in fact popular ones that could seriously challenge socialism. Absent from his theory is any discussion of the normative as opposed to functional superiority of a particular myth.

In some ways Mariátegui's work seems very prescient. His two main themes—the relationship between the global and local in former colonies, and the material and cultural dimensions of indigenous oppression and resistance—are just as relevant today. His faith in the myth of socialist revolution, on the other hand, may seem somewhat anachronistic to contemporary readers. It reflects the optimism of the 1920s, the period just after the Russian Revolution when social democratic parties, the general strike, and factory occupations seemed like potent tools for transforming Europe. Even as Marxism and socialism continued to exert a great deal of influence, a subsequent generation of theorists tried to expand the notion of the revolutionary subject and to rethink the concept of liberation itself.

PHILOSOPHY OF LIBERATION

The philosophy of liberation was part of a broad intellectual current in Latin America that included liberation theology (Gutierrez), liberation pedagogy (Illich, Freire), and the critique of neoclassical economics (Frank, Faleto, Cardoso). The figures associated with the philosophy of liberation were primarily Latin American academics, including Arturo Andrés Roig, Horacio Cerutti Guldberg, Augusto Salazar Bondy, Leopoldo Zea, and Enrique Dussel.[37] Some of the key works were published in two philosophical journals: *Nuevo mundo* and *Revista de filosofía latinoamericana*. In these journals, philosophers engaged in a long-running debate about whether there could be such a thing as a distinctively Latin American philosophy, given the economic and cultural dependence on Europe and, increasingly, the United States. The turmoil of the 1960s and 1970s, including both the proliferation of new social movements and the "national security" dictatorships in Argentina, Brazil, Chile, and Paraguay also influenced debates about the possibility of national, popular revolution.[38] Although the thinkers involved in these debates differed on a number of issues, they shared a point of departure: they all criticized the abstract universalism of Western philosophy for its tendency to privilege dominant European interests and identities, while masking its own implication in violence, exclusion, and domination.[39] From this core premise, however, the figures associated with the philosophy of liberation developed in different directions, which reflected different philosophical influences: Marxism (Bondy), phenomenology (Dussel), and historicism (Zea).[40] Some enthusiastically embraced indigenous or national-popular movements; others called for Marxist-inspired revolution; and a few identified conservative, Catholic values as the basis of an authentic, Latin American alternative to materialism and modernity.

Despite these differences, it is still worthwhile to try to identify the core features of the philosophy of liberation before exploring the work of any particular exponent in detail. Creating such an ideal type is a sort of distortion because it minimizes differences between thinkers and overlooks nuances of any individual work. Nevertheless, it is useful to identify commonalities because it reminds us that a related set of arguments emerged out of a particular historical, regional, and intellectual context. The philosophy of liberation formed a distinctive discourse with its own vocabulary and concerns. One of the key insights of the philosophy of liberation is the situated character of knowledge.

There are four key principles that characterize most of the work associated with the label "philosophy of liberation." First, the philosophy of liberation starts from a distinctive point of departure: the standpoint of the marginal or the oppressed. Formulated in a more abstract fashion, it holds that critical insight emerges from the position of exteriority vis-à-vis any totalizing system. In the case of the global world system, Latin America and other less economically developed countries form a periphery and the interests and culture of this periphery are marginal compared to the economic interests and cultural production of the core. According to the philosophy of liberation, the marginal position of Latin Americans positions them in a way that makes them particularly able to recognize the violent, exclusionary underside of modernity. The same logic of exteriority applies domestically and in the domain of interpersonal relations. A person who is poor, hungry, or homeless is an outsider whose very existence questions the logic of the dominant system and the subject's privileged place within it.

The three other themes are, in a sense, different dimensions or implications of the first. The philosophy of liberation is an ethical and political theory and not simply a philosophical reflection on perspectivalism. As the term "liberation" suggests, it is oriented toward social transformation and reflects on the theoretical and practical basis of emancipation. The philosophy of liberation emphasizes national-popular movements as potential agents of change. "The people" plays a structural role that is similar to Marx's proletariat; that is, it is a group that has been the carrier of historical contradictions and therefore potentially has an interest in radical change. Nevertheless, the emphasis on the popular is also a departure from Marxism because it does not locate politicization of identity primarily in the process of production. For some thinkers in this tradition, the source of critical insight into modernity comes from indigenous cultural traditions (pre-Columbian thought or practices); for others the experience of dispossession or marginality varies in different contexts (e.g., the feminine in a macho culture, the Hispano-American in a Eurocentric culture). The crucial assumption is that marginality is identified as the basis of a certain kind of moral insight.

The philosophy of liberation was also influenced by dependency theory, which was very prominent in the 1970s. Dependency theory identified global capitalism as a hierarchical, structured world system that benefited core countries (usually former colonial powers, with the United States, a former colony, belatedly joining the club) at the expense of peripheral countries (mostly former colonies).[41] Even after dependency theory lost favor in economic circles, Enrique Dussel continued to insist that its basic premise was insightful. Dussel emphasizes that the relationship between core and peripheral countries consists primarily of the extraction of surplus value from the latter for the former. He argues that this "essence" or basic logic is disguised by the varying phenomenal forms that the extraction of surplus takes: slavery, trade, debt payment, or profit of multinational corporations.[42]

The final component of the philosophy of liberation is its critique of modernity.[43] Of course modernity can mean many things, including global capitalism, Enlightenment philosophy, secularism, science, industrialization, and individualism, to name just a few. There are two dimensions of this critique of modernity. One is simply the idea that the values and practices brought to Latin America by the Spanish conquistadores cannot be understood simply as civilization, progress, and prosperity. The violent conquest and the hierarchical, exploitative system that it set up revealed the hypocrisy of the European values of equality, universalism, and rationality. European "civilization" cannot simply be dismissed because it is deeply and inevitably part of Latin American history, but the traditional creole and mestizo narrative that celebrates this history must be tempered by the recognition that the Spanish brought more barbarism than civilization. The philosophical version of this point is that the value system of modernity was not simply the autonomous achievement of Europe but was instead a myth that emerged in response to Europe's bloody encounter with the New World.[44]

DUSSEL'S LEVINASIAN MARXISM

Enrique Dussel (b. 1934) is the figure most associated with the philosophy of liberation. Dussel was trained in philosophy in Argentina in the 1950s, with a particular focus on Thomism, natural law theory, and Catholic theology. As a student, he was also affiliated with the Christian Democratic Party and the Catholic Action social movement. After completing his doctoral dissertation in Madrid on "The Common Good in the Modern Thomist School of the 16th Century," he lived in Israel before moving to France and Germany to study history and theology.[45] In his first book, *A History of the Church in Latin America: Colonialism to Liberation (1492–1979)*, he pioneered a distinctive approach to Church history.[46] In the 1960s he also began intensive study of twentieth-century continental philosophy, focused on the work of Sartre, Gadamer, Ricoeur, Heidegger, and especially Levinas. After his return to Argentina in 1967, he began work on a multivolume study called the *Filosofía ética latino-americana*. This work reflected his interest in the relationship between totality and exteriority as well as the political and ethical consequences of responsibility for the other. Dussel concluded that one aspect of ethical obligation was a profound transformation of the structures of neoimperialism and capitalism.[47] In order to explore the economic aspects of the problem of liberation, Dussel wrote a three-volume study of the concepts of living labor and surplus value in Marx.[48]

Dussel's work has been the subject of fairly extensive scholarly debate both within and outside of Latin America, and this scholarly debate provides a useful point of departure for understanding the strengths and weaknesses of his approach. Dussel is extremely prolific, having written books and essays on topics as diverse as discourse ethics, church history, theology, and the character of modernity. It is beyond the scope of this chapter to provide an overview of his numerous contributions; we will focus on *Philosophy of Liberation (Filosofía de la liberación)*, his best-known work.[49]

In *Philosophy of Liberation*, Dussel articulates what he calls a "barbarian philosophy."[50] He appropriates a term that was used frequently in the eighteenth and nineteenth century to describe non-European cultures and to legitimize the European conquest of the Americas. The term "barbarian philosophy" draws attention to the marginal, peripheral, nonrational position of exteriority that he identifies as the most potent location for a critique of contemporary politics and its dominant form of legitimation. *Philosophy of Liberation*, however, is much more than simply a philosophical critique of Eurocentrism. Dussel attempts to outline an expansive theory that encompasses domination in the domains of gender/sexuality, pedagogy, religion, and economics as well.

Dussel introduces his philosophy of liberation in terms that are familiar to any reader of Emmanuel Levinas. He begins with the concept of proximity, which he describes as the concrete, immediate connection to the other person and the basis of responsibility. He uses the example of nursing (breast-feeding) as the paradigmatic illustration of a proximate relationship to the other that is a response to another's need, a primal social bond that interpolates us as interconnected not isolated individuals.[51] Proximity is also achieved in more reciprocal interactions such as the kiss between lovers or the dialogue between friends.[52] Using a phenomenological approach, he describes a form of recognition that is not simply a projection of the same (the self) or an instrumental use of the other. Although Dussel does not call these relationships natural or authentic, such a notion of nonexploitative mutuality is the basis of his philosophy of liberation.

The concepts of exteriority and totality also play an important role in the theoretical structure of the book. His use of the term "totality" slides between a descriptive and a normative sense. In the descriptive mode, totality refers to the world as a whole. He explains, "We comprehend or embrace the world as a totality. This totality is present in every concrete human act. To discover that this sense-thing is a table is possible because the one who discovers it can relate it to other things and interpret it as a table. Without the a priori whole, it is impossible to make sense out of anything."[53] This seems to suggest totality is something akin to a horizon of interpretation. It is the whole which makes possible the comprehension of parts. Later in the text, however, Dussel uses totality in a more normative, critical vein that evokes Levinas's use of the same term in his book *Totality and Infinity*. Dussel argues that "Totality, the system, tends to totalize itself, to center itself, and to attempt—temporally—to eternalize its present structure. Spatially it attempts to include within itself all possible exteriority."[54] Totality here signifies the tendency to assimilate difference into the logic of the same. He elaborates by describing "totalizing totality" as the violent assimilation of anything alien. Given Dussel's focus on the European conquest of the Americas as the defining moment of modernity, it is clear that Western colonialism and its violent destruction or instrumental control of alien peoples is the paradigmatic illustration of the logic of totality.

Exteriority, then, is the perspective or position that is not wholly within the totality and therefore can be the basis of critique. According to Dussel, exteriority is meant to signify "the ambit whence other persons, as free and not conditioned by one's own system and not as part of one's own world, reveal themselves."[55] To take the most concrete illustration, Latin America is in a position of exteriority vis-à-vis the centers of economic and cultural power in the United States and Europe. This place beyond the horizon of the totality is a privileged locus for assessing the limitations, contradictions, and irrationalities of the dominant worldview. Dussel claims that the poor in the Third World are most likely to challenge the view that capitalism, colonialism, and globalism are beneficial to all parties in these hierarchical relations. Similarly, the woman in a patriarchal society or the student in authoritarian pedagogical relations recognizes the system of order for what it is: a system of power. Exteriority is the key concept of the philosophy of liberation because it provides a theoretical rationale for privileging the standpoint of the oppressed peoples, peripheral countries, and marginalized voices. Dussel defends a version of the position that others have labeled the epistemic privilege of the oppressed.

The concept of absolute exteriority is also troubling and Dussel recognizes its limitations. In fact, he immediately modifies the concept and calls it "interior transcendentality." This term signals the fact that a position that is completely beyond totality is incomprehensible. He explains, "The category of exteriority . . . is misunderstood when what is 'beyond' the ontological horizon of the system is thought of in an absolute, total way without any participation in the interior of the system."[56] This means that most subject positions simultaneously find themselves both inside and outside different dimensions of power relations. There is no single system or totality but rather a number of overlapping and often reinforcing (but also different and contradictory) systems. This means that a man might find himself identifying with the logic of the patriarchal gender system while inhabiting a position of exteriority vis-à-vis capitalist economic relations or Eurocentric cultural meanings. Rather than emphasizing the contradictory and differential dimensions of power and resistance, however Dussel tends to treat the dyad totality (or system, *proyecto*)/exteriority as abstract categories. He frequently refers to "the system" or "the totality" in the singular. The source that disrupts the system/totality may have different anthropological characteristics ("the ebony face of the African slave . . . the yellow face of the Chinese coolies"), but these different manifestations reflect what he calls "the face."[57]

Given this abstract, essentialist way of framing totality and exteriority, Dussel leaves himself open to poststructuralist criticisms of theories that grant epistemic privilege to the oppressed. The core of this criticism is that approaches that emphasize marginality as a privileged standpoint also essentialize and homogenize this identity in a way that itself can be exclusionary and oppressive. In *States of Injury*, for example, Wendy Brown suggests that identity politics can be a form of *ressentiment* that instrumentalizes powerlessness or dispossession in an effort to assume a position of moral superiority.[58] She uses the term "wounded attachments" to describe a politics that is invested in its own marginality because it provides a coherent identity and privileged standpoint. In so far as these wounded attachments attain coherence by politicizing exclusion from an ostensible universal, they are reproducing rather than challenging the dominant political logic.[59] According to Brown, feminist standpoint theory is particularly flawed because it is premised on the contradiction that women are both socially constructed by patriarchy and that simultaneously they can be the source of essential truths. Moreover, the standpoint theory requires a universal category of women as its basis and this category is itself constructed and exclusionary.[60]

Does this critique of American identity politics apply to Latin American philosophy of liberation? Initially it appears as if the two have little in common. American identity politics tends to be more individualistic, to emphasize race or ethnicity and to be less concerned with class. In contrast, the philosophy of liberation as a political movement has affinities with national-populist forms of socialism. Nevertheless, Wendy Brown's core critique of feminist standpoint theory is a relevant challenge to any theory that privileges exteriority as a basis of critique. She explains that standpoint theory "requires suspending recognition that women's 'experience' is thoroughly constructed, historically and culturally varied, and interpreted without end."[61] In other words, the epistemic privilege of the disempowered (women, people living in peripheral countries, racial minorities, etc.) is based on the untenable assumption that their identities and insights are not constructed by dominant social structures.

Ofelia Schutte's *Cultural Identity and Social Liberation in Latin American Thought* is an early work that introduces this line of criticism; moreover, it focuses specifically on the limitations of Dussel's concept of exteriority. Although Schutte is sympathetic to the goal of the philosophy of liberation, she notes that Dussel's approach has at least two disturbing features.[62] First, she argues that his philosophy identifies alterity or otherness as a privileged basis for absolute authority. In his search for a purified source of perspective and critique, Dussel privileges exteriority, a term that describes the metaphysical essence of concrete modalities of oppression. According to Schutte, this essence comes to mark a new foundational source of knowledge. Furthermore, for Schutte, totality and exteriority are dualistic concepts that evoke the theological notions of good and evil.

There are numerous examples of totalizing language in *Philosophy of Liberation*. For example, Dussel claims that "metaphysical proximity materializes unequivocally before the face of the oppressed."[63] But of course, the moment of face-to-face exposure is nothing if not equivocal. Depending on one's political ideology, religious training, and personal experience, one may encounter a homeless person and perceive him as a threat, a vagrant, a child of god, a bearer of social critique, a victim, a lazy parasite or one may simply not perceive him at all. The same is true of any of the marginal figures that Dussel invokes. Dussel is not unaware of this problem and introduces concepts such as "alienation" and "the mask," which is "fashioned by the system to hide the other's entreaty."[64] The problem is that the concept of the mask implies that there is an essence or truth hidden behind the mask. It denies the possibility that subject and mask are mutually constitutive of one another and that unmasking may be a process of creation rather than discovery.

Dussel's theoretical absolutism also has problematic political consequences. Schutte argues that Dussel's philosophy of liberation is similar to the structure of Leninism because it identifies the poor and working class as the carriers of a critique that they themselves do not understand. Liberation, then, requires the leadership of a vanguard party or at least an intellectual with privileged access to the metaphysical/historical insight that is needed to guide the people in their struggle.

There are passages in *Philosophy of Liberation* that lend themselves to this reading. For example, Dussel writes, "A people alone cannot liberate itself . . . It is because of this that the critical mentality of the organic intellectual, of critical communities or political parties, is indispensable so that a people acquire a critical mentality . . . Philosophy has much to do in this field."[65] He puts it even more explicitly later in the text when he insists,

> The most oppressed classes do not always have the most acute critical awareness, but such awareness can be reached by classes that, although objectively not the most oppressed, are the ones upon whom ideological contradictions weigh the heaviest.[66]

Not surprisingly, he identifies the philosopher as particularly well-positioned to "express the criticism of the people."[67] Political liberation requires leadership, but it is worth asking whether all forms of leadership are equivalent to Leninism, or whether a comparison with Gramsci's organic intellectual is more apt. Schutte claims that the structure of Dussel's analysis is similar in structure to that used by "some of the most fanatic ideologies in modern history."[68] But there are also at least two important differences between Dussel and Lenin. First, Dussel's concept of exteriority differs from the Marxist-Leninist idea of class because it privileges exteriority in general rather than a particular position such as the proletariat. Since exteriority could describe a potentially unlimited number of positions, it could be the basis for criticizing any totalizing system, including a workers' state. Leninism identifies the proletariat as the agent of historical change and assumes that the end of class oppression is the end of all oppression. Its categories do not allow for the possibility that this new stage could also solidify into a totality that needs to be criticized from another position. Dussel, on the other hand, sees the oppression as diffuse and complete liberation as impossible.

In Dussel's more recent work, he places less emphasis on leadership and more stress on institutions as spheres of democratic legitimacy. In *Twenty Theses on Politics* (published in English in 2008), he invokes Hannah Arendt's understanding of power as that which emerges when people act together, something distinctive from violence, force or authority.[69] He also modifies his earlier approach to leadership:

> Liberation praxis is not solipsistic—that is, it is not created by a single and inspired subject: the leader. . . . Liberation praxis is *always* an intersubjective

community act of reciprocal consensus, which does not reject leadership . . .
but definitively abandons vanguardism. It is a "rearguard" action by
the *people* itself, which educates social movements about its democratic
autonomy, its political evolution, and about being responsible for its
destiny.[70]

In *Twenty Theses*, Dussel explains that even the Gramscian organic intellectual
is not a leader in the traditional sense but rather "a promoter, an organizer, and
a light that illuminates the path constructed, unfolded, and perfected by the
people."[71] This passage makes it clear that Dussel has taken his critics seriously.
Twenty Theses on Politics was published in Spanish in 2006, over thirty years
after *Philosophy of Liberation*, and places greater emphasis on the politics, as
opposed to the philosophy, of liberation.

A second difference between Dussel's philosophy of liberation and totali-
tarian variants of Marxism is their respective attitudes toward history. As Hannah Arendt pointed out in *The Origins of Totalitarianism*, totalitarianism
typically relies on historical inevitability as a mode of legitimation. In a particularly reductionist version of dialectics, history guarantees that the end justifies
the means. This, however, is clearly not Dussel's view. Dussel has no concept of
historical progress. In fact, he criticizes dialectics precisely because of its potentially totalizing character.[72] He worries that the moment of difference in dialectics is ultimately subsumed into a synthetic whole and therefore loses its alterity.
Instead, he calls for an alternative "analectical method." According to Dussel,
the term "analectic" comes from the Greek prefix *ano-*, or 'beyond.' It signals
the need to look "beyond the horizon of totality."[73] It is another way of describing the moment of irreducible exteriority that provides insight into structures of domination.[74]

Dussel uses the concept of exteriority as a way of characterizing the logic of
critique without privileging any individual critical perspective. This approach is
much closer to Levinas than to Lenin.[75] But even without the specter of totalitarianism haunting the philosophy of liberation, it is still worth reflecting on
the validity of the concept of exteriority and its usefulness for political praxis.
Ofelia Schutte argues that the concept of exteriority is based on the uncon-
vincing premise that there exists a place external to the system of domination
(the totality).[76] For example, Schutte challenges Dussel's claim that the pre-
school child is exterior to the system of pedagogical domination of the school
system. Since small children are already deeply socialized and disciplined both
literally and metaphorically, they do not encounter the school system from
some position of natural innocence or primal freedom. In fact, some have suggested that the natural child idealized in Rousseau's *Émile* (1762) was itself socially constructed through pedagogy.[77] This example reminds us that absolute

exteriority simply does not exist. Each of the figures that Dussel mentions—the poor, the Latin American, the indigenous person, the woman—might be better understood as inhabiting a differential position within a system of power rather than a position outside of it. To argue that the woman/poor/peripheral person is a constituted through power relations and also is a source of meaning and truth outside of such power relations does entail a logical contradiction.[78] Furthermore, Schutte is right that the abstract logic of "exteriority" can be an evasion of the concrete and complex analysis of actual social relations of domination. From the perspective of contemporary feminist theory, for example, calling "woman" exterior to macho-patriarchy (Dussel's term) does not really advance a debate that has engaged in rich reflections about themes such as the disciplinary effects of essentialism, universalism/difference, legal remedies, intersectionality, sex/gender, and performativity.

These criticisms of standpoint theory are convincing, but we think they point toward the need to modify the theory rather than to reject it entirely. Dussel himself recognizes that total exteriority is conceptually impossible. He warns, "The category of exteriority, as said above, is misunderstood when what is 'beyond' the ontological horizon of the system is thought of in an absolute, total way without any participation in the interior of the system. To avoid this misunderstanding, exteriority must be understood as transcendentality interior to the system."[79] He explains that no person is entirely a reflection of the system of domination, but neither are they ever completely outside of it. This more modest account of exteriority helps resolve the apparent logical contradiction above. Given that subject positions are themselves produced by social, economic and discursive structures (what Dussel calls the totality), they cannot be sources of pure, uncontaminated, essential knowledge. Nevertheless, certain positions are the sites of particularly acute contradictions that can reveal the irrationality and impossibility of the system. For example, the unemployed person or underdeveloped country may experience the negative effects of a system based on "free competition" between individuals and groups with vastly different resources and power. Although these positions are not exterior to the capitalist world system, the people inhabiting these marginal positions are likely to see and evaluate the system differently than those who claim most of the benefits. This is really no more controversial than saying that the people at the bottom often see domination where those at the top see functional differentiation, meritocracy, or the natural order of things. Interpreted in this way, "exteriority" is more akin to perspectivalism rather than a foundationalist, essentialist epistemic privilege of the oppressed. The consequence for philosophical practice is not to authorize the philosopher to speak for the poor but instead to remind her to listen to them. It is an inversion of Rawls's veil of ignorance, in other words, a demand that moral reasoning requires the fullest possible knowledge of the concrete consequences for the weak and disempowered. The concepts of the other, the face, and exteriority can be read as reminders that this knowledge cannot be acquired through abstract reflection but through experience and exposure that potentially disrupts certainty, identity, and ideology.

The problem with *Philosophy of Liberation*, in our view, is not the validity of this critical perspectivalism but rather the difficulty of deducing any particular political program from its key tenets.[80] A critique of global capitalism could lead to a number of very different solutions including national corporatism, anarchism, autarky, state socialism, or libertarian forms of the free market, among others. To decide among these requires both a normative framework and an empirical analysis of political economy. Not surprisingly, *Philosophy of Liberation* is somewhat thin when it comes to political praxis. Dussel endorses a series of proposals that include calls for self-determination, the right to work, and a culture that fosters human dignity. Given the extremely unequal distribution of capital, he concludes that an egalitarian society requires a "total economic revolution" and "a new mode of production" that will emerge through the leadership of the popular classes.[81]

Although Dussel uses a very different theoretical vocabulary, he ends up embracing a position that is not too different from Mariátegui. Both conclude that the conquest of the Americas with its cultural alienation and economic dispossession has created a system of hyperexploitation that cannot be reformed. Although Dussel was dismissive of Marx early in his career, he came to hold the view that "a new mode of production is necessary in dependent nations."[82] He notes that there are three different models of economic liberation. The first is essentially the mainstream economic idea of development, or what he calls "dependent capitalism," for example, the hope that investment by transnational corporations will lead to economic growth. The second is independent capitalism, which tried to achieve growth through the leadership of the national bourgeoisie. The third model, which he endorses, involves "leadership by the popular classes." He calls this socialism and concludes that "the system of capitalist enterprise, with hereditary capital on the part of some and the sale of their labor on the part of others . . . can no longer be permitted in the periphery."[83] He leaves it to the philosophy of economics, however, to clarify what type of economic structures would take its place and how the transition would be brought about.

Dussel's philosophy of liberation falls into the category that Marx derisively called "utopian socialism." It is based primarily on a normative argument and clearly reflects a religious concern with the "wretched of the earth." Although this concern manifests itself in support of socialism, it does not include a detailed analysis of the structures of capitalism or the social forces most likely to bring about radical change. *Twenty Theses on Politics* introduces the concept of the people, a term that Dussel uses to describe the "moment of negativity"—the excluded whose struggle for inclusion drives the process of democratization.[84] Dussel also wrote a multivolume study of Marx, a work that is not so much a departure from Dussel's earlier approach as a creative interpretation that identifies similarities between it and Marx. The study of Marx focused on a painstaking reconstruction of the early drafts of Marx's *Capital* that revealed the importance of an undertheorized Marxian concept: living labor. According to Dussel, living labor is a form of exteriority that cannot be absorbed by the totality of capital.[85] Unlike labor power, which is the source of value for capital, living labor is the nonalienated form that is its constitutive outside. In spite of this nuanced contribution to Marxist scholarship, Dussel still remains very resistant to what we take to be the key aspect of Marx's approach, his materialism. Marx's innovation was his commitment to a materialist method that illuminated the contradictions of capital and the social forces that were the primary bearers of this antagonism. Since Dussel's philosophy of liberation suffers from excessive abstraction and Mariátegui's variant, as suggested above, was too dismissive of normativity, it makes sense to bring the two thinkers together.

CONCLUSION

Although Mariátegui and Dussel are not usually seen as part of the same theoretical tradition, each one provides a way of resolving some of the problems in the other's approach.[86] Dussel's *Philosophy of Liberation* lacks a materialist analysis of economic conditions and oppositional social forces. In his *Ética de la Liberación en la edad de globalización y de la exclusión*, he has begun to rectify this by focusing on the capitalist world system that structures the inequalities between central and peripheral countries.[87] Nevertheless, Dussel's work still emphasizes that liberation is inspired by a quasi-mystical ethical force that is made incarnate and accessible through the face of the poor, the slum-dweller, the campesino. But perhaps this is precisely the myth that is most politically potent today. Many people living in the global periphery experience capitalism not only as exploited workers but also as the unemployed, indebted migrants, marginal entrepreneurs, indigenous peasants, dependent clients, workers in the informal economy, and homemakers making homes in the favelas.

One of the most visible and influential resistance movements of the past two decades has employed precisely this language. The declarations, letters, and essays of the Zapatista spokesman Subcomandante Marcos (see Chapter 5) read like a page from *Philosophy of Liberation*. In "Other Intellectuals," Marcos urges supporters "to embrace the other, to learn about themselves through it, and to come to know the indigenous, the worker, the campesino, the young person, the woman, the child, the old one, the teacher, the student, the employee, the homosexual, the lesbian, the transgendered person, the sex worker, the street vendor, the small shopkeeper, the Christian base, the street worker, the other."[88] When the Zapatistas relaunched their movement in 2006, they described it as "the other campaign." This was, in part, a reference to their decision not to participate in Mexico's presidential election, instead opting for other political tactics. But it was also a way of emphasizing connections between their own distinctive struggle to control their land and the other forms of dispossession experienced by urban workers, residents of informal settlements, immigrants, and the poor, both in Mexico and throughout the world.

As the experience of the Zapatistas has shown, there are difficulties that stem from using the concept of "the other" as the basis of a new political subjectivity. As a movement becomes more inclusive, it also has to find ways of reconciling diverse factions, establishing priorities, and acting together. Socialist history and theory are filled with passionate debates about the costs and benefits of building alliances with other classes.[89] But the idea of "the other" in the philosophy of liberation is not a naive assumption that all of the various forms of oppression and exploitation can be absorbed into one political movement or agenda. Sexism and homophobia are not precisely the same as economic exploitation or cultural erasure, but the logic of critique in one area is analogous to the other. Each structure must be assessed from the perspective of those who bear the burdens rather than simply of those who enjoy the benefits.

Mariátegui's work, however, still has two important lessons for the philosophy of liberation. The first is a cautious attitude toward the lingering traces of naive moralism in the philosophy of liberation. Mariátegui was dismissive of any solution to the "Indian question" that relied on the good intentions of elites and the neutrality of the state. The philosophy of liberation becomes utopian (in the negative sense) when it seems to rely on a conversion experience whereby elites, confronted with the "eyes of the poor," eschew their own economic interests and champion those of the poor. Instead, it makes more sense to see Dussel's emphasis on "encounter" and "proximity" as phenomenological descriptions of the moment that enables people from diverse subaltern positions to achieve solidarity. From this perspective, change occurs not when the elite (or imperialist countries) miraculously recognize their responsibility for the poor/peripheral, but rather when the latter recognize their responsibility for one another and become capable of demanding political change and creating alternatives.

The second lesson that emerges from Mariátegui's work comes from one of his least appreciated insights: the intriguing moment when he admits the illusory nature of universal laws and principles but still affirms that "one must propose a faith, a myth, an action."[90] This insight is similar to the political reading of the "empty signifier" developed by Ernesto Laclau, who began his career as a scholar of Latin American Marxism. According to Laclau, universals such as democracy, the people, freedom, law, and justice can never achieve a stable, fixed, definitive meaning.[91] They are empty signifiers that mark our aspirations and frame our political activities, but they are always vulnerable to, and available for, reconfiguration. Freedom can mean the free market or the collective self-government of the community. Mariátegui recognized that this antifoundationalist insight would be sterile and depoliticizing if it led to satisfaction with perpetual critique. As he put it, "Humanity resists following a truth that it does not believe absolute and supreme."[92] Action is much more difficult if one acknowledges the contingencies and complexities of one's available choices. These two theorists insist upon balancing aspirational visions with critical insight. Because we believe in the necessity for change without the illusion of purity, we can recognize and accept the philosophy of liberation as a myth, perhaps a salutary one.

Conclusion

Gandhi and the Critique
of Western Civilization

HIND SWARAJ

Hind Swaraj (Indian Home Rule) is widely considered the most concise and forceful statement of Gandhi's political theory. It contains an explanation of British domination in India, an analysis of the meaning of *swaraj* (self-rule), a discussion of political strategy, and, perhaps most notoriously, a critique of Western civilization. Not content to merely condemn the excesses of British colonialism, Gandhi criticizes the colonial state's proudest achievements: technology, parliamentary government, the railway system, public education, modern medicine, and the judicial system.[1] Like Jamal al-Din al-Afghani twenty years earlier and Jalal Al-e Ahmad fifty years later, Gandhi castigates Western civilization for its materialism, individualism, and immorality. He calls Western civilization a disease and suggests that the cure is to be found in the traditional Indian practice of self-mastery.

Gandhi composed the book in just ten days while traveling by ship from England to South Africa. It seems somehow fitting that the book was written on a ship, because of its cosmopolitan character. At first it might seem strange to characterize *Hind Swaraj* as cosmopolitan, given its status as a foundational text of the Indian nationalist movement and, of course, its seemingly Manichaean distinction between Western and Indian civilizations. Gandhi's essay, however, points to another cosmopolitanism, one that emerges in opposition to the illusory universalism of Western civilization. Gandhi points out that "civilization" is a normative concept that is invoked to distinguish good from bad and superior from inferior. According to Gandhi, the West recognizes material comfort as the primary marker of civilization but this value system, far from being universal, is the product of a particular time and place. It emerged historically with the growth of commerce and industrialization. True civilization for Gandhi is good conduct, which involves duty, self-control, and morality.[2]

Like many writers before him, Gandhi uses the term "civilization" both as a normative ideal and a descriptive term that is more or less synonymous with culture.[3] He argues that Indian civilization (culture) has been particularly effective at preserving the values of civilization (good conduct/morality), but he never suggests that Indian civilization is the only way to reinforce these positive values. He notes that both Islam and Hinduism are antithetical to the value system of Western civilization, and even the English themselves are portrayed as victims of Western civilization rather than agents who are individually responsible for it.[4] *Hind Swaraj* is a nationalistic text but it also presents a universalistic theory. Western industrial civilization is depicted as particularism that masquerades as universal, an aberration that has corrupted the spiritual values embedded in its own traditions as well as the traditions of its colonies. *Hind Swaraj* is a paradigmatic example of colonial critique; it demystifies European civilization, describes an alternative set of values, and asserts the universality of these values.

The first step of colonial critique is *demystification*. This involves showing that the West is not superior in absolute terms but rather it is superior only in terms of the criteria that it sets for itself. Yet in a colonial state it becomes difficult to see that law courts and railroads are not the only possible symbols of civilization. During the period of British domination, the West's criteria for superiority became so deeply ingrained in political discourse and practice that these criteria began to seem natural and inevitable. Demystification or denaturalization is part of the process of penetrating colonial ideology and undermining the legitimacy of the colonial system.

The problem with demystification is that it seems to run into an insurmountable problem: the fact of European power. In other words, the basis of European "superiority" isn't really its greater capacity for freedom and justice but rather its military strength and economic resources. Might makes a strong claim upon right, and no amount of demystification can change this. Gandhi confronts this argument directly and makes the controversial claim that "the English have not taken India; we have given it to them."[5] He explains that the British East India Company was a trading company and Indians welcomed it because they desired imported goods and the prosperity that could come from trade. Similarly, the British soldiers were welcomed by Indian princes who sought external allies in their struggles with domestic rivals. He concludes that the English, "a nation of shopkeepers," could not possibly hold India by the sword; the Indians are enslaved by their own avarice and disunity. The implication is that political unity and spiritual renewal are the bases for independence.[6]

In addition to questioning the universal validity of European norms, critics also argue that the colonists fail in their own terms. They point out that the European colonists valued liberty but engaged in coercion; the colonists claimed to bring civilization but cemented their rule by engaging in brutal violence. Gandhi rejects some Western values quite forcefully, but others he tries to reclaim and reconfigure.[7] Justice and freedom, for example, are values shared by everyone; the problem stems from the way that these values have become sutured to institutions and practices that undermine them. For example, he criticizes the legal system not because he underestimates the importance of impartial justice, but rather because he thinks that the adversarial structure of the court system is divisive: it actually "advances quarrels" rather than solving them. When he attacks the British parliament as a prostitute and a sterile woman, he is not expressing opposition to popular self-government. Instead, his point is that parliament does not effectively achieve popular government.[8] It is a vehicle for advancing the careers of prominent men rather than fostering deliberation and providing leadership. There is an inevitable gap between any abstract ideal such as freedom or justice and the particular practices that embody these ideals. By attacking parliament, the legal system, the railroads, and even modern medicine, Gandhi is trying to remind his readers that these distinctively modern practices are not the only ways to achieve health, justice, and self-rule.

Demystification, however, is not enough. Colonial critics such as Gandhi also wanted to recover precolonial practices and ideas that had been denigrated and undermined by the colonists in order to use them as resources for renewal and resistance. We call this second element of anticolonial critique "reversal." It has also been described as "reverse orientalism."[9] "Reversal" describes attempts to undermine power relations by valorizing the cultural markers that the colonial system has denigrated as inferior.[10] An illustration of this is Gandhi's depiction of Indian civilization as more spiritual and less materialist than the West. According to Gandhi, "The tendency of Indian civilization is to elevate the moral being, that of Western civilization is to propagate immorality. The latter is godless, the former is based on a belief in God."[11] Many colonial critics have advanced some version of this argument. Even Tagore, who is usually remembered as an opponent of Gandhi's nationalist rhetoric, depicted Eastern and Western civilization in Orientalist terms. In his essays, he contrasted the more active, acquisitive, individualist West with the more imaginative, spiritual, communal East.[12] Al-e Ahmad's *Gharbzadeghi* is another forceful articulation of the logic of reversal. Césaire and Senghor redefined blackness, not rejecting racial categories, but instead revaluing them. Jean-Paul Sartre's endorsement of negritude in his essay "Black Orpheus" (1948) claims that the redefinition of particular identities is "the moment of separation or negativity: this anti-racist racism is the only road that will lead to the abolition of racial differences."[13]

Most colonial critics claim that their own precolonial culture is a source of alternative and superior values. Of course, there are political as well as theoretical reasons for this move. As Partha Chatterjee pointed out, this tactic was very effective at mobilizing the common people who often felt little connection with Westernized native elites.[14] The critics of colonialism discussed in this book could be divided into two groups, or perhaps more appropriately located along a continuum based on whether they argued that the alternative values were embedded in history or created through struggle. The Ayatollah Khomeini, for example, located the source of renewal in the past, even as he refashioned traditional religious texts in order to restructure the present. Frantz Fanon, on the other hand, recognized that nationalist consciousness encouraged pride and fostered anticolonial mobilization, but he worried that it would undermine the long-term goal of building a more just society. According to Fanon, fostering strong bonds based on religion, ethnicity, or nationalism could strengthen indigenous elites and undermine the solidarity of oppressed peoples. In the conclusion to *Wretched of the Earth*, he urged, "Let us try to create the whole man, whom Europe has been incapable of bringing to triumphant birth."[15] Where would Gandhi stand on this continuum? There are moments in *Hind Swaraj* in which Gandhi seems deeply embedded in the moment of reversal.[16] His rejection of the symbols of modernity is strongly worded. He argues that railways spread disease, exacerbate famines, and encourage communal conflict. He characterizes lawyers as parasites who encourage conflict in order to enrich themselves. Even modern medicine is not immune to his criticism. He claims that it does little more than provide palliatives that encourage people to indulge in sloth and gluttony. In the final pages of the book he calls on his readers to use the English language rarely, to give up their professions and "take up a handloom," and to repent for the sin of encouraging European civilization.[17] While Gandhi is careful to emphasize that the target of his criticism is not the English people but their civilization, he certainly does not point to some cultural synthesis or dialectical synthesis as the solution.

The opposition between the corrupt materialist Western civilization and the spiritual, moral Indian civilization, however, is not as absolute as it initially appears. Unlike most other commentators, Gandhi did not identify "East" and "West" as geographical markers of a clash of civilizations. Instead, he saw the difference as temporal rather than geographical. He argued that Asia and Europe had shared fundamental spiritual values until Europe experienced a decline of civilization brought about by the industrial revolution.

This allowed him to affirm the unity of mankind while still criticizing Western civilization.[18]

There are other ways that the text subverts its own Manichaeanism. For example, *Hind Swaraj* is written as a dialogue, and the character that clearly articulates Gandhi's own views is a newspaper editor. As Anthony Parel points out, it is interesting that Gandhi chooses the distinctively European figure of the newspaper editor rather than a more traditional Indian character such as a guru.[19] It is significant in part because it seems to contradict his critical assessment of newspapers in the text itself. In *Hind Swaraj* Gandhi argues that one of the weaknesses of the parliamentary system is that it depends on informed voters, yet the voters rely on the distorted, capricious, and partisan information that they read in newspapers.[20] Gandhi criticized newspapers, yet he also relied on them to circulate his critique of Western civilization. This could be a performative contradiction or it could be a way of reminding the reader that a simple return to tradition is neither possible nor advisable. A strident theoretical critique might be useful in dismantling the assemblage linking materialism/individualism/rationalism to freedom/equality/justice, yet a pragmatic approach might be needed to reconstruct an alternative.

In the guise of "the editor," Gandhi appears not so much an antimodernist as a critical traditionalist. This term comes from Bhikhu Parekh's influential study *Colonialism, Tradition, and Reform: An Analysis of Gandhi's Political Discourse.* Parekh situates Gandhi in the context of other British responses to colonial rule. He identifies four main alternatives: modernism, traditionalism, critical modernism, and critical traditionalism. According to Parekh, critical modernists believed that the basic principles of Indian civilization were worth preserving but these principles could only be safeguarded through extensive modernization.[21] They aspired to a "creative synthesis" of modern scientific culture, Indian moral values, and European political institutions. In *Hind Swaraj* Gandhi clearly rejects this approach. He obviously shares little of the critical modernists' enthusiasm for scientific culture or British political institutions. He also recognized the tension between the Hindu emphasis on mastering desire and the scientific/materialist emphasis on mastering nature in order to fulfill constantly expanding desires. Parekh defines critical traditionalism as rooted in the view that "a civilization was an organic whole and could not be judged in terms of criteria derived from outside it."[22] This meant that Indian civilization could not be judged by European standards, nor would it be possible to use Britain as a model for reform. But critical traditionalists realized that some reform was necessary. British rule made it impossible to continue to avoid addressing the causes of India's weakness. This opened up discussions about the caste system, Hindu-Muslim relations, sectarianism, and economic exploitation.

Critical traditionalism was a response to British rule, but one that sought reformist solutions in Indian sources.

Critical traditionalism sounds like the best label for Gandhi's own thought, except for the fact that *Hind Swaraj* so obviously draws on European ideas and authors. In the appendix Gandhi suggests that readers who want to explore his arguments in more depth should consult works by Tolstoy, Thoreau, Mazzini, Plato, Maine, and Ruskin. Edward Carpenter's *Civilisation: Its Causes and Cure* (1889) is one of the few books referenced in the text.[23] It is obvious that these works were not included in the bibliography merely in an attempt to gain scholarly legitimacy or cultural legibility. The impact of these authors is very pronounced in the text. Gandhi's explanation of British rule in India, for example, bears a striking resemblance to Tolstoy's analysis in his "Letter to a Hindu." In the letter, Tolstoy argued that a commercial company could not enslave a nation of two hundred million people. According to Tolstoy, the English did not enslave the Indians but rather the Indians enslaved themselves. Furthermore, the Indians acquiesced to their own subordination by recognizing force as "the fundamental principle of the social order."[24] In *Hind Swaraj* Gandhi advances a similar argument. The Reader asks "why was India lost?" and the Editor answers, "The English have not taken India; we have given it to them."[25] According to the Editor, Indians consent to British rule largely because they believe that the development of commerce is in their self-interest. In other words, it is the Indians' embrace of the materialist values of Western civilization that is the cause of their own domination.

Gandhi's critique of Western civilization also closely echoes some of the arguments advanced in Edward Carpenter's *Civilisation*.[26] Compared to Tolstoy, Thoreau, and Gandhi himself, Edward Carpenter's reputation has not proved enduring. He was a Fabian socialist, university extension teacher, gentleman farmer and gay activist, and his book made a strong impression on Gandhi. Carpenter emphasized that the term "civilization" has two meanings. It can be used as a normative concept synonymous with "ennobling."[27] Alternatively, it can be an analytic concept that describes a specific historical stage characterized by alienable private property, social classes based on material possessions, and the institution of the state. While Carpenter did not endorse the "noble savage" theory, he tried to show that civilization in the later sense is far from ennobling.[28] He called it a disease and he used the term both metaphorically and literally. He argued that barbarians were much less likely to become physically or mentally sick. Carpenter also criticized science, another sacred symbol of the superiority of modern civilization.

Gandhi incorporates all of these points into *Hind Swaraj*. Like Carpenter, he argues that modern civilization creates the pathologies that modern medicine purports to cure. But rather than curing the sick body, medicine often enables it to survive in its pathological state. More important, however, is the impact Carpenter's general approach to the concept of civilization had on Gandhi. The idea that civilization is a historical stage marked by economic development is by no means Carpenter's original idea. John Stuart Mill made the same distinction between civilization understood as moral development and civilization understood as economic development.[29] It dates back at least as far as the Scottish Enlightenment when conjectural historians like Adam Ferguson and John Millar divided historical development into four stages: hunting, herding, farming, and commerce. For the Scots, these stages also tracked the progress of moral and political development from savagery to barbarism and finally to civilization.[30] For Carpenter and Gandhi, on the other hand, the expansion of commercial/industrial society is just the reverse; it ushers in a new kind of barbarism.

Gandhi's critique of Western civilization is similar to the analysis advanced by the European romantic-radicals who he cites as well as other anticolonial writers whose work he was not familiar with. By pointing to the similarities we do not mean to diminish the significance of Gandhi's work. It is an original and powerful synthesis. Furthermore, we agree with Anthony Parel that the Hindu sources of his thought are also very important.[31] In fact, Indian ideas are also embedded in the "Western" texts in a way that makes it difficult to distinguish the original. Edward Carpenter traveled to India before writing *Civilisation: Its Causes and Cures*, and he identified Hinduism as an inspiration for his ideas. Tolstoy was a voracious reader of Hindu and Buddhist religious texts, which he cited as an influence on his own Christian socialism. So it would be equally plausible to conclude that European anti-Enlightenment thought was derived, in part, from non-Western sources.

One implication, however, is that we cannot describe Gandhi as a traditionalist or even as a critical traditionalist, as defined by Parekh. Gandhi borrowed freely, explicitly, and enthusiastically from Western sources in order to develop his critique of Western civilization. *Hind Swaraj* describes a clash of civilizations, but the text also subverts this image by drawing on European authors who were critical of their own civilization. This suggests that perhaps there are multiple civilizations within both East and West and that cross-cultural dialogue and learning is possible.

OCCIDENTALISM

Gandhi may not be a traditionalist but he seems to fit the definition of an occidentalist, a term popularized by Ian Buruma and Avishai Margalit in their book *Occidentalism* (2004). They use the term "occidentalism" to describe the romantic critique of Western civilization that emerged in the late nineteenth century and flourished in a more virulent form in the Muslim world in the twentieth century. They argue that occidentalism was "born in Europe" but was adopted in Third World countries where it turned into a "hateful caricature."[32]

What exactly are the tropes of occidentalism? According to Buruma and Margalit, they include hostility to the city, commerce, scientific rationality, and secularism. These are all prominent themes in Gandhi's writings.[33] He calls Western civilization "irreligion."[34] His critiques of commerce, science, technology, and industrialization are more far-reaching than those found in the writings of Islamists like Yusuf al-Qaradawi and Sayyid Qutb. In *Hind Swaraj* he argues that studying the sciences (geography, algebra, astronomy) is not very useful because it neither helps the student control his desires nor understand his duties.[35] Antiurbanism is less explicit but seems to be a corollary of his depiction of the rural village as the center of cultural and moral life. The independent rural village also plays a prominent role in his writings on economic theory, where he promotes self-sufficient rural production as a model for economic life.[36]

It is surprising that Buruma and Margalit did not include Gandhi in their study. The most likely explanation is that Gandhi doesn't fit well with the subtext of their argument.[37] The book's subtitle, *The West in the Eyes of Its Enemies*, points toward their concern with the ideological motivation behind terrorism. The first substantive chapter opens with a description of 9/11, and the later chapters focus on the ideology embraced by Muslim terrorists. While Buruma and Margalit acknowledge that occidentalism is a broader ideology with varied geographical and intellectual roots, their goal is clearly to link the critique of Western civilization to the ideology of political Islam and the practices of terrorism and violence. Gandhi's writings encourage us to question this link.

The occidentalism that worries Buruma and Margalit is the variant that not only criticizes the West but also dehumanizes and demonizes it. But even according to these narrower criteria, *Hind Swaraj* seems at least partially to fit. Gandhi's vivid description of the British parliament as a "sterile woman and a prostitute"[38] is highly unflattering. And consider the following depiction of Western civilization:

> This civilization is such that one has only to be patient and it will be self-destroyed. According to the teaching of Mahomed this would be considered a Satanic civilization. Hinduism calls it a black Age. . . . It is eating into the vitals of the English nation.[39]

Gandhi demonizes Western civilization when he describes it as "evil," but he is careful not to dehumanize the English people. He insists that the English "are not inherently immoral" and therefore deserve sympathy rather than blame.[40]

The subtext of *Occidentalism* is that theoretical critiques of Western civilization incite and legitimize violent and fanatic politics. But the link is never clearly spelled out. Anti-Enlightenment and romantic thinkers embraced varied political goals, from anarchism (Tolstoy) to participatory democracy (Rousseau) to utopian socialism (Fourier) to Nazism (Heidegger). In the colonial context we also see a variety of different political programs linked to the critique of Western civilization. Political context and intellectual context (e.g., the ensemble of other political and ethical ideas of the colonized society) also inform the way that the critique of Western civilization influences political practice. Gandhi's nonviolence (or *ahimsa*), for example, is a doctrine with deep roots in Hindu religious teaching. Hindu thinkers disapproved of violence for several reasons; they believed that it violated the sacred character of life; it stirred up negative emotions such as anger and hate; and it corrupted the soul, thereby undermining spiritual progress.[41]

Occidentalism may not necessarily entail violence, but it is a prominent motif in colonial critique. Buruma and Margalit also recognize the connection between hostility to the West and opposition to colonialism. They acknowledge that to Asians, the West meant colonialism and this means it also connoted domination[42] Yet we want to resist the conclusion that occidentalism is the essence of anticolonial political theory. We are troubled by the concept of occidentalism for two main reasons. First, it conflates political theories and political programs in a way that obscures rather than illuminates the connection between them. In some cases, anticolonial and anti-Western ideas legitimate and inspire violent resistance movements, including those that use terrorism, but this connection involves a political process of articulation that is not determined by the content of the ideas themselves. Political opportunities, social forces, and material factors also influence political strategies, and sometimes theories are developed retrospectively to provide a language for explaining, criticizing, and legitimizing them. This does not mean that ideas are irrelevant to politics. It seems that the strong tradition of nonviolence in Hinduism was an important influence on Gandhi's political tactics and the movement he led, but, as his own assassination reminds us, other Hindus interpreted the principles of nonviolence differently.

The second problem with the term occidentalism is the way that it misleadingly suggests a parallel between that concept and Orientalism. In his pathbreaking book, Edward Said argued that the Orient was the constitutive outside of the West. According to Said, by representing the Orient as irrational, sensual, and violent, Orientalism served to establish the superior rationality of the Occident.[43] Buruma and Margalit suggest that Occidentalism is something similar.

The image of a calculating, atomizing, alienating, dominating West becomes the marker of a stable and superior identity for the Third World, but there is an important difference between the two discourses. According to Said, Orientalism was not just an academic discipline that produced expert knowledge through the study of linguistics, anthropology, literature, and religion, but also a stable and recurring set of images that served to define, dominate, and restructure the Middle East. In other words, it was a set of ideas that was tightly linked to the exercise of power. In the case of Occidentalism, the power relations are exactly the reverse. Occidentalism does not have the status of expert knowledge about the West, nor does it have institutional links to structures of domination. Instead, the critique of Western civilization is usually a discourse of resistance, part of what we earlier called the logic of reversal: an attempt to reassert the autonomy and legitimacy of religions, cultures, or places that had been denigrated and dominated.

One reason why we have addressed the concept of occidentalism in some depth is that this type of critique of Western civilization is a thread than runs through many of the texts that we have discussed in this book. These critiques are not identical. Some variants are more inspired by Marxism, focus on the material bases of exploitation, and look to changes in the mode of production for solutions. Others emphasize cultural or spiritual renewal as the foundation of new political institutions, ethical dispositions, and communal unity. But most converge on the conclusion that European civilization, or in a more contemporary idiom, *liberal capitalist democracy*, fails to realize its own aspirations to universalism, freedom, and equality. Looking at the history of colonialism and its contemporary legacies makes this easier to recognize. Moreover, these arguments are not simply historical relics that emerged during the anticolonial wars of the twentieth century and disappeared after independence. There are echoes of them in the philosophy of liberation, in indigenous critiques of neo-liberalism and globalization, and some strands of Islamism today.

How convincing is this critique?

THE POSTCOLONIAL MESSAGE

To address this question we want to turn to the response made by one of Gandhi's opponents: Manabendra Nath Roy. M. N. Roy (born Narendranath Bhattacharya in 1887) was a Bengali intellectual, founder of the Indian Communist party, and a leader of Comintern. After fleeing Stalinist Russia in 1930, he was imprisoned by the British government in India. Later he moved away from orthodox Marxism and developed a theory of radical democratic humanism. He was also a vocal critic of Gandhi.[44]

In the 1920s Roy published a series of articles and pamphlets criticizing Gandhi's vision of *swaraj*. First, he argued that Gandhi's economic program would be unable to end rural misery. Second, he insisted that Gandhi's emphasis on social harmony and aversion to class conflict would reinforce existing inequalities. Third, he criticized Gandhi's reactionary view of history as rooted in nostalgia for an imaginary past that never existed and could not solve contemporary problems.[45] Roy's most detailed criticism of Gandhism, however, was developed in a series of essays that he wrote in jail and later published as *India's Message*. In the title essay, Roy attacks Gandhi's cultural nationalism and exposes its unintended consequences.[46]

Roy himself was no "reverse orientalist." He was unconvinced by the rhetoric of other critics of colonialism such as Gandhi who celebrated India's moral and spiritual superiority. In "India's Message," Roy insists that India is no more spiritual than the West. He points to the rich tradition of idealist philosophy and religious mysticism in Europe and concludes that metaphysical speculation may take different forms but is not the exclusive possession of any particular culture. In both East and West, "love, truth, goodness, etc." are affirmed in theory and ignored in practice.[47] According to Roy, Gandhi's suggestion that Indians have remained more faithful to these ideals is wishful thinking, or, more accurately, a dogmatic assertion. Roy notes that even a cursory look at the historical record shows that Gandhi is wrong. Rather than love and renunciation, Indian history is full of caste violence, the subordination of women, and exploitation of the peasantry.

Roy challenges the accuracy of Gandhi's view of India and worries that Gandhi's followers will learn the wrong lessons from this romantic depiction. Roy is most concerned with its ideological and political effects of these misconceptions. He is particularly critical of Gandhi's view of history, with its explicit aversion to historical progress and economic development. According to Roy, "The Gandhist utopia is a static society."[48] The consequence of this stasis is to naturalize hierarchy, inequality, and injustice. Furthermore, the cult of nonviolence entails acceptance of the more indirect forms of coercion that guarantee and perpetuate exploitation.[49]

In spite of these flaws, Roy argues that the appeal of Gandhism for the masses is understandable. Gandhism is expressed in a familiar religious idiom; it celebrates rather than denigrates their image of themselves; and it identifies an external source of their problems. The reasons for Gandhi's popularity in the West are somewhat less obvious. According to Roy, his appeal stems in part from the allure of "moralizing mysticism" and in part from its functionality, for example, the way that the doctrine of self-denial breeds docile workers rather than revolutionaries.[50]

There are a number of lessons that we can draw from Roy's scathing critique in "India's Message," even if we are not convinced by his most polemical formulations. It alerts us to the dangers of nostalgia and romanticism, which may entail an essentialist and uncritical picture of indigenous traditions. Second, an essentialist picture can have conservative political effects, as noted above. Finally, it reminds us that instead of searching for a "postcolonial message" we should recognize that there are multiple postcolonial messages. Roy's critique of cultural essentialism, written in the 1930s, was reiterated in very similar terms in the early 1960s by Fanon and again in the 1980s by Ngugi. All three made the argument that the rhetoric of reversal—negritude, Indian spirituality, cultural authenticity—could easily be mobilized by indigenous elites to legitimize their continued exploitation of the masses. Whereas Ngugi explicitly drew on Fanon, the link between Fanon and Roy is simply the fact that they both thought deeply about the relationship between colonialism, nationalism, and class power.

CONCLUSION: UNSTABLE GROUNDS

Political theories of decolonization are forced to address one of the most intractable issues in political theory, the problem of foundations. In order to legitimize a break with the past and a vision of the future, founders must act in the name of a people that does not yet exist. They must turn either to the past or to the future in order to perform a kind of alchemy, that of transforming people into *a* people. Both strategies entail certain dangers. Relying on an imagined community from the precolonial past naturalizes the people and may end up justifying parochialism and exclusion. Founding a polity for the new man and citizen may justify the pursuit of certain collective goods at the expense of individual freedom. Postcolonial regimes have not always managed to achieve self-rule or even stability, but this is not necessarily due to theoretical shortcomings. Instead, as all of the chapters in this book demonstrate, the attempt to envision and the ability to create a decolonized regime, population, identity, economy and ethic are certainly influenced by colonial legacies. This is theorizing that is happening upon unstable grounds. Yet this instability in this case is an opening, an opportunity to break from the past and create a new form of politics in the future. These theories of decolonization are also unstable in the sense that they are often contradictory and impractical. The project of decolonization is too multifaceted to have only one answer and too overarching to approach with anything less than very big ideas. A concise program would soon be revealed as irrelevant. A reorganization of structures of power is necessarily ambitious.

Finally, these are unstable grounds because decolonization is a tentative achievement at best, and a victory can quickly become failure as time progresses.

For example, Fanon saw nationalism, which was a tool for the mobilization of the masses, become a hindrance to achieving full citizenship later on. The vehement support demanded by new leadership in order to achieve stability often left populations vulnerable to the whims of their new protectors (who sometimes are not so protective of the people). Political independence could become a vehicle for obscuring continued expropriation of resources from a country. These unstable grounds are the foundation of our time, continuing to inspire and frustrate our freedom to act.

NOTES

INTRODUCTION

1. Two works that have started this project are David Jefferess, *Postcolonial Resistance: Culture, Liberation, and Transformation* (Toronto: University of Toronto Press, 2008) and Helen M. Hintjens, *Alternatives to Independence: Explorations in Post-Colonial Relations* (Aldershot, UK, and Brookfield, VT: Dartmouth, 1995). Jefferess is interested in how the cultural terms of postcolonial theory can change our ideas of resistance. Hintjens explores how the continued economic and political exploitation of former colonies challenges the idea of independence.

2. These texts have largely focused on the extent to which each canonical thinker's works have contained pro- or anticolonial sentiments. See Jennifer Pitts, *A Turn to Empire: The Rise of Imperial Liberalism in Britain and France* (Princeton, NJ: Princeton University Press, 2005) and "Empire and Democracy: Tocqueville and the Algerian Question," *Journal of Political Philosophy* 8, no. 3 (2000); Uday Singh Mehta, *Liberalism and Empire: A Study in Nineteenth-Century British Liberal Thought* (Chicago: University of Chicago Press, 1999); Fred Whelan, *Edmund Burke and India: Political Morality and Empire* (Pittsburgh: University of Pittsburgh Press, 1997); Margaret Kohn and Daniel I. O'Neill, "A Tale of Two Indias: Burke and Mill on Empire and Slavery in the West Indies and America," *Political Theory* 34, no. 2 (2006); Sankar Muthu, *Enlightenment Against Empire* (Princeton, NJ: Princeton University Press, 2003); and Emmanuel Chukwudi Eze, "The Color of Reason: The Idea of 'Race' in Kant's Anthropology," in *Postcolonial African Philosophy: A Critical Reader*, ed. Emmanuel Chukwudi Eze (Oxford: Blackwell, 1997); Margaret Kohn, "Empire's Law: Tocqueville on Colonialism and the State of Exception," *Canadian Journal of Political Science* 41, no. 2 (June 2008): 255–78.

3. For instance see Deepika Bahri, "Coming to Terms with the Postcolonial," in *Between the Lines: South Asians and Postcoloniality*, ed. Deepika Bahri and Mary Vasudeva (Philadelphia: Temple University Press, 1996); Bill Ashcroft, Gareth Griffiths, and Helen Tiffin, "Introduction" to *The Empire Writes Back: Theory and Practice in Post-Colonial Literatures*, 2nd ed.(London: Routledge, 2002); Leela Gandhi, *Postcolonial Theory: A Critical Introduction* (New York:

Columbia University Press, 1998); and Robert Young, "Editorial: Ideologies of the Postcolonial," *Interventions* 1, no. 1 (1998): 4–8.

4. Frantz Fanon, *Black Skin, White Masks* (New York: Grove Press, 2002). Originally published in Paris, 1952, as *Peau noire, masques blancs*.

5. See Robert Malley, *The Call from Algeria: Third Worldism, Revolution, and the Turn to Islam* (Berkeley: University of California Press, 1996); Odd Arne Westad, *The Global Cold War: Third World Interventions and the Making of Our Times* (Cambridge: Cambridge University Press, 2007); and Vijay Prashad, *The Darker Nations: A People's History of the Third World* (New York: The New Press, 2007).

6. For example, see Paul Gilroy, *Postcolonial Melancholia* (New York: Columbia University Press, 2005).

7. Ashcroft et al., *The Empire Writes Back*. See Chandra Talpade Mohanty, "Under Western Eyes: Feminist Scholarship and Colonial Discourses," *Feminist Review* 30 (1988); Sara Suleri, "Women Skin Deep: Feminism and the Postcolonial Condition," *Critical Inquiry* 18 (1992); and Trinh T. Minh-ha, *When the Moon Waxes Red: Representation, Gender and Cultural Politics* (New York: Routledge, 1991).

8. Edward Said's works *Orientalism* (New York: Pantheon, 1978; republished in 2003 by Penguin Modern Classics as *Orientalism: Western Conceptions of the Orient*) and *Culture and Imperialism* (New York: Alfred A. Knopf, 1993) paved the way. Thomas Patterson's *Inventing Western Civilization* (New York: Monthly Review Press, 1997) is a concise statement of this argument. See also Chatterjee, *Nationalist Thought and the Colonial World: A Derivative Discourse?* (London: Zed Books, 1986); *The Nation and Its Fragments: Colonial and Postcolonial Histories* (Princeton, NJ: Princeton University Press, 1993); and Dipesh Chakrabarty, *Provincializing Europe: Postcolonial Thought and Historical Difference* (Princeton, NJ: Princeton University Press, 2000).

9. The scope of work in both of these areas is enormous. Paul Gilroy's work was seminal for understanding identity politics in a postcolonial context. See *"There Ain't No Black in the Union Jack": The Cultural Politics of Race and Nation* (Chicago: University of Chicago Press, 1991); *The Black Atlantic: Modernity and Double Consciousness* (New York: Verso Press, 1993); *After Empire: Melancholia or Convivial Culture?* (New York: Routledge, 2004); and *Against Race: Imagining Political Culture Beyond the Color Line* (Cambridge, MA: Harvard University Press, 2000). Postcolonial studies also significantly changed analyses of identity construction and power as exemplified in Anne McClintock's *Imperial Leather: Race, Gender and Sexuality in the Colonial Contest* (New York: Routledge, 1995) and Laura Ann Stoler, *Carnal Knowledge and Imperial Power: Race and the Intimate in Colonial Rule* (Berkeley: University of California Press, 2002). Examples of the discourse analysis directly or indirectly inspired by Edward Said's work include works such as *Bodies and Voices: The Force-Field of Representation and Discourse in Colonial and Postcolonial Studies* (Amsterdam: Rodopi Press, 2008); Laura Chrisman and Patrick Williams, eds., *Colonial Discourse and Post-Colonial Theory: A Reader* (Hemel Hempstead, UK: Harvester Wheatsheaf, 1994); Leo Ching, *The Disavowal*

and the Obsessional: Colonial Discourse East and West (Durham, NC: Duke University Press, 1995); and Lisa Wedeen, *Ambiguities of Domination: Politics, Rhetoric, and Symbols in Contemporary Syria* (Chicago: University of Chicago Press, 1999).

10. See Ann Douglass, "Periodizing the American Century: Modernism, Postmodernism, and Postcolonialism in the Cold War Context," *Modernism/Modernity* 5, no. 3 (1998): 71–98, and Sanjay Seth, "A 'Postcolonial' World?" in *Contending Images of World Politics*, ed. Greg Fry and Jacinta O'Hagan, eds. (London: Macmillan, and New York: St. Martin's Press, 2000), 214–26, for thoughtful discussions of whether the twentieth century should be characterized as postcolonial. Such work contrasts with original work by historians about decolonization that studied the process of the formal transfer of power such as two volumes edited by Prosser Gifford and Wm. Roger Louis, *The Transfer of Power in Africa: Decolonization 1940–1960* (New Haven, CT: Yale University Press, 1982) and *Decolonization and African Independence: The Transfers of Power, 1960–1980* (New Haven, CT: Yale University Press, 1988). These works contain valuable historical information for those interested in the process of decolonization as a not yet completed endeavor.

11. Collections of historical scholarship influenced by postcolonial critique include Gyan Prakash, ed., *After Colonialism: Imperial Histories and Postcolonial Displacements* (Princeton, NJ: Princeton University Press, 1995); Gregory Blue, Martin Bunton, and Ralph Crozier, eds., *Colonialism and the Modern World: Selected Studies* (Armonk, NY: M. E. Sharpe, 2002); and Antoinette Burton, ed., *After the Imperial Turn: Thinking With and Through the Nation* (Durham, NC: Duke University Press, 2003). An interesting attempt to provide quantitative measurements that reveal more about colonial history is Bouda Etemad, *Possessing the World: Taking the Measurements of Colonisation from the Eighteenth to the Twentieth Century*, trans. Andrene Everson (New York: Berghahn Books, 2007).

12. Although we do not see this as a work of comparative political theory, we are grateful to scholars of CPT who have played an important role in introducing the political theory of non-Western thinkers to the field. See for example Roxanne Euben's work including: "Premodern, Antimodern or Postmodern? Islamic and Western Critiques of Modernity," *Review of Politics* 59, no. 3 (1997); *Enemy in the Mirror: Islamic Fundamentalism and the Limits of Modern Rationalism: A Work of Comparative Political Theory* (Princeton, NJ: Princeton University Press, 1999); "Killing (for) Politics: Jihad, Martyrdom, and Political Action," *Political Theory* 30, no. 1 (2001).

13. On postcolonialism and legality see Jean Comaroff and John Comaroff, eds., *Law and Disorder in the Postcolony* (Chicago: University of Chicago Press, 2006), and Nasser Hussain, *Jurisprudence of the Emergency: Colonialism and the Rule of Law* (Ann Arbor: University of Michigan Press, 2003). For analysis of the postcolonial state see Eqbal Ahmad's essays, "From Potato Sack to Potato Mash: The Contemporary Crisis of the Third World" and "Postcolonial Systems of Power" in Carollee Bengelsdorf, Margaret Cerullo, and Yogesh Chandrani, eds., *The Selected Writings of Eqbal Ahmad* (New York: Columbia University

Press, 2006); Crawford Young, *The African Colonial State in Comparative Perspective* (New Haven, CT: Yale University Press, 1994); and Hamza Alavi, "The State in Postcolonial Societies: Pakistan and Bangladesh," *New Left Review* I, no. 74 (July–August 1972). In the field of anthropology, there has been an explosion of works addressing power and culture in postcolonial regimes such as Achille Mbembe, *On the Postcolony* (Berkeley: University of California Press, 2001) and James Ferguson, *Global Shadows: Africa in the Neoliberal World Order* (Durham, NC: Duke University Press, 2006).

14. More works are addressing the underlying similarities and differences between colonization and economic globalization. See Anthony King, *Urbanism, Colonialism, and the World Economy: Cultural and Spatial Foundations of the World Urban System* (London: Routledge, 1990); Arif Dirlik, *The Postcolonial Aura: Third World Criticism in the Age of Global Capitalism* (Boulder, CO: Westview Press, 1997); and a collection edited by Gary Backhaus and John Murungi, *Colonial and Global Interfacings: Imperial Hegemonies and Democratizing Resistances* (Newcastle-upon-Tyne, UK: Cambridge Scholars Publishing, 2007). Two works that consider the vocabulary of globalization and colonialism are Manfred Steger, *Globalism: The New Market Ideology* (Lanham, MD: Rowman and Littlefield, 2002), and Ulrich Beck, *What is Globalization?* (Cambridge, UK: Polity Press, 2000).

15. Two recent works are related to this endeavor. Duncan Ivison's *Postcolonial Liberalism* (Cambridge: Cambridge University Press, 2002) tries to reimagine the perimeters of liberalism through an engagement with postcolonial critiques of identity and exclusion. A new collection of essays edited by Nalini Persram, *Postcolonialism and Political Theory* (Lanham, MD: Lexington Books, 2008), is centered on issues of power in postcolonial theory, with a special focus upon epistemology.

16. Many commentators have raised the point that Orientalism seems to suggest that scholarly work on other cultures is impossible. Joshua Teitelbaum and Meir Litvak write, "In our experience this has led to a crippling timidity amongst non-Muslim or non-Arab students." In "Students, Teachers, and Edward Said: Taking Stock of Orientalism," *The Middle East Review of International Affairs* 10 (March 2006).

17. Anne McClintock, "The Angel of Progress: Pitfalls of the Term 'Post-Colonialism,'" *Social Text* 31/32 (1992): 84–98.

18. Diana Brydon, "Introduction," *Postcolonialism: Critical Concepts in Literary and Cultural Studies*, Vol. 1, ed. Diana Brydon (London: Routledge, 2000), 2.

19. The life work of Mohandas Gandhi has been exceptional in attracting the lens of scholarly interpretation in the discipline of political theory. For instance, Bhikhu Parekh's *Gandhi's Political Philosophy: A Critical Examination* (South Bend, IN: University of Notre Dame Press, 1989) provides an excellent example of how nontraditional political theorizing can be critically approached to reveal astute critiques of not only colonialism as such, but also Western conceptions of modernity and progress. Manfred Steger has also written an engaging study of the complexities of Gandhi's political thinking and strategies, *Gandhi's Dilemma: Nonviolent Principles and Nationalist Power* (New York:

Palgrave Macmillan, 2000), and Ronald J. Terchek has significantly contributed to our understanding of Gandhi's political philosophy with his volume, *Gandhi: Struggling for Autonomy* (Lanham, MD: Rowman and Littlefield, 1998).

20. In chapter 1 we argue that many anti-colonial leaders initially embraced liberalism but became disillusioned. In *Decolonization and the Evolution of International Human Rights*, Roland Burke shows that the language of human rights was very popular at the Bandung conference and had an important impact on the Development of the international human rights agenda. The book also documents a split within the anticolonial movement over the respective importance of self-determination versus individual rights.

21. Michael Freeden, *Ideologies and Political Theory: A Conceptual Approach* (Oxford: Oxford University Press, 1996).

CHAPTER 1

1. Hobsbawm, "Introduction: Introducing Traditions," in *The Invention of Tradition*, ed. By Eric Hobsbawm and Terence Ranger (Cambridge: Cambridge University Press, 1992) and Rogers Smith, *Stories of Peoplehood: The Politics and Morals of Group Membership* (Cambridge: Cambridge University Press, 2003).

2. Karl Marx, "The Future Results of British Rule in India," *Marx and Engels: Collected Works* (New York: International Publishers, 1975–2005), 12: 217. First published in *New-York Daily Tribune*, August 8, 1853.

3. John Locke, *Second Treatise of Government*, ed. C. B. Macpherson (Indianapolis, IN: Hackett, 1980), 29. Though not quite so absolute, similar ideas about historical progress persisted well into the twentieth century. Developmental theorists always placed different regions of the world in an earlier period on the European (and American) time line, the implication being that ultimately the rest of the world would catch up with proper direction by American elites. See Nils Gilman, *Mandarins of the Future: Modernization Theory in Cold War America* (Baltimore, MD: Johns Hopkins University Press, 2004) for an excellent discussion for the historical assumptions behind development theory.

4. Jacques Derrida, "Declarations of Independence," *New Political Science* 7, no. 1 (1986): 10. See Bonnie Honig, "Declarations of Independence: Arendt and Derrida on the Problem of Founding a Republic," *American Political Science Review* 85, no. 1 (March 1991): 97–113, for an excellent discussion of the problem of founding. More recently, Lisa Disch has also taken on the problem of founding mythologies and our interpretations of them in an unpublished paper, "How Could Arendt Valorize the American Revolution and Revile the French?"

5. Derrida, "Declarations of Independence," 10.

6. On the paradox of founding, see Bonnie Honig, "Between Decisionism and Deliberation," American Political Science Review 101 (2007): 1–17; Jason Frank, *Constituent Moments: Enacting the People in Postrevolutionary America* (Durham, NC: Duke University Press, 2010).

7. See Michael Rogin's "The Two Declarations of Independence," *Representations* 55 (Summer 1996): 13–30. The last in the litany of abuses wrought by the king (George III) is that he has "excited domestic insurrections amongst us."

8. Exemplary of this project are the following works: Richard Hofstadter, *The Paranoid Style of American Politics and Other Essays* (New York: Alfred A. Knopf, 1965); Michael Paul Rogin's *Fathers and Children: Andrew Jackson and the Subjugation of the American Indian* (New York: Alfred A. Knopf, 1975) and *Subversive Genealogy: The Art and Politics of Herman Melville*(Berkeley: University of California Press, 1985); and George Shulman, *American Prophecy: Race and Redemption in American Political Culture* (Minneapolis: University of Minnesota Press, 2008).

9. Hannah Arendt, *Between Past and Future: Eight Exercises in Political Thought* (New York: Viking Press, 1968), 11.

10. Léopold Sédar Senghor, *The Foundations of "Africanité" or "Négritude" and "Arabité,"* trans. by Mercer Cook (Paris: Présence Africaine, 1971), 7.

11. Partha Chatterjee, *Nationalist Thought and the Colonial World: A Derivative Discourse* (Minneapolis: University of Minnesota Press, 1993; originally published in 1986) and *The Nation and Its Fragments: Colonial and Postcolonial Histories* (Princeton, NJ: Princeton University Press, 1993).

12. Rabindranath Tagore, *Nationalism* (Madras: Macmillan Press, 1976 [1916]).

13. Sir Thomas Munro, "On the Ultimate Aim of British Rule in India," 1824. Reprinted in *Indian Constitutional Documents 1757–1947*, 3rd ed., ed. Anil Chandra Banerjee (Calcutta: A. Mukherjee and Co., 1961), 1: 206–7. For more discussion of Indian penal law and colonialism, see Keally McBride, "Macaulay to Malimath: Postcolonialism, Punishment and the Police in India." Paper presented at University of Chicago Law School, May 2008.

14. Quoted in Martin Meredith, *The Fate of Africa: A History of Independence* (New York: Public Affairs, 2006), 11.

15. Manela's book *The Wilsonian Moment* begins with this story. *The Wilsonian Moment: Self-Determination and the International Origins of Anticolonial Nationalism* (New York: Oxford University Press, 2007).

16. Quoted in Manela, 71.

17. The Egyptians were not immune to playing the race card themselves. As Manela elaborates, they pointed out their own cultural superiority in contrast to the cultures of Africa.

18. Quoted in Manela, 149.

19. Vijay Prashad, *The Darker Nations: A People's History of the Third World* (New York: The New Press, 2007), 21.

20. Quoted in Bernard Porter, "Trying to Make Decolonisation Look Good," *London Review of Books* (August 2, 2007), 6.

21. See Chapter 3, "The 'Tide of History' versus the Laws of the Republic," in Todd Shepard, *The Invention of Decolonization: The Algerian War and the Remaking of France* (Ithaca, NY: Cornell University Press, 2006).

22. Kwame Anthony Appiah, *In My Father's House: Africa in the Philosophy of Culture* (New York: Oxford University Press, 1992), 30.

23. Frantz Fanon, *A Dying Colonialism*, trans. Haakon Chevalier (New York: Grove Weidenfeld, 1965), 47.

24. Michael Lambert, "From Citizenship to *Négritude*: Making a Difference in Elite Ideologies of Colonized Francophone West Africa," *Comparative Studies in Society and History* 35, no. 2 (1993): 241–42.

25. See Lambert, footnote, 242.

26. G. Wesley Johnson, *The Emergence of Black Politics in Senegal: The Struggle for Power in the Four Communes, 1900–1920* (Stanford, CA: Stanford University Press, 1971), 81.

27. Johnson, *The Emergence of Black Politics in Senegal*, 82–84.

28. One study placed the number of black Africans in the French Army during World War I at 161,250, meaning that their presence was indeed critical for the country's strategic position. See Charles Balesi, "West African Influence on the French Army of World War One," in *Double Impact: France and Africa in the Age of Imperialism*, ed. G. Wesley Johnson (Westport, CT: Greenwood Press, 1985), 104, fn. 32.

29. Quoted in Robert W. July, *The Origins of Modern African Thought: Its Development in West Africa During the Nineteenth and Twentieth Centuries* (New York: Frederick A. Praeger, 1967), 410–11.

30. A. James Arnold, *Modernism and Negritude: The Poetry and Poetics of Aimé Césaire* (Cambridge, MA: Harvard University Press, 1981). Ch. 2, "Césaire and Modernism," documents these influences extensively.

31. See Gary Wilder, *The French Imperial Nation-State: Colonial Humanism and Negritude Between the Two World Wars* (Chicago: University of Chicago Press, 2005), Chapter 6, for an extensive discussion of how *L'Étudiant Noir* compares with previous publications by students from the French empire in Paris.

32. Interview with René Depestre reprinted in Robin D. G. Kelley, "A Poetics of Postcolonialism," introduction to Aimé Césaire, *Discourse on Colonialism*, trans. Joan Pinkham (New York: Monthly Review Press, 2000), 88.

33. Ibid., 84.

34. Edna Stevens takes the view that negritude is an extension of tropes about Africans made by Europeans. See "Negritude and the Noble Savage," *The Journal of Modern African Studies* 11, no. 1 (1973): 91–104. Senghor's archeological evidence can be found in *The Foundations of "Africanité" or "Négritude" and "Arabité,"* trans. Mercer Cook (Paris: Présence Africaine, 1967), 9–36.

35. Irving Leonard Markovitz, *Léopold Sédar Senghor and the Politics of Negritude* (New York: Atheneum, 1969), 42.

36. Suzanne Césaire, "Surrealism and Us: 1943," quoted in Robin D. G. Kelley, "A Poetics of Postcolonialism," in Césaire, *Discourse on Colonialism*, 15.

37. Colin Dayan, "Out of Defeat: Aimé Césaire's Miraculous Words," *Boston Review* (September–October 2008).

38. Frantz Fanon, *Toward the African Revolution*, trans. Haakon Chevalier (New York: Grove Press, 1967), 27.

39. Walter Benjamin, "Surrealism," in *Reflections: Essays, Aphorisms, Autobiographical Writings*, trans. Edmund Jephcott, ed. Peter Demetz (New York: Harcourt Brace Jovanovich, 1978), 189.

40. *Senghor: Prose and Poetry*, ed. and trans. by John Reed and Clive Wake (London: Oxford University Press, 1965), 29.

41. Ibid.

42. *Prose and Poetry*, 32.

43. Wilder, *The French Imperial Nation-State*, 201, 203.

44. Chatterjee, *Nationalist Thought and the Colonial World*, 30.
45. Quoted in Dayan, "Out of Defeat."

Chapter 2

1. "Iran's Landmark Revolution," in *The Selected Writings of Eqbal Ahmad*, ed. Carollee Bengelsdorf, Margaret Cerullo, and Yogesh Chandrani (New York: Columbia University Press, 2006), 81–82.
2. See Nikki R. Keddie, *Modern Iran: Roots and Results of Revolution* (New Haven, CT: Yale University Press, 2006).
3. Following the dominant approach in contemporary scholarship, we are using the term "Islamism" to refer to ideas and movements that are often labeled fundamentalist. For a discussion of this issue that informed our choice of terminology, see Roxanne L. Euben and Muhammad Quasim Zaman, eds., *Princeton Readings in Political Thought* (Princeton, NJ: Princeton University Press, 2009).
4. Bernard Lewis, "The Roots of Muslim Rage," *Atlantic Monthly* 266, no. 3 (1990): 47–60. Lewis argues that it is hypocritical of Muslims to object to imperialism, given their own history of conquest and empire. The true issue, he argues is not imperialism per se but Western dominance over Islam. Furthermore, he claims that the Muslim critique of imperialism, despite its political language, actually relies on a religious opposition between believers and infidels and reflects a religious obligation to defend and promote the faith. According to Lewis, Western imperialism simply cannot be the cause of contemporary attitudes, since it was comparatively benign to begin with and is now part of the remote past. In other strands of the academic literature, however, the connection between Islam and imperialism is well established. For a recent version of this argument, see Mahmood Mamdani, *Good Muslim, Bad Muslim: America, the Cold War, and the Roots of Terror* (New York: Pantheon, 2004).
5. For a reading of Khomeini's Islamic fundamentalism as a distinctively modern movement, see Sami Zubaida, *Islam, the People, and the State: Political Ideas and Movements in the Middle East*, 3rd ed. (London: I. B. Tauris, and New York: St. Martin's Press, 2009. Originally published London: Routledge, 1989).
6. Bobby Sayyid, *A Fundamental Fear: Eurocentrism and the Emergence of Islamism* (London and New York: Zed Books, 1997).
7. See Philip Khoury, "Islamic Revivalism and the Crisis of the Secular State in the Arab World: A Historical Appraisal," in *Arab Resources: The Transformation of a Society*, ed. Ibrahim Ibrahim (London: Croom Helm, 1983).
   In a similar vein, Michael M. J. Fischer explained the politicization of Islam in Iran: "Islam became an umbrella language of moral protest." See "Becoming Mollah: Reflections on Iranian Clerics in a Revolutionary Age," *Iranian Studies* 13, no. 1–4 (1980): 83–117.
8. Bassam Tibi, *The Crisis of Modern Islam* (Salt Lake City: University of Utah Press, 1988).
9. Sayyid, *A Fundamental Fear*, 93.
10. Al-Afghani, Shariati, Al-e Ahmad, and Khomeini all come from Iran, one of the countries in the Middle East that was not directly colonized, although its

bank, taxation system, and foreign trade were controlled by Britain. Following Bobby Sayyid, we use the term "postcolonialism" in the broader sense to describe (as he puts it) "the period following the de-colonization of European rule. In the case of Egypt, post-colonial refers to the coup that brought Nasser and the Free Officers to power in 1953, and not the period following Egypt's nominal independence in 1922. The beginning of the post-colonial period varies from place to place, but for the majority of Muslim communities, it refers to the period from 1947–61, during which most of the present-day Muslim states gained some form of real autonomy from imperial centres" (Sayyid, *A Fundamental Fear*, 82).

11. Afghani is something of an exception. Although he was born and raised in Iran, he adopted the name "al-Afghani" in order to suggest that he was from Afghanistan, which would increase his influence in the Sunni world. He spent most of his life in India, France, Turkey, and Egypt and had particularly strong influence on Islamic thought in Egypt. See Nikki R. Keddie, *Sayyid Jamāl ad-Dīn"al-Afghani"*: *A Political Biography* (Berkeley: University of California Press, 1968).

12. For an excellent introduction to their work based on primary texts, see Euben and Zaman, eds., *Princeton Readings in Political Thought*.

13. A second reason for choosing these Iranian figures over the influential Egyptian Islamists is that we thought that Sayyid Qutb's work is already well known to political theorists because of the influence of Roxanne Euben's pathbreaking study *Enemy in the Mirror: Islamic Fundamentalism and the Limits of Modern Rationalism* (Princeton, NJ: Princeton University Press, 1999).

14. See the Conclusion to this book.

15. Zubaida, *Islam, the People, and the State*.

16. There are debates about the best terms for the different strands of Arabic and Islamic political thought. Hisham Sharabi prefers the term "Islamic Reformism" to describe the position formulated by Afghani and developed by Abduh. See Hisham Sharabi, *Arab Intellectuals and the West: The Formative Years, 1875–1914* (Baltimore: Johns Hopkins University Press, 1970). The most common term is probably "Islamic modernism." See Charles Adams, *Islam and Modernism in Egypt: A Study of the Modern Reform Movement Inaugurated by Muhammad 'Abduh* (London: Russell and Russell, 1968).

17. One of the classic secondary sources is Albert Hourani's *Arabic Thought in the Liberal Age: 1798–1939* (London: Oxford University Press, 1962).

18. See Keddie, *Sayyid Jamāl ad-Dīn"al-Afghani."*

19. On the term "fundamentalist," see Sayyid, *A Fundamental Fear*, and Ervand Abrahamian, *Khomeinism: Essays on the Islamic Republic* (Berkeley: University of California Press, 1993).

20. See Nikki R. Keddie, *Religion and Rebellion in Iran: The Tobacco Protest of 1891–1892* (London: Cass, 1966), 15–27.

21. Keddie, *An Islamic Response to Imperialism*.

22. See Ian Buruma and Avishai Margalit, *Occidentalism: The West in the Eyes of Its Enemies* (New York: Penguin Press, 2004); Stuart Hall and Bram Gieben, eds., *Formations of Modernity* (Cambridge, UK: Polity Press, 1992); Cemil Aydin,

"Between Occidentalism and the Global Left: Islamist Critiques of the West in Turkey," *Comparative Studies of South Asia, Africa, and the Middle East* 26, no. 3 (2006): 446–61.

23. One example of this approach was the Khayr al-Dīn, *The Surest Path*, trans. Leon Carl Brown (Cambridge, MA: Harvard University Press, 1967).

24. Binnaz Toprak, *Islam and Political Development in Turkey* (Leiden: E. J. Brill, 1981).

25. Sayyid Jamāl ad-Dīn al-Afghani, "Answer of Jamāl ad-Dīn to Renan" in Keddie, *An Islamic Response to Imperialism*, 181–87. Originally published in *Journal des Débats*, May 18, 1883. This section draws on text previously published in Margaret Kohn, "Afghani on Empire, Islam and Civilization," *Political Theory* 37, no. 3 (2009): 398–422. For an alternative view, see Elie Kedourie, *Afghani and 'Abduh: An Essay on Religious Unbelief and Political Activism in Modern Islam* (London: Cass, 1966).

26. Afghani, "The Truth about the Neicheri Sect," 141.

27. Many of Afghani's most explicitly antiimperialist articles were published in a pan-Islamic Arabic newspaper, *al-'Urwa al-Wuthqā*. Some of these have been translated into French. See "Pages choisies de Djamal al-din al-Afghani," trans. Marcel Colombe, *Orient* 21–25 (1961–1963).

28. See Hamid Enayat, *Modern Islamic Political Thought* (Austin: University of Texas Press, 1982); Anouar Abdel-Maleki, *Contemporary Arabic Political Thought* (London: Zed Books, 1984); and Euben, *Enemy in the Mirror*.

29. Nikki R. Keddie, *Modern Iran: Roots and Results of Revolution* (New Haven, CT: Yale University Press, 2003), 179. Updated edition published 2006.

30. Not only his father, but also an older brother, two brothers-in-law, and a nephew were religious leaders. The biographical information is drawn from Hamid Algar's introduction to the English translation of *Gharbzadegi*. See Jalal al-i Ahmad, *Occidentosis: A Plague from the West*, trans. R. Campbell (Berkeley: Mizan Press, 1984).

31. There is some controversy about Al-e Ahmad's embrace of Islam near the end of his life. In 1964 Al-e Ahmad went on a pilgrimage to Mecca and wrote an account titled *Khasi dar miquā*. See Brad Hanson, "The 'Westoxication' of Iran: Depictions and Reactions of Behrangi, Al-e Ahmad, and Shariati," *International Journal of Middle East Studies* 15, no. 1 (1983): 9.

32. Ahmad, *Occidentosis*, 28.

33. Ibid.

34. Ahmad, *Occidentosis*, 124.

35. There are exceptions. For example, he writes, "Thus if in the West, through the inexorable logic of technology (and of capitalism), that is, as a consequence of mechanosis, specialization has replaced character . . ." (133)

36. Ahmad, *Occidentosis*, 59.

37. Ahmad, *Occidentosis*, 56.

38. Ahmad, *Occidentosis*, 57.

39. Ahmad, *Occidentosis*, 61.

40. Ahmad, *Occidentosis*, 73.

41. Ahmad, *Occidentosis*, 58.

42. Ibid.
43. Keddie, *Modern Iran*, 178.
44. Ali Shariati, *From Where Shall We Begin & The Machine in the Captivity of Machinism*, trans. Fatollah Marjani (Houston, TX: Free Islamic Literatures, 1980).
45. Shariati, *From Where Shall We Begin*, 17.
46. Shariati, *From Where Shall We Begin*, 19, 20.
47. Shariati, *From Where Shall We Begin*, 22.
48. Shariati, *From Where Shall We Begin*, 25.
49. Shariati, *From Where Shall We Begin*, 26.
50. Ali Shariati, *An Approach to the Understanding of Islam*, trans. Venus Kaivantash (Tehran: Hamdami Publishers, 1979).
51. This is a Quranic term that Shariati suggests is evidence that the common people are the basis of Islamic society. See Ali Shariati, *On the Sociology of Islam*, trans. Hamid Algar (Berkeley: Mizan Press, 1979), 49.
52. Shariati, *On the Sociology of Islam*.
53. Shariati, *From Where Shall We Begin*, 30.
54. Shariati, however, emphasized that his approach to these issues differed from Marxism. See Ali Shariati, *Marxism and Other Western Fallacies*, trans. R. Campbell (Berkeley: Mizan Press, 1980).
55. See also Susan Buck-Morss, *Thinking Past Terror: Islamism and Critical Theory on the Left* (London: Verso, 2003).
56. Shariati, *From Where Shall We Begin*, 48.
57. Shariati, *From Where Shall We Begin*, 51.
58. See for example Michel Foucault, "What Are the Iranians Dreaming About?" in *Foucault and the Iranian Revolution*, ed. Janet Afary and Kevin B. Anderson (Chicago: University of Chicago Press, 2005).
59. Abrahamian, *Khomeinism*, 23.
60. For an excellent analysis of Khomeini's political theory, see Shahrough Akhavi, "Islam, Politics and Society in the Thought of Ayatullah Khomeini, Ayatullah Taliqani and Ali Shariati," *Middle Eastern Studies* 24, no. 4 (1988): 404–31. This article also highlights the critique of imperialism in another Persian-Islamic thinker, Ayatullah Taliqani, who argued that class conflict is not inevitable but is instead a project of imperialism (410).
61. Abrahamian, *Khomeinism*. For a fascinating analysis of the relationship between modernism and traditionalism in Sunni thought, see Shahrough Akhavi, "The Dialectic in Contemporary Egyptian Social Thought: The Scripturalist and Modernist Discourses of Sayyid Qutb and Hasan Hanafi," *International Journal of Middle East Studies* 29, no. 3 (August 1997): 377–401
62. "Islam and Politics" in *The Selected Writings of Eqbal Ahmad*, ed. Carollee Bengelsdorf, Margaret Cerullo, and Yogesh Chandrani (New York: Columbia University Press, 2006), 177–78.
63. *Islam and Revolution: Writings and Declarations of Imam Khomeini*, trans, and annotated by Hamid Algar (Berkeley, CA: Mizan Press, 1981), 68.
64. *Islam and Revolution*, 28.
65. *Islam and Revolution*, 30.

66. *Islam and Revolution*, 33.
67. *Islam and Revolution*, 28.
68. *Islam and Revolution*, 58.
69. *Islam and Revolution*, 31.
70. Khomeini's position on the Constitution was not entirely consistent. At some points he suggested that it was a good idea that was distorted by secularists and imperialist influence. See Abrahamian, *Khomeinism*, 93.
71. Abrahamian, *Khomeinism*, 54.
72. Abrahamian, *Khomeinism*, 49.
73. Abrahamian, *Khomeinism*, 115.
74. Abrahamian, *Khomeinism*, 74.
75. Abrahamian, *Khomeinism*, 47.
76. For an analysis of the Iranian revolution that situates it in the context of other revolutionary and antiimperialist movements, see Said Amir Arjomand, "Iran's Islamic Revolution in Comparative Perspective," *World Politics* 38, no. 3 (1986): 383–414.
77. The clerical establishment was well situated to play this role for four reasons: it was not associated with the Pahlavi regime; it had a strong institutional network that was autonomous from the state apparatus; it had the symbolic capital that came from association with Islam; and it had not been decimated by SAVAK the way that leftist groups had been. See Keddie, *Modern Iran*.
78. Khomeini used the term "*gharbzadegi*" in his writings.
79. This is the core of Bobby Sayyid's analysis of Islamism in Sunni areas. See *A Fundamental Fear*.
80. Bernard Lewis, "The Roots of Muslim Rage," *Atlantic Monthly* 266, no. 3 (1990): 47–60.
81. It is now widely accepted that the CIA was involved in the 1953 overthrow of Mosaddeq, the democratically elected prime minister of Iran who proposed nationalizing the oil industry. See Keddie, *Modern Iran*, 128–30.
82. See for example Uday Singh Mehta, *Liberalism and Empire: A Study in Nineteenth-Century British Liberal Thought* (Chicago: University of Chicago Press, 1999); Jennifer Pitts, *A Turn to Empire: The Rise of Liberalism in Britain and France* (Princeton, NJ: Princeton University Press, 2005).
83. For an interesting argument that cultural and ethnic essentialism are products of democratic mobilization in new nation-states, see Clifford Geertz, "The Integrative Revolution: Primordial Sentiments and Civil Politics in the New States," in *Old Societies and New States: The Quest for Modernity in Asia and Africa*, ed. Clifford Geertz (New York: The Free Press of Glencoe, 1963).

Chapter 3

1. Hannah Arendt, *On Revolution* (New York: Viking, 1963), 42–43.
2. John Locke, *Second Treatise of Government*, ed. C. B. Macpherson (Indianapolis, IN: Hackett, 1980), 113.
3. Ibid.
4. "In an effort to distance liberal democracy from the populist fanaticism associated with Hitlerism and Stalinism, this 'democratic theory' described—and

prescribed—a thoroughly domesticated, normalized kind of democracy, a democracy in which a clear division of labor existed between politicians and citizens, in which significant ideological conflicts were abated, and in which government could distribute its benefits to an eagerly consuming public." Jeffrey C. Isaac, *Democracy in Dark Times* (Ithaca, NY: Cornell University Press, 1998), 39.

5. See for example Jason Frank, "Publius and Political Imagination," *Political Theory* 37, no. 1 (2009): 69–98; and his *Constituent Moments: Enacting the People in Postrevolutionary America* (Durham, NC: Duke University Press, 2010); Pauline Ochoa, *The Time of the People* (University Park: Pennsylvania State University Press, forthcoming). Bruce Ackerman's two-volume *We the People* (Cambridge, MA: Belknap Press, 1991) also engages in a reconsideration of revolution, democracy, and institutionalism.

6. See Peter Calvert, *Revolution and Counter-Revolution* (Minneapolis: University of Minnesota Press, 1990); John Dunn, "Understanding Revolutions" in John Dunn, *Rethinking Modern Political Theory: Essays 1979–83* (Cambridge: Cambridge University Press, 1985); Barrington Moore Jr., *Social Origins of Dictatorship and Democracy: Lord and Peasant in the Making of the Modern World* (New York: Penguin Books, 1969); Theda Skocpol, *States and Social Revolutions: A Comparative Analysis of France, Russia and China* (Cambridge: Cambridge University Press, 1979).

7. Slavoj Zizek's introductory essay to Mao Tse-Tung, *On Practice and Contradiction* (London: Verso Press, 2007), explores these issues in a provocative manner.

8. Arendt, *On Revolution*, 33.

9. Ibid.

10. Arendt, *On Revolution*, 57.

11. At this stage, France governed what it termed French Indochina (Indochine); the area that would become Vietnam was three different areas: Tonkin (Bac Bo), Annam (Trung Bo), and Cichinchina (Nam Bo).

12. Pierre Brocheux, *Ho Chi Minh: A Biography*, trans. Claire Duiker (Cambridge: Cambridge University Press, 2007), 9.

13. "Zoology," *Le Paria*, vol. 2. Quoted in Jean Lacouture, *Ho Chi Minh*, trans. Peter Wiles (London: Allen Lane Press, 1968), 28.

14. Pierre Brocheux reports in his biography that two teachers had particular influence on the young student. Hoang Thong introduced him to "Chinese translations of the works of Jean-Jacques Rousseau and Montesquieu," while Le Van Mien, a product of the École Coloniale and the École Nationale Supérieure des Beaux-Arts, instructed him in French history and culture. Pp. 6–7.

15. Ho spent many years in Moscow after leaving Paris, studying Leninist revolutionary methods.

16. Alexander Woodside, "History, Structure and Revolution in Vietnam," *International Political Science Review* 10, no. 2 (1989): 143–57.

17. Woodside, 149.

18. In Peter DeCaro, *Rhetoric of Revolt: Ho Chi Minh's Discourse for Revolution* (Westport, CT: Praeger, 2003), 29.

19. See George Dutton, *The Tay Son Uprising: Society and Rebellion in Eighteenth-Century Vietnam* (Honolulu: University of Hawaii Press, 2006).

20. Daniel Gardner, trans., *The Four Books: The Basic Teachings of the Later Confucian Tradition* (Indianapolis, IN: Hackett, 2007).

21. Ho Chi Minh, *Down with Colonialism!* ed. Walden Bello (London: Verso Books, 2007), 98.

22. Mark Philip Bradley also notes the influence of Confucian values of self-cultivation in the Vietnamese revolution. In "Becoming Van Minh: Civilizational Discourse and Visions of the Self in Twentieth-Century Vietnam," *Journal of World History* 15, no. 1 (2004): 65–83, he remarks, "But as colonial subjects for whom French conquest had raised urgent questions about what it meant to be Vietnamese, radicals in Vietnam came to the emancipatory potentialities of civilizational thinking as a space not only for the collective imaginings of a future postcolonial state but also for working out new concepts of personhood" (67).

23. Ho Chi Minh, *Down with Colonialism!* 159.

24. Ho Chi Minh, *Down with Colonialism!* 154.

25. Ho Chi Minh, *Down with Colonialism!* 73.

26. Brocheux, *Ho Chi Minh*, 99.

27. Ho Chi Minh, *Down with Colonialism!* 72.

28. Brocheux, *Ho Chi Minh*, 136.

29. Ho Chi Minh, *Down with Colonialism!* 54–55.

30. Ho Chi Minh, *Down with Colonialism!* 72.

31. Ho Chi Minh, *Down with Colonialism!* 156.

32. Ho Chi Minh, *Down with Colonialism!* Italics in translation.

33. See Brocheux, 149–83 especially.

34. There are several excellent collections of essays that respond to the life and afterlife of the ideas of Fanon. See *Fanon: A Critical Reader*, ed. Lewis R. Gordon, T. Denean Sharpley-Whiting, and Renée T. White (Malden, MA: Blackwell, 1996); *Fanon: Critical Perspectives*, ed. Anthony Alessandrini (New York: Routledge, 1999); and *Rethinking Fanon: The Continuing Dialogue*, ed. Nigel Gibson (Amherst, NY: Humanity Books, 1999).

35. Henry Louis Gates Jr., "Critical Fanonism," *Critical Inquiry* 17 (1991): 457–70.

36. Frantz Fanon, *The Wretched of the Earth*, trans. Richard Philcox (New York: Grove Press, 2004), 2 (hereafter WE).

37. WE, 19.

38. WE, 22.

39. For example see Lewis Gordon, "Fanon's Tragic Revolutionary Violence," *Fanon: A Critical Reader* (Oxford: Blackwell, 1996): 297–308; Elizabeth Frazer and Kimberly Hutchings, "On Politics and Violence: Arendt Contra Fanon," *Contemporary Political Theory* 7 (2008): 90–108; Adele Jinadu, *Fanon: In Search of the African Revolution* (London: Routledge and Kegan Paul, 1986).

40. Joan Cocks, *Passion and Paradox: Intellectuals Confront the National Question* (Princeton, NJ: Princeton University Press, 2002), 64.

41. WE, 72.

42. Ibid.

43. WE, 88.

44. WE, 89.

45. WE, 62.
46. WE, 140.
47. Ibid.
48. WE, 127.
49. WE, 124.
50. WE, 181.
51. A more extreme version of this argument is found in Eldridge Cleaver's *Soul on Ice* (1968). Fanon's work in some way lays the foundation for this very disturbing exploration of subjugation, liberation, and sexuality.
52. One of the most skillful aspects of the recreation of the Algerian revolution in *The Battle of Algiers* is that the film captures this aspect of Fanon's analysis, lingering upon women as they dress in different styles, cut their hair, apply makeup or wrap themselves in traditional dress in service of the revolution. See "The Making of *The Battle of Algiers*" in *The Selected Writings of Eqbal Ahmad.*
53. Fanon, *A Dying Colonialism*, 37–38.
54. Fanon, *Dying Colonialism*, 44.
55. Fanon, *Dying Colonialism*, 45.
56. Fanon, *Dying Colonialism*, 47.
57. Fanon, *Dying Colonialism*, 54.
58. Fanon, *Dying Colonialism*, 50.
59. Fanon, *Dying Colonialism*. Italics in translation.
60. Fanon, *Dying Colonialism*, 59.
61. This gendering of Fanon's revolutionary transformation deserves much more exploration than the scope of this book allows here.
62. Interestingly, the Committee has recently become a place where Palestinian people and statehood are discussed. For more information and full texts of reports and meetings, go to http://www.un.org/Depts/dpi/decolonization/main.htm.

CHAPTER 4

1. The issue of forced labor was controversial because the detainees argued that they had not been convicted of any crime and therefore could not be punished by hard labor. They claimed that they were equivalent to prisoners of war under the Geneva Convention and could not be forced to work. See Josiah Mwangi Kariuki, *Mau Mau Detainee: The Account by a Kenyan African of His Experiences in Detention Camps, 1953–1960* (Nairobi: Oxford University Press, 1975).
2. Caroline Elkins, *Imperial Reckoning: The Untold Story of Britain's Gulag in Kenya* (New York: Henry Holt, 2005), 347.
3. Elkins, *Imperial Reckoning*, 429.
4. There has been a debate in the scholarly literature about the portrayal of the Mau Mau rebellion and its significance for Kenyan history. See Bruce J. Berman, "Nationalism, Ethnicity, and Modernity: The Paradox of Mau Mau," *Canadian Journal of African Studies* 25, no. 2 (1991): 181–206; John Lonsdale, "Mau Maus of the Mind: Making Mau Mau and Remaking Kenya," *The Journal of African History* 31 (1990): 393–421.

5. Clement Fatovic, "Emergency Action as Jurisprudential Miracle," paper presented at the American Political Science Association Meeting, August 2006.
6. Giorgio Agamben, *The State of Exception*, trans. Kevin Attell (Chicago: University of Chicago Press, 2005).
7. Giorgio Agamben, *Homo Sacer: Sovereign Power and Bare Life*, trans. Daniel Heller-Roazen (Stanford, CA: Stanford University Press, 1995); William E. Scheuerman, *Between the Norm and the Exception: The Frankfurt School and the Rule of Law* (Cambridge, MA: MIT Press, 1997); Ellen Kennedy, *Constitutional Failure: Carl Schmitt in Weimar* (Durham, NC: Duke University Press, 2004).
8. Nasser Hussain, *The Jurisprudence of Emergency* (Ann Arbor: University of Michigan Press, 2003).
9. Rande Kostal, *A Jurisprudence of Power: Victorian Empire and the Rule of Law* (Oxford: Oxford University Press, 2005).
10. There are several exceptions, including Hussain, *The Jurisprudence of Emergency* and Kostal, *A Jurisprudence of Power*.
11. For a general discussion of the political theory that emerges in Ngugi's writing, see M. S. C. Okolo, *African Literature as Political Philosophy* (Dakar, Senegal: CODESRIA Books, 2007).
12. See Margaret Kohn and Daniel O'Neill, "A Tale of Two Indias: Burke and Mill on Racism and Slavery in the West Indies and Americas," *Political Theory* 34 (2006).
13. Ngugi's analysis of postcolonial Kenya bears a striking resemblance to Mbembe's. In *Petals of Blood* he advances the view that independence has done little more than put a black mask on the face of neocolonial exploitation. Although African elites now run the government and have a share of economic privilege, the basic political structure of *commandement* and the economic system of imperial capitalism remain unchanged. But Ngugi's analysis of the colonial *régime d'exception* has distinctive elements that are worth considering in some detail.
14. *Weep Not, Child* was Ngugi's first published novel (London: Heinemann, 1964). His second published novel, *The River Between*, was written first (London: Heinemann, 1965).
15. The colonial state implemented a series of measures to ensure that peasant cultivators were forced into the wage economy where they would have to work for low wages on white farms. First, the government established reserves limiting the areas where Kikuyu could live. Those who couldn't gain access to the limited supply of land were forced into wage labor. Second, the government enacted a hut tax that amounted to the equivalent of two months' worth of African wages. To ensure the docility of labor, they also implemented a pass system according to which anyone outside of the reserves without a valid labor contract could be fined or imprisoned. See Bruce Berman, *Control and Crisis in Colonial Kenya: The Dialectic of Domination* (London: James Currey, and Athens: Ohio State University Press, 1990).
16. Lynn M. Thomas, *Politics of the Womb: Women, Reproduction, and the State in Kenya* (Berkeley: University of California Press, 2003).

17. See E. Adriaan et al., eds., *Sovereignty, Legitimacy, and Power in West African Societies: Perspectives from Legal Anthropology* (Hamburg: Lit Verlag, 1998).

18. Mahmood Mamdani, *Citizen and Subject: Contemporary Africa and the Legacy of Late Colonialism* (Princeton, NJ: Princeton University Press, 1996).

19. Martin Chanock, *Law, Custom, and Social Order: The Colonial Experience in Malawi and Zambia* (Portsmouth, NH: Heinemann, 1998; first published 1985 by Cambridge University Press).

20. Mamdani, *Citizen and Subject*, 37–61.

21. Jomo Kenyatta, *Facing Mount Kenya: The Tribal Life of the Gikuyu* (Nairobi: Heinemann, 1978).

22. John Lonsdale and Bruce Berman, "Coping with the Contradictions: The Development of the Colonial State in Kenya, 1895–1914," *Journal of African History* 20 (1979): 487–505; and Berman, *Control and Crisis in Colonial Kenya*, 368.

23. Ngugi, *Weep Not, Child*, 84–85.

24. The scholarly consensus is that Kenyatta was not a supporter of the Mau Mau. There is also evidence that the judge (Ransley Thacker) was bribed to ensure a conviction despite the paucity of evidence. See John Lonsdale, "Kenyatta's Trials: Breaking and Making an African Nationalist," in *The Moral World of the Law*, ed. Peter Cross (Cambridge: Cambridge University Press, 2007), 196–239.

25. Ngugi's third novel, *A Grain of Wheat*, also explores the psychological and political consequences of the Emergency. This time, however, the story is set on the eve of Kenyan independence, and Ngugi draws attention to the political challenges faced by the postcolonial state. Like *Weep Not, Child*, it shows how the Emergency undermined precolonial social and political practices without providing viable alternatives.

26. David Cook and Michael Okenimpke, *Ngugi wa Thiong'o: An Exploration of His Writings*, 2nd ed. (Oxford: James Currey, 1997), 172.

27. Ngugi wa Thiong'o and Micere Githae Mugo, *The Trial of Dedan Kimathi* (London and Nairobi: Heinemann, 1977), 23.

28. Ngugi and Micere, *The Trial of Dedan Kimathi*, 25.

29. Ibid.

30. To translate Kimathi's argument into the language of European legal theory, his position is a radicalization of the well-known position of Dicey, who advanced a political understanding of the rule of law (e.g., parliamentary supremacy) and challenged the German concept of *rechtstaat*, a formal notion that rulers are bound by the laws that they make. For an excellent discussion of this issue, see Franz Neumann, *The Rule of Law: Political Theory and the Legal System in Modern Society* (Heidelberg and Dover: Berg, 1986); Judith N. Shklar, "Political Theory and the Rule of Law," in *The Rule of Law: Ideal or Ideology*, ed. Allan C. Hutchinson and Patrick Monahan (Toronto: Carswell, 1987); H. L. A. Hart, *The Concept of Law*, 2nd ed. (Oxford: Oxford University Press, 1994; originally published 1961).

31. Ngugi and Micere, *The Trial of Dedan Kimathi*, 25–26.

32. Ngugi and Micere, *The Trial of Dedan Kimathi*, 32.

33. Ngugi and Micere, *The Trial of Dedan Kimathi*, 34.

34. In *Detained*, Ngugi explains that the motive for his arrest was not the critical views contained in his English language novels but rather his involvement in the Kamiriithu Community Education and Cultural Centre. Together with the villagers, he wrote and produced a play that told the story of Kenyan history from the perspective of peasants and workers. When government officials heard about this project, they withdrew the permit for public performance, razed the cultural center to the ground, and arrested Ngugi.

35. Ngugi wa Thiong'o, *Detained: A Writer's Prison Diary* (Nairobi and London: Heinemann, 1981), 4.

36. Ngugi, *Detained*, 32–33.

37. Ngugi, *Detained*, 40.

38. Yash P. Ghai and P. McAuslan, *Public Law and Political Change in Kenya: A Study of the Legal Framework of Government from Colonial Times to the Present* (New York and Nairobi: Oxford University Press, 1970).

39. These examples are cited in Ngugi, *Detained*, 44–45.

40. Mamdani, *Citizen and Subject*, 63–64.

41. Ngugi, *Detained*, 19.

42. Ngugi, *Detained*, 19.

43. Ngugi, *Detained*, 13.

44. Achille Mbembe, *On the Postcolony* (Berkeley: University of California Press, 2001).

45. For an interesting, thoughtful analysis and critique of social contract theory, see Carole Pateman, *The Sexual Contract* (Cambridge, UK: Polity Press, 1988). See also Charles Mills, *The Racial Contract* (Ithaca, NY: Cornell University Press, 1997).

46. Debra Baumgold, *Hobbes's Political Theory* (Cambridge: Cambridge University Press, 1988), 94.

47. See, for example, Alexis de Tocqueville, *Writings on Empire and Slavery*, ed. Jennifer Pitts (Baltimore, MD: Johns Hopkins University Press, 2001).

48. Mbembe, *On the Postcolony*, 25.

49. Some contemporary theorists—most notably Giorgio Agamben—have argued that the liberal state is actually no different than the colonial state. It too is based on creating and excluding bare life that can be killed without being murdered. This is a provocative argument that takes us beyond the scope of this book. See Agamben, *Homo Sacer: Sovereign Power and Bare Life* (cited in note 7 above). For a fuller discussion of these issues, see Paul Passavant, "The Contradictory State of Giorgio Agamben," *Political Theory* 35, no. 2 (2007): 147–74.

50. It is beyond the scope of this essay to intervene in the debate about whether social contract theory can realize its own normative aspirations in the context of the liberal polity. For an interesting debate about this issue, see Carole Pateman and Charles Mills, *Contract and Domination* (New York: Polity, 2007).

51. Mbembe, *On the Postcolony*, 25.

52. See for example W. F. Finlason, *The history of the Jamaica Case founded upon official or authentic documents, and containing an account of the debates in*

Parliament and the Criminal Prosecutions arising out of the case (London: Chapman and Hall, 1868).

53. Mill was an outspoken critic in Parliament of the use of martial law in the colonies. He also took a very vocal and controversial role in criticizing the government for failing to prosecute John Edward Eyre, the colonial governor of Jamaica, for atrocities committed against blacks during a state of emergency. See Kostal, *A Jurisprudence of Power: Victorian Empire and the Rule of Law* (cited in note 9 above).

54. Mbembe, *On the Postcolony*, 31.

55. Mbembe, *On the Postcolony*, 28.

56. See Adam Hochschild, *King Leopold's Ghost: A Story of Greed, Terror, and Heroism in Colonial Africa* (New York: Houghton Mifflin, 1998).

57. Alexis de Tocqueville, "Essay on Algeria," in *Writings on Empire and Slavery*, ed. Pitts.

58. Mbembe, *On the Postcolony*, 46.

59. See also David Scott, "Colonial Governmentality," *Social Text* 43 (1995): 191–220.

60. Rodrick Mukumbira, "White Farmers Win Case Against Zimbabwe Land Grabs," *Associated Press*, November 28, 2008. See also Mahmood Mamdani, "Lessons of Zimbabwe," *London Review of Books*, December 4, 2008.

61. Kostal, *A Jurisprudence of Power*; Kohn and O'Neill, "A Tale of Two Indias," 192–228; and Hussain, *The Jurisprudence of Emergency*.

62. Jacques Derrida, "The Force of Law: The Mystical Foundation of Authority," *Cardozo Law Review* 11, nos. 5–6 (July/August 1990): 919–1045.

63. See Agamben, *State of Exception*, 39.

64. This analysis was influenced by Fanon and is most apparent in Ngugi wa Thiong'o, *Petals of Blood* (New York: Penguin, 2005).

65. Cass Sunstein, "Social and Economic Rights? Lessons from South Africa," John M. Olin Law & Economics Working Paper no. 124 (Chicago, 2001); Heinz Klug, *Constituting Democracy: Law, Globalism, and South Africa's Political Reconstruction* (Cambridge, MA: Cambridge University Press, 2000).

CHAPTER 5

1. L. Cotlua, S. Vermeulen, R. Leonard, and J. Keeley, 2009, *Land Grab or Development Opportunity? Agricultural Investment and International Land Deals in Africa*. IIED/FAO/IFAD London.

2. Javier Blas, "UN Warns of Food Neocolonialism," August 18, 2008. http://www.ft.com/cms/s/0/3d3ede92-6e02-11dd-b5df-0000779fd18c.html.

3. Reported in Vivienne Walt, "The Breadbasket of South Korea," *Time*, November 23, 2008. http://www.time.com/time/world/article/0,8599,1861145,00.html.

4. For an excellent analysis of the impact of the Daewoo deal on Madagascar's political system, see Chris Chida, "Agricultural Investment or Extraction: Daewoo and Political Instability in Madagascar." Unpublished paper on file with Keally McBride.

5. BBC News, "Madagascar Leader Axes Land Deal," March 19, 2009. Accessed January 10, 2009. http://news.bbc.co.uk/2/hi/africa/7952628.stm.

6. John Locke, *Second Treatise of Government*, ed. C. B. Macpherson (Indianapolis, IN: Hackett, 1980); Henri Lefebvre, *The Production of Space*, trans. Donald Nicholson-Smith (Cambridge, MA: Blackwell, 1991); Raymond Williams, *The Country and the City* (Oxford: Oxford University Press, 1973).

7. Carl Schmitt, *The Nomos of the Earth in the International Law of the Jus Publicum Europaeum*, trans. G. L. Ulmen (New York: Telos Publishing, 2006), 86.

8. For discussions of territory and colonization see James Tully, *Public Philosophy in a New Key*, vol. 2, *Imperialism and Civic Freedom* (Cambridge: Cambridge University Press, 2008); Richard Tuck, *The Rights of War and Peace: Political Thought and the International Order from Grotius to Kant* (Oxford: Oxford University Press, 1999); *Political Theory and the Rights of Indigenous Peoples*, ed. Duncan Ivison, Paul Patton, and Will Sanders (Cambridge: Cambridge University Press, 2000). For descriptions of the geographical and representational elements of colonialism, see William Cronon, *Changes in the Land: Indians, Colonists and the Ecology of New England* (New York: Hill and Wang, 1983); Neil Smith, *American Empire: Roosevelt's Geographer and the Prelude to Globalization* (Berkeley: University of California Press, 2003); and John Zarobell, *Empire of Landscape: Space and Ideology in Colonial Algeria* (University Park: Pennsylvania State University Press, 2010).

9. Cited in Burke A. Hendrix, *Ownership, Authority, and Self-Determination* (University Park: Pennsylvania State University Press, 2008), 179. See also Michael Dodson, "Land Rights and Social Justice," in *Our Land Is Our Life: Land Rights: Past, Present and Future*, ed. Galarrwuy Yunupingu (Queensland: University of Queensland Press, 1997); Vine Deloria Jr., *God Is Red: A Native View of Religion*. Thirtieth anniversary edition (Golden, CO: Fulcrum, 2003).

10. In other cases, however, the legal system did assign alienable property rights to indigenous peoples in order to make it possible for them to sell their lands to settlers. See Robert A. Williams, *The American Indian in Western Legal Thought: The Discourses of Conquest* (Oxford: Oxford University Press, 1992). For a different take on some of these same cases about indigenous ownership of land, see James Tully, *Strange Multiplicity: Constitutionalism in an Age of Diversity* (Cambridge: Cambridge University Press, 1995).

11. See David Armitage, "John Locke, Carolina, and the Two Treatises of Government," *Political Theory* 32 (2004): 602–27; Peter Brooks and Paul Gewirtz, eds., *Law's Stories: Narrative and Rhetoric in the Law* (New Haven, CT: Yale University Press, 1996); Vine Deloria Jr. and David E. Wilkins, *Tribes, Treaties and Constitutional Tribulations* (Austin: University of Texas Press, 1999); Sidney L. Harring, *Crow Dog's Case: American Indian Sovereignty, Tribal Law, and United States Law in the Nineteenth Century* (Cambridge: Cambridge University Press, 1994); Anthony Pagden, "Human Rights, Natural Rights, and Europe's Imperial Legacy," *Political Theory* 31, no. 2 (2003): 171–99; and Keally McBride, "Stories of Our Ancestors," unpublished paper.

12. See Tully, *Imperialism and Civic Freedom*; and Armitage, "John Locke, Carolina, and the Two Treatises of Government."

13. James Tully, "The Struggles of Indigenous Peoples for and of Freedom," in *Political Theory and the Rights of Indigenous Peoples*, 36–59.

14. See Carole Pateman, "The Settler Contract," in Carole Pateman and Charles Mills, *Contract and Domination* (Cambridge, UK: Polity Press, 2007), 35–78.
15. For instance Harring (1994); Pateman (2007); and William Cronon, *Changes in the Land: Indians, Colonists, and the Ecology of New England* (New York: Hill and Wang, 1983).
16. Ivison et al., "Introduction," *Political Theory and the Rights of Indigenous Peoples*, 5.
17. Göran Therborn, "Roads to Modernity: Revolutionary and Other," foreword, in *Revolution in the Making of the Modern World: Social Identities, Globalization and Modernity*, ed. John Foran, David Lane, and Andreja Zivkovic (New York: Routledge, 2008), xvi.
18. Ibid.
19. Mariátegui, 21.
20. Mariátegui, 35.
21. Frantz Fanon, *The Wretched of the Earth*, trans Richard Philcox (New York: Grove Press, 2004 [1961]), 5.
22. Mahmood Mamdani, "Lessons of Zimbabwe," in *The London Review of Books*, December 4, 2008.
23. See Robert Blackey, "Fanon and Cabral: A Contrast in Theories of Revolution for Africa," *The Journal of Modern African Studies* 12, no. 2 (1974): 191–209. Also, Charles F. Peterson, *DuBois, Fanon, Cabral: The Margins of Elite Anti-Colonial Leadership* (Lanham, MD: Lexington Books, 2007), examines Fanon and Cabral's similar attempt to empower, not simply mobilize the populations of Algeria and Guinea. For more on this topic, see Chapter 3, "Self-Determination Reconsidered."
24. Amílcar Cabral, *Unity and Struggle: Speeches and Writings of Amílcar Cabral* (New York: Monthly Review Press, 1979), 124.
25. Cabral, *Unity and Struggle*, 126.
26. Cabral, *Unity and Struggle*, 129–30.
27. Cabral, *Unity and Struggle*, 130, 134.
28. See his essay, "Destroy the Economy of the Enemy and Build Our Own Economy," in *Unity and Struggle*, 239–42.
29. Cabral, *Unity and Struggle*, 136.
30. Cabral, *Unity and Struggle*, 31, 32.
31. Courtney Jung, *The Moral Force of Indigenous Politics: Critical Liberalism and the Zapatistas* (Cambridge: Cambridge University Press, 2008), 3.
32. See for example Nancy Fraser, "From Redistribution to Recognition? Dilemmas of Justice in a 'Postsocialist' Age," in *Justice Interruptus: Critical Reflections on the "Postsocialist" Condition* (New York: Routledge, 1997).
33. Jung, *The Moral Force of Indigenous Politics*, 23.
34. The *foco* theory of revolution is the belief that radical leadership can create revolutionary conditions even when the population is not inclined toward uprising.
35. This account is supported by a number of different sources. See Mihalis Mentinis, *Zapatistas: The Chiapas Revolt and What It Means for Radical Politics* (London and Ann Arbor, MI: Pluto Press, 2006); John Gibler, *Mexico Unconquered: Chronicles of Power and Revolt* (San Francisco: City Lights Books,

2009); and Neil Harvey, *The Chiapas Rebellion: The Struggle for Land and Democracy* (Durham, NC: Duke University Press, 1998).

36. Karen Kampwirth, "Marching with the Taliban or Dancing with the Zapatistas? Revolution after the Cold War," in *The Future of Revolutions: Rethinking Radical Change in the Age of Globalization*, ed. John Foran (London: Zed Books, 2003), 227–41.

37. Walter D. Mignolo, *The Darker Side of the Renaissance: Literacy, Territoriality, and Colonization*, 2nd ed. First published 1995 (Ann Arbor: University of Michigan Press, 2003), 260.

38. Subcomandante Insurgente Marcos, *Our Word Is Our Weapon: Selected Writings*, ed. Juana Ponce de León (New York: Seven Stories Press, 2001), 27.

39. Quoted in Marcos, *Our Word Is Our Weapon*, 78.

40. Sarah Washbrook, "The Chiapas Uprising of 1994: Historical Antecedents and Political Consequences," in *Rural Chiapas Ten Years After the Zapatista Uprising*, ed. Sarah Washbrook (New York Routledge, 2007), 1–33.

41. Gemma van der Haar, "Land Reform, the State, and the Zapatista Uprising in Chiapas." In Washbrook, *Rural Chiapas*, 68–91.

42. Patricia Huntington, "Challenging the Colonial Contract: The Zapatistas' Insurgent Imagination," *Rethinking Marxism* 12, no. 3 (2000): 58–80.

43. Marcos, *Our Word*, 23.

44. Marcos, *Our Word*, 46.

45. "Interview: Subcommandante Marcos by Medea Benjamin," in *First World, Ha Ha Ha! The Zapatista Challenge*, ed. Elaine Katzenberger (San Francisco: City Lights Books, 1995), 57–70.

46. Marcos, quoted in Luis Lorenzano, "Zapatismo: Recomposition of Labour, Radical Democracy and Revolutionary Project," in *Zapatista!: Reinventing Revolution in Mexico*, ed. John Holloway and Eloina Pelaez (London: Pluto Press, 1998), 126–58.

47. Marcos, *Our Word*, 276.

48. Marcos, *Our Word*, 283.

Chapter 6

1. See Mabel Moraña, Enrique Dussel, and Carlos A. Jáuregui, eds., *Coloniality at Large: Latin America and the Postcolonial Debate* (Durham, NC: Duke University Press, 2008).

2. J. Jorge Klor de Alva, "Colonialism and Postcolonialism as (Latin) American Mirages," *Colonial Latin American Review* 1, no. 1–2 (1992): 233–45.

3. Walter D. Mignolo, *The Idea of Latin America* (Malden, MA: Blackwell, 2005).

4. Mignolo, *The Idea of Latin America*, 7.

5. Patricia D'Allemand, "José Carlos Mariátegui: Culture and Nation," in *Postcolonial Perspectives on the Cultures of Latin America and Lusophone Africa*, ed. Robin Fiddian (Liverpool, UK: Liverpool Press, 2000), 79.

6. Walter D. Mignolo, "La razón postcolonial: herencias coloniales y teorías postcoloniales," *Revista Chilena de Literatura* 47 (1995): 91–141; Eduardo Mendieta, *Global Fragments: Latinamericanisms, Globalizations, and Critical Theory* (Albany: State University of New York Press, 2008).

7. See for example Peter Hulme, *Colonial Encounters: Europe and the Native Caribbean, 1492–1797* (London and New York: Routledge, 1992). First published London: Methuen, 1986.

8. Walter D. Mignolo, "The Geopolitics of Knowledge and the Colonial Difference," in *Coloniality at Large*, ed. Moraña et al.

9. See Tzvetan Todorov, *The Conquest of America: The Question of the Other*, trans. Richard Howard (New York: Harper and Row, 1984).

10. V. I. Lenin, *The Development of Capitalism in Russia* (Moscow, 1956); Antonio Gramsci, "The Southern Question," *The Modern Prince and Other Writings* (New York: International Publishers, 1959). Cited in Michael Hechter, *The Celtic Fringe in British National Development*, new ed. (New Brunswick, NJ: Transaction, 1999). Originally published as *Internal Colonialism: The Celtic Fringe in British National Development, 1536–1966* (Berkeley: University of California Press, 1975).

11. For an introduction to both figures, see Ofelia Schutte, *Cultural Identity and Social Liberation in Latin American Thought* (Albany: State University of New York Press, 1993).

12. See Leela Gandhi, *Postcolonial Theory* (New York: Columbia University Press, 1998).

13. For an overview, see Robert J. C. Young, *Postcolonialism: An Historical Introduction* (Malden, MA: Blackwell, 2001): 193–216; Sheldon B. Liss, ed., *Marxist Thought in Latin America* (Berkeley: University of California Press, 1984).

14. See Marc Becker, *Mariátegui and Latin American Marxist Theory* (Athens, OH: Ohio University Center for International Studies, 1993); Robert Paris, "El Marxismo de Mariátegui," in *Mariategui y los orígenes del marxismo latinoamericano* (Mexico: Sigolo XXI, 1978).

15. Mariátegui's life is recounted in Jorge Basadre's introduction to *Seven Interpretive Essays on Peruvian Reality*, trans. Marjory Urquidi (Austin: University of Texas Press, 1971). See also Marc Becker, *Mariátegui and Latin American Marxist Theory* (Athens: Ohio University Center for International Studies, 1993).

16. See Patricia D'Allemand, "Art and Culture in the Discourse of José Carlos Mariátegui," *Travesía* 3, no. 1–2 (1994): 299–312.

17. Mariátegui, *Seven Essays*, 8–9.

18. In "The Indigenous Question" (*Amauta*, July–August 1929, 95), he also claimed, "the colonization of Latin America by the white race has had, as is easy to prove, only retarding and depressive effects in the life of the indigenous races."

19. Mariátegui, *Seven Essays*, 36.

20. Mariátegui, "The Indigenous Question."

21. Mariátegui, *Seven Essays*, 36.

22. Mariátegui, *Seven Essays*, 60, 73.

23. Mariátegui, *Seven Essays*, 59.

24. Mariátegui, *Seven Essays*, 58.

25. According to Mariátegui "the colonizer was not guilty of having brought an inferior race—this was the customary reproach of sociologists of fifty years ago—but of having brought slaves" (*Seven Essays*, 38).

26. For Mariátegui it is possible because the Peruvian peasantry is different from the European peasantry. After the enclosures and the introduction of commercial farming, the European peasantry had been fragmented into a rural proletariat, a class of small proprietors, and an urban proletariat; in feudal Peru, the indigenous peasantry maintained its class identity and was further cemented by cultural traditions.

27. Mariátegui, *Seven Essays*, 29. Mariátegui does not consider that socialism, too, is a version of "the white man's civilization." For a discussion of this issue, see Partha Chatterjee, *Nationalist Thought and the Colonial World: A Derivative Discourse?* (Minneapolis: University of Minnesota Press, 1993).

28. See particularly "El hombre y el mito," *Obra Política* (Mexico: Ediciones Era: 1979), 308–11.

29. Jose Mariátegui, *The Heroic and Creative Meaning of Socialism: Selected Essays of José Carlos Mariátegui*, 142–43.

30. Mariátegui, *The Heroic and Creative Meaning of Socialism*, 142–43.

31. Mariátegui, *The Heroic and Creative Meaning of Socialism*, 145.

32. Zeev Sternhell, with Mario Sznajder and Maia Aheri, *The Birth of Fascist Ideology: From Cultural Rebellion to Political Revolution*, trans. David Maisel (Princeton, NJ: Princeton University Press, 1994). Originally published in 1989.

33. Mariátegui, *The Heroic and Creative Meaning of Socialism*, 143–44.

34. Ofelia Schutte convincingly argues that Mariátegui is influenced by Nietzsche. See Schutte, "Nietzsche, Mariátegui, and Socialism: A Case of 'Nietzschean Marxism' in Peru?" *Social Thought and Practice* 14, no. 1 (1988): 71–85.

35. Mariátegui, *The Heroic and Creative Meaning of Socialism*, 144.

36. José Mariátegui, "Gandhi," in *The Heroic and Creative Meaning of Socialism*, 49.

37. Ofelia Schutte, *Cultural Identity and Social Liberation in Latin American Thought* (Albany: State University of New York Press, 1993); Hugo Biagini, "Contemporary Argentinian Philosophy," in *Philosophy and Literature in Latin America: A Critical Assessment of the Current Situation*, ed. Jorge J. E. Gracia and Mireya Camurati (Albany: State University of New York Press, 1989).

38. See Enrique Dussel, "Philosophy in Latin America in the Twentieth Century: Problems and Currents," *Latin American Philosophy: Issues, Currents, Debates*, ed. Eduardo Mendieta (Bloomington: Indiana University Press, 2003), 30.

39. Horacio Cerutti Guldberg, "Actual Situation and Perspectives of Latin American Philosophy for Liberation," *The Philosophical Forum* 20 (1988–1989): 43–61.

40. Dussel, "Philosophy in Latin America," 30–33.

41. Enrique Dussel, "The 'World-System': Europe as 'Center' and Its 'Periphery,' beyond Eurocentrism," in *Latin America and Postmodernity: A Contemporary Reader*, ed. Pedro Lange-Churión and Eduardo Mendieta (Amherst, NY: Humanity Books, 2001).

42. For a different view that emphasizes the distinctiveness of the Marxist approach, which locates the core economic logic in the capitalist mode of production, see Ernesto Laclau, *Politics and Ideology in Marxist Theory: Capitalism, Fascism, Populism* (London: Verso, 1979).

43. Fred R. Dallmayr, "The Underside of Modernity: Adorno, Heidegger, and Dussel," *Constellations* 11, no. 1 (2004): 102–20. Enrique Dussel, *The Invention of*

the Americas: Eclipse of "the Other" and the Myth of Modernity, trans. Michael Barber (New York: Continuum, 1995).

44. Enrique Dussel, "Eurocentrism and Modernity (Introduction to the Frankfurt Lectures)," *Boundary* 2, no. 3 (1993): 65–76.

45. For an excellent overview of Enrique Dussel's life and work, see Eduardo Mendieta, *Global Fragments: Latinamericanisms, Globalizations, and Critical Theory* (Albany: State University of New York Press, 2008).

46. Enrique Dussel, *A History of the Church in Latin America: Colonialism to Liberation, 1492–1979* (Grand Rapids, MI: Wm. B. Eerdmans, 1981).

47. Much of this biographical background is drawn from Linda Martín Alcoff and Eduardo Mendieta, eds., *Thinking from the Underside of History: Enrique Dussel's Philosophy of Liberation* (New York: Rowman and Littlefield, 2000).

48. Only one volume has been translated into English: Enrique Dussel, *Towards an Unknown Marx: A Commentary on the Manuscripts of 1861–1863* (London: Routledge, 2001).

49. Although his major six-volume study *Filosofía ética latino-americana* has not been translated into English, *Philosophy of Liberation* is a summary and synthesis of the key themes of the longer work. The reading presented in this chapter is based mostly on the essays and books that are available in English, but is supplemented by translations and summaries of Spanish-language materials. We would like to thank Ange J. Martinez for her help.

50. Enrique Dussel, *Philosophy of Liberation*, trans. Aquilina Martinez and Christine Morkovsky (Eugene, OR: Wipf & Stock, 2003), 14. Originally published 1985.

51. Dussel, *Philosophy of Liberation*, 18.

52. Dussel, *Philosophy of Liberation*, 19.

53. Dussel, *Philosophy of Liberation*, 27.

54. Dussel, *Philosophy of Liberation*, 49.

55. Dussel, *Philosophy of Liberation*, 40.

56. Dussel, *Philosophy of Liberation*, 47.

57. Dussel, *Philosophy of Liberation*, 44.

58. Wendy Brown, *States of Injury: Power and Freedom in Late Modernity* (Princeton, NJ: Princeton University Press, 1995), 45.

59. Brown, *States of Injury*, 65.

60. Brown, *States of Injury*, 41.

61. Brown, *States of Injury*, 41.

62. Schutte, *Cultural Identity and Social Liberation*, 178.

63. Dussel, *Philosophy of Liberation*, 20.

64. Dussel, *Philosophy of Liberation*, 62.

65. Dussel, *Philosophy of Liberation*, 94.

66. Dussel, *Philosophy of Liberation*, 135.

67. Dussel, *Philosophy of Liberation*, 125.

68. Dussel, *Philosophy of Liberation*, 179.

69. Enrique Dussel, *Twenty Theses on Politics*, trans. George Ciccariello-Maher (Durham, NC: Duke University Press, 2008), 40.

70. Dussel, *Twenty Theses on Politics*, 98.

71. Dussel, *Twenty Theses on Politics*, 98.
72. In fact, the very few times that he uses the term "history" it seems to be almost a synonym for "facticity," a term that signals the importance of concrete, situated knowledge.
73. Dussel, *Philosophy of Liberation*, 158.
74. George Ciccariello-Maher, "Exteriority Against Totality: Enrique Dussel's Ana-Dialectical Method," a paper presented at the Western Political Science Association Meeting, 2010.
75. On this topic, see Michael Barber's *Ethical Hermeneutics: Rationality in Enrique Dussel's Philosophy of Liberation* (New York: Fordham University Press, 1998).
76. Schutte, *Cultural Identity and Social Liberation*, 189.
77. In an interesting variant of this claim, Clarissa Hayward shows how the nonauthoritarian pedagogy employed in many elite suburban schools reflects a class logic—for example, the assumption that it is appropriate to train "future leaders" (but no future manual and service workers) in an ethos of creativity, teamwork and problem solving. See Hayward, *De-facing Power* (Cambridge: Cambridge University Press, 2000).
78. Brown, *States of Injury*.
79. Dussel, *Philosophy of Liberation*, 47.
80. Other commentators have drawn attention to a similar problem in the work of Emmanuel Levinas. See Simon Critchley, "Five Problems in Levinas's View of Politics and the Sketch of a Solution to them," *Political Theory* 32, no. 2 (2004): 172–85.
81. Dussel, *Philosophy of Liberation*, 151.
82. Dussel, *The Philosophy of Liberation*, 150.
83. Dussel, *The Philosophy of Liberation*, 151.
84. Dussel, *Twenty Theses on Politics*, 72–81.
85. Mario Sáenz, "Living Labor and the Materiality of Life," in Alcoff and Mendieta, eds., *Thinking from the Underside of History*, 215.
86. Although Dussel does not reference Mariátegui in his early work, he does mention Mariátegui's contribution in *El Último Marx (1863–1882) y La Liberación Latinoamerican: Un comentario a la tercera y a la cuarta redacción de "El capital"* (Mexico: Siglo Veintiuno, 1990), 278–83. In *Twenty Theses on Politics*, Dussel mentions Mariátegui's populism as consistent with his own depiction of "the pueblo" as a subject of liberation (74).
87. See also Eduardo Mendieta, "Ethics for an Age of Globalization and Exclusion," *Philosophy and Social Criticism* 25, no. 2 (1999): 115–21.
88. Subcomandante Insurgente Marcos, *The Speed of Dreams: Selected Writings 2001–2007*, ed. Canek Pena-Vargas and Greg Ruggiero (San Francisco: City Lights, 2005), 344.
89. One famous example is the debate between Eduard Bernstein and Rosa Luxemburg. See Eduard Bernstein, *Evolutionary Socialism* (New York: Schocken, 1965); Rosa Luxemburg, *Reform or Revolution and Other Writings* (Dover, 2006). For a rational choice version of this argument, see Adam Przeworski, *Capitalism or Social Democracy* (Cambridge: Cambridge University Press, 1986).

90. Mariátegui, *The Heroic and Creative Meaning of Socialism*, 144.
91. Ernesto Laclau and Chantal Mouffe, *Hegemony and Socialist Strategy: Towards a Radical Democratic Politics* (London: Verso, 1985). Ernesto Laclau, *Emancipation(s)* (London: Verso, 1996).
92. Mariátegui, *The Heroic and Creative Meaning of Socialism*, 144.

CONCLUSION

1. Mohandas Gandhi, *'Hind Swaraj' and Other Writings*, ed. Anthony Parel. Centenary edition (Cambridge: Cambridge University Press, 2009).
2. Gandhi, *Hind Swaraj*, 67–68.
3. John Stuart Mill, "Civilisation," in *Essays on Politics and Society*, ed. John M. Robson (Toronto: University of Toronto Press, 1977).
4. Gandhi, *Hind Swaraj*, 37–38.
5. Gandhi, *Hind Swaraj*, 39.
6. Gandhi, *Hind Swaraj*, 41.
7. See Manfred B. Steger, *Gandhi's Dilemma: Nonviolent Principles and Nationalist Power* (New York: Palgrave Macmillan, 2000).
8. In *Hind Swaraj* Gandhi endorses government by a "few good men" (31). His other writings, however, defend a decentralized democracy. See M. K. Gandhi, *Democracy, Real and Deceptive* (Ahmedabad, India: Navajivan, 1961). See also Thomas Pantham, "Thinking with Mahatma Gandhi: Beyond Liberal Democracy," *Political Theory* 11, no. 2 (1983): 165–88; Ronald Terchek, *Gandhi: Struggling for Autonomy* (New York: Rowman and Littlefield, 1998).
9. Lila Abu-Lughod, "Writing Against Culture," *Feminist Anthropology: A Reader* (Wiley-Blackwell, 2006), 157.
10. Richard Fox, *Gandhian Utopia: Experiments with Culture* (Boston: Beacon Press, 1989), 90–103.
11. Gandhi, *Hind Swaraj*, 71.
12. Unlike Gandhi, however, Tagore called for a synthesis of Eastern and Western ideas rather than a rejection of the latter. See Stephen N. Hay, *Asian Ideas of East and West: Tagore and His Critics in Japan, China and India* (Cambridge, MA: Harvard University Press, 1970), p. 21.
13. Jean-Paul Sartre, *Black Orpheus*, trans. S. W. Allen (Paris: Présence Africaine, 1976).
14. Partha Chatterjee, *Nationalist Thought and the Colonial World: A Derivative Discourse* (London: Zed Books, 1986); for a similar argument, see Clifford Geertz, ed., *Old Societies and New States: The Quest for Modernity in Asia and Africa* (New York: Free Press of Glencoe, 1963).
15. Frantz Fanon, *The Wretched of the Earth* (New York: Grove Press, 1963), 313.
16. Partha Chatterjee calls this the "moment of manouevre." Chatterjee has identified it as a necessary feature in the development of national consciousness; we would modify this claim slightly to suggest that it is a necessary feature of anti-colonial thought. In India this expressed itself in nationalism, whereas in other parts of the world it took the form of pan-Islamic or pan-African oppositional consciousness. See Chatterjee, *Nationalist Thought and the Colonial World*, 85–130.

17. Gandhi, *Hind Swaraj*, 116–18.
18. Bhikhu Parekh, *Colonialism, Tradition, and Reform: An Analysis of Gandhi's Political Discourse* (Thousand Oaks, CA: Sage, 1989), 82.
19. Anthony Parel, "Introduction," *Hind Swaraj*.
20. Gandhi, *Hind Swaraj*, 32–33.
21. Parekh, *Colonialism, Tradition, and Reform*, 68.
22. Parekh, *Colonialism, Tradition, and Reform*, 72.
23. Gandhi, *Hind Swaraj*, 34.
24. Leo Tolstoy, "A Letter to a Hindu," http://www.gutenberg.org/etext/7176, accessed December 2009.
25. Gandhi, *Hind Swaraj*, 39.
26. Edward Carpenter, *Civilisation: Its Cause and Cure*. Originally published 1889; enlarged edition of *Civilisation: Its Cause and Cure and Other Essays* (New York: Charles Scribner's Sons, 1921).
27. Gandhi, *Hind Swaraj*, 18.
28. Edward Carpenter, *Civilisation: Its Causes and Cure*, 22.
29. Mill, "Civilisation."
30. See Christopher J. Berry, *Social Theory of the Scottish Enlightenment* (Edinburgh: Edinburgh University Press, 1997).
31. Anthony J. Parel, *Gandhi's Philosophy and the Quest for Harmony* (Cambridge: Cambridge University Press, 2006).
32. Ian Buruma and Avishai Margalit, *Occidentalism: The West in the Eyes of Its Enemies* (New York: Penguin Press, 2004), 6.
33. Gandhi continued to defend his critique of civilization decades after it was originally published. For example, in 1921 he wrote, "The booklet [*Hind Swaraj*] is a severe condemnation of 'modern civilization.' It was written in 1908. My conviction is deeper today than even. I feel that if India would discard 'modern civilization,' she can only gain by doing so." He clarifies, however, that he is not actively working to destroy machinery, railroads or hospitals. He distinguishes between his personal practice which still aspires to the same vision of *swaraj* and his political activity that focuses on more practical short-term goals that are consistent with the wishes of the people of India. In National Gandhi Museum, ed., *Gandhiji on Hind Swaraj and Select Views of Others* (New Delhi: National Gandhi Museum, 2009), 59.
34. Gandhi, *Hind Swaraj*, 37.
35. Gandhi, *Hind Swaraj*, 101–102.
36. M. K. Gandhi, "Letter to Nehru," in *Hind Swaraj*, 150.
37. Akeel Bilgrami, "Occidentalism, the Very Idea: An Essay on Enlightenment and Enchantment," *Critical Inquiry* 32 (Spring 2006): 381–411.
38. Gandhi, *Hind Swaraj*, 30.
39. Gandhi, *Hind Swaraj*, 37–38.
40. Gandhi, *Hind Swaraj*, 38.
41. Parekh, *Colonialism, Tradition, and Reform*.
42. Buruma and Margalit, *Occidentalism*, 3.
43. Edward Said, *Orientalism* (New York: Pantheon, 1978; republished in 2003 by Penguin Modern Classics as *Orientalism: Western Conceptions of the Orient*).

44. Dennis Dalton, *Mahatma Gandhi: Nonviolent Power in Action* (New York: Columbia University Press, 2001), 63–91.

45. Dalton, *Mahatma Gandhi*, 63–65.

46. Manabendra Nath [M. N.] Roy, *India's Message*, Vol. Two (Calcutta: Renaissance Publishers, Ltd., 1950).

47. Roy, *India's Message*, 219.

48. Roy, *India's Message*, 217.

49. Roy, *India's Message*, 215.

50. Roy, *India's Message*, 210.

SELECTED BIBLIOGRAPHY

Abrahamian, Ervand. 1993. *Khomeinism: Essays on the Islamic Republic*. Berkeley: University of California Press.

Abu-Lughod, Lila. 2006. "Writing Against Culture." In *Feminist Anthropology: A Reader*, edited by Ellen Lewin. Malden, MA: Wiley-Blackwell.

Ackerman, Bruce. 1991. *We the People*. 2 vols. Cambridge, MA: Belknap Press.

Adams, Charles. 1968. *Islam and Modernism in Egypt: A Study of the Modern Reform Movement Inaugurated by Muhammad 'Abduh*. London: Russell and Russell.

Adriaan, E., et al., eds. *Sovereignty, Legitimacy, and Power in West African Societies: Perspectives from Legal Anthropology* (Hamburg: Lit Verlag, 1998).

Al-Afghani, Sayyid Jamal ad-Din. 1983. "Answer of Jamāl ad-Dīn to Renan." In Nikki Keddie, *An Islamic Response to Imperialism: Political and Religious Writings of Sayyid Jamal ad-Din "al-Afghani,"* 181–87. Berkeley: University of California Press.

———. 1961–1963. "Pages choisies de Djamal al-din al-Afghani." Translated by Marcel Colombe. *Orient* 21–25.

Agamben, Giorgio. 1995. *Homo Sacer: Sovereign Power and Bare Life*. Translated by Daniel Heller-Roazen. Stanford, CA: Stanford University Press.

———. 2005. *State of Exception*. Translated by Kevin Attell. Chicago: University of Chicago Press.

Ahmad, Eqbal. 2006a. "From Potato Sack to Potato Mash: The Contemporary Crisis of the Third World." In *The Selected Writings of Eqbal Ahmad*, edited by Carollee Bengelsdorf, Margaret Cerullo, and Yogesh Chandrani. New York: Columbia University Press.

———. 2006b. "Islam and Politics." In *The Selected Writings of Eqbal Ahmad*, edited by Carollee Bengelsdorf, Margaret Cerullo, and Yogesh Chandrani, 160–78. New York: Columbia University Press.

———. 2006c. "The Making of *The Battle of Algiers*." In *The Selected Writings of Eqbal Ahmad*, edited by Carollee Bengelsdorf, Margaret Cerullo, and Yogesh Chandrani, 160–78. New York: Columbia University Press.

———. 2006d. "Postcolonial Systems of Power." In *The Selected Writings of Eqbal Ahmad*, edited by Carollee Bengelsdorf, Margaret Cerullo, and Yogesh Chandrani, 128–41. New York: Columbia University Press.

Ahmad, Jalal al-i. 1984. *Occidentosis: A Plague from the West*. Translated by R. Campbell. Berkeley: Mizan Press.

Akhavi, Shahrough. 1988. "Islam, Politics and Society in the Thought of Ayatullah Khomeini, Ayatullah Taliqani and Ali Shariati." *Middle Eastern Studies* 24 (4): 404–31.

———. 1997. "The Dialectic in Contemporary Egyptian Social Thought: The Scripturalist and Modernist Discourses of Sayyid Qutb and Hasan Hanafi." *International Journal of Middle East Studies* 29 (3): 377–401.

Alavi, Hamza. 1972. "The State in Postcolonial Societies: Pakistan and Bangladesh." *The New Left Review* I (74): 59–81.

Alcoff, Linda Martín, and Eduardo Mendieta, eds. 2000. *Thinking from the Underside of History: Enrique Dussel's Philosophy of Liberation*. Second edition. Lanham, MD: Rowman and Littlefield.

al-Dīn, Khayr. 1967. *Surest Path: The Political Treatise of a Nineteenth-Century Muslim Statesman*. Translated by Leon Carl Brown. Cambridge, MA: Harvard University Press.

Alessandrini, Anthony, ed. 1999. *Fanon: Critical Perspectives*. New York: Routledge.

Arendt, Hannah. 1954. *Between Past and Future: Eight Exercises in Political Thought*. New York: Penguin Books.

———. 1963. *On Revolution*. New York: Viking.

Arjomand, Amir. 1986. "Iran's Islamic Revolution in Comparative Perspective." *World Politics* 38 (3): 383–414.

Armitage, David. 2004. "John Locke, Carolina, and the Two Treatises of Government." *Political Theory* 32 (5): 602–27.

Arnold, James. 1981. *Modernism and Negritude: The Poetry and Poetics of Aimé Césaire*. Cambridge, MA: Harvard University Press.

Ashcroft, Bill, Gareth Griffiths, and Helen Tiffin. 2002. *The Empire Writes Back: Theory and Practice in Postcolonial Literatures*. Second edition. London: Routledge. Originally published 1989.

Aydin, Cemil. 2006. "Between Occidentalism and the Global Left: Islamist Critiques of the West in Turkey." *Comparative Studies of South Asia, Africa, and the Middle East* 26 (3): 446–61.

Backhaus, Gary, and John Murungi, eds. 2007. *Colonial and Global Interfacings: Imperial Hegemonies and Democratizing Resistances*. Newcastle-upon-Tyne, UK: Cambridge Scholars Publishing.

Bahri, Deepika. 1996. "Coming to Terms with the Postcolonial." In *Between the Lines: South Asians and Postcoloniality*, edited by Deepika Bahri and Mary Vasudeva, 137–64. Philadelphia: Temple University Press.

Balesi, Charles. 1985. "West African Influence on the French Army of World War One." In *Double Impact: France and Africa in the Age of Imperialism*, edited by G. Wesley Johnson. Westport, CT: Greenwood Press.

Barber, Michael. 1998. *Ethical Hermeneutics: Rationality in Enrique Dussel's Philosophy of Liberation*. New York: Fordham University Press.

Basadre, Jorge. 1971. Introduction to *Seven Interpretive Essays on Peruvian Reality*. Translated by Marjory Urquidi. Austin: University of Texas Press.

Baumgold, Debra. 1988. *Hobbes's Political Theory*. Cambridge: Cambridge University Press.

BBC News, March 19, 2009. "Madagascar Leader axes Land Deal." Accessed January 10, 2009. http://news.bbc.co.uk/2/hi/africa/7952628.stm.

Beck, Ulrich. 2000. *What Is Globalization?* Cambridge, UK: Polity Press.

Becker, Marc. 1993. *Mariategui and Latin American Marxist Theory*. Athens: Ohio University Center for International Studies.

Benjamin, Medea. 1995. "Interview: Subcommandante Marcos by Medea Benjamin." In *First World, Ha Ha Ha! The Zapatista Challenge*, edited by Elaine Katzenberger, 57–70. San Francisco: City Lights Books.

Benjamin, Walter. 1978. "Surrealism." In *Reflections: Essays, Aphorisms, Autobiographical Writings*, translated by Edmund Jephcott, edited by Peter Demetz. New York: Schocken Books.

Berman, Bruce. 1990. *Control and Crisis in Colonial Kenya: The Dialectic of Domination*. London: James Currey.

———. 1991. "Nationalism, Ethnicity, and Modernity: The Paradox of Mau Mau." *Canadian Journal of African Studies* 25 (2): 181–206.

Berry, Christopher J. 1997. *Social Theory of the Scottish Enlightenment*. Edinburgh: Edinburgh University Press.

Bernstein, Eduard. 1965. *Evolutionary Socialism*. New York: Schocken Books.

Biagini, Hugo. 1989. "Contemporary Argentinian Philosophy." In *Philosophy and Literature in Latin America*, edited by Jorge J. E. Gracia and Mireya Camurati. Albany: State University of New York Press.

Bilgrami, Akeel. 2006. "Occidentalism, the Very Idea: An Essay on Enlightenment and Enchantment." *Critical Inquiry* 32 (3): 381–411.

Blackey, Robert. 1974. "Fanon and Cabral: A Contrast in Theories of Revolution for Africa." *The Journal of Modern African Studies* 12 (2): 191–209.

Blas, Javier. "UN Warns of Food Neocolonialism." August 18, 2008. http://www.ft.com/cms/s/0/3d3ede92-6e02-11dd-b5df-0000779fd18c.html.

Blue, Gregory, Martin Bunton and Ralph Crozier, eds. 2002. *Colonialism and the Modern World: Selected Studies*. London and Armonk, NY: M. E. Sharpe.

Borch, Merete F., Eva R. Knudsen, Martin Leer, and Bruce C. Ross, eds. 2008. *Bodies and Voices: The Force-Field of Representation and Discourse in Colonial and Postcolonial Studies*. Amsterdam: Rodopi Press.

Bradley, Mark Philip. 2004. "Becoming Van Minh: Civilizational Discourse and Visions of the Self in Twentieth-Century Vietnam." *Journal of World History* 15 (1): 65–83.

Brocheux, Pierre. 2007. *Ho Chi Minh: A Biography*. Translated by Claire Duiker. Cambridge: Cambridge University Press.

Brooks, Peter, and Paul Gewirtz, eds. 1996. *Law's Stories: Narrative and Rhetoric in the Law*. New Haven, CT: Yale University Press.

Brown, Wendy. 1995. *States of Injury: Power and Freedom in Late Modernity*. Princeton, NJ: Princeton University Press.

Brydon, Diana. 2000. "Introduction," *Postcolonialism: Critical Concepts in Literary and Cultural Studies*, Vol. 1., edited by Diana Brydon, London: Routledge.

Buck-Morss, Susan. 2003. *Thinking Past Terror: Islamism and Critical Theory on the Left*. London: Verso.

Burke, Roland. 2010. *Decolonization and the Evolution of International Human Rights*. Philadelphia: University of Pennsylvania Press.

Buruma, Ian, and Avishai Margalit. 2004. *Occidentalism: The West in the Eyes of Its Enemies*. New York: Penguin Press.

Cabral, Amílcar. 1979. *Unity and Struggle: Speeches and Writings of Amílcar Cabral*. New York: Monthly Review Press.

Calvert, Peter. 1990. *Revolution and Counter-Revolution*. Minneapolis: University of Minnesota Press.

Carpenter, Edward. 2004. *Civilisation: Its Cause and Cure and Other Essays*. Whitefish: Kessinger Publishing.

Césaire, Aimé. 2000. *Discourse on Colonialism*. Translated by Joan Pinkham. Introduction by Robin D. G. Kelley. New York: Monthly Review Press.

Chakrabarty, Dipesh. 2000. *Provincializing Europe*. Princeton, NJ: Princeton University Press.

Chanock, Martin. 1985. *Law, Custom, and Social Order: The Colonial Experience in Malawi and Zambia*. Cambridge: Cambridge University Press.

Chatterjee, Partha. 1986. *Nationalist Thought and the Colonial World: A Derivative Discourse*. London: Zed Books.

———. 1993a. *The Nation and Its Fragments: Colonial and Postcolonial Histories*. Princeton, NJ: Princeton University Press.

———. 1993b. *Nationalist Thought and the Colonial World: A Derivative Discourse*. Minneapolis: University of Minnesota Press.

Ching, Leo. 1995. *The Disavowal and the Obsessional: Colonial Discourse East and West*. Durham, NC: Duke University Press.

Chrisman, Laura and Patrick Williams, eds. 1994. *Colonial Discourse and Post-Colonial Theory: A Reader*. Upper Saddle River, NJ: Pearson Professional Education.

Cocks, Joan. 2002. *Passion and Paradox: Intellectuals Confront the National Question*. Princeton, NJ: Princeton University Press.

Comaroff, Jean and John Comaroff, eds. 2006. *Law and Disorder in the Postcolony*. Chicago: University of Chicago Press.

Connell, Raewyn. 2007. *Southern Theory: The Global Dynamics of Knowledge in Social Science*. Cambridge, UK: Polity Press.

Cook, David, and Michael Okenimpke. 1997. *Ngugi wa Thiong'o: An Exploration of His Writings*. Oxford: James Currey.

Cook, Mercer, trans. 1967. *The Foundations of "Africanité" or "Négritude" and "Arabité."* Paris: Présence Africaine.

Cotula, Lorenzo, Sonja Vermeulen, Rebeca Leonard, and James Keeley. 2009. *Land Grab or Development Opportunity? Agricultural Investment and International Land Deals in Africa*. London: IIED/FAO/IFAD.

Critchley, Simon. 2004. "Five Problems in Levinas's View of Politics and the Sketch of a Solution to Them." *Political Theory* 32 (2): 172–85.

Cronon, William. 1983. *Changes in the Land: Indians, Colonists and the Ecology of New England*. New York: Hill and Wang.

D'Allemand, Patricia. 1994. "Art and Culture in the Discourse of José Carlos Mariátegui." *Travesía* 3 (1–2): 299–312.

———. 2000. "José Carlos Mariátegui: Culture and Nation." In *Postcolonial Perspectives on the Cultures of Latin America and Lusophone Africa*, ed. Robin Fiddian, 79–102. Liverpool: Liverpool Press.

Dallmayr, Fred R. 2004. "The Underside of Modernity: Adorno, Heidegger, and Dussel." *Constellations* 11 (1): 102–20.

Dalton, Dennis. 2001. *Mahatma Gandhi: Nonviolent power in action*. New York: Columbia University Press.

Dayan, Colin. "Out of Defeat: Aimé Césaire's Miraculous Words." *Boston Review*. September/October 2008.

DeCaro, Peter. 2003. *Rhetoric of Revolt: Ho Chi Minh's Rhetoric of Revolution*. Westport, CT: Praeger.

Deloria, Vine, Jr. 2003. *God Is Red: A Native View of Religion*. Golden, CO: Fulcrum.

Deloria, Vine, Jr., and David E. Wilkins. 1999. *Tribes, Treaties and Constitutional Tribulations*. Austin: University of Texas Press.

Derrida, Jacques. 1986. "Declarations of Independence." *New Political Science* 7 (1): 7–15.

———. 1990. "The Force of Law: The Mystical Foundation of Authority." *Cardozo Law Review* 11 (5–6): 919–1045.

Dodson, Micahel. 1997. "Land Rights and Social Justice." In *Our Land Is Our Life: Land Rights: Past, Present and Future*, edited by Galarrwuy Yunupingu. Queensland: University of Queensland Press.

Dirlik, Arif. 1997. *The Postcolonial Aura: Third World Criticism in the Age of Global Capitalism*. Boulder, CO: Westview Press.

Douglass, Ann. 1998. "Periodizing the American Century: Modernism, Postmodernism, and Postcolonialism in the Cold War Context." *Modernism/Modernity* 5 (3): 71–98.

Dunn, John. 1985. "Understanding Revolutions." In John Dunn, *Rethinking Modern Political Theory: Essays 1979–83*, 68–86. Cambridge: Cambridge University Press.

Dussel, Enrique. 1981. *History of the Church in Latin America:Colonialism to Liberation, 1492–1997*. Grand Rapids, MI: Wm. B. Erdmans.

———. 1985. *The Philosophy of Liberation*. Trans. Aquilina Martinez and Christine Morkovsky. Eugene, OR: Wipf & Stock.

———. 1990. *El Ultimo Marx (1863–1882) Y La Liberacion Latinoamericana: Un comentario a la tercera y a la cuarta redaccion de "El capital."* Delegacion Coyoacan: Sigolo Veintiuno Editores.

———. 1993. "Eurocentrism and Modernity (Introduction to the Frankfurt Lectures)." *Boundary* 20 (3): 65–76.

———. 1995. *The Invention of the Americas: Eclipse of "the other" and the Myth of Modernity*. Translated by Michael Barber. New York: Continuum.

———. 2001a. "The "World-System": Europe as "Center" and Its "Periphery," beyond Eurocentrism." In *Latin America and Postmodernity*, edited by Pedro Lange-Churión and Eduardo Mendieta. Amherst, NY: Humanity Books.

———. 2001b. *Towards an Unknown Marx: A Commentary on the Manuscripts of 1861–1863*. London: Routledge.

———. 2003a. "Philosophy in Latin America in the Twentieth Century: Problems and Currents." In *Latin American Philosophy: Currents, Issues, Debates*, edited by Eduardo Mendieta. Bloomington: Indiana University Press.

———. 2003b. *Beyond Philosophy: Ethics, History, Marxism and Liberation Theology*. Edited by Eduardo Mendieta. Lanham, MD: Rowman and Littlefield.

———. 2008. *Twenty Theses on Politics*. Translated by George Ciccariello-Maher. Durham, NC: Duke University Press.

Dutton, George. 2006. *The Tay Son Uprising: Society and Rebellion in 18th Century Vietnam*. Honolulu: University of Hawaii Press.

Elkins, Caroline. 2005. *Imperial Reckoning: The Untold Story of Britain's Gulag in Kenya*. New York: Henry Holt.

Enayat, Hamid. 1982. *Modern Islamic Political Thought*. Austin: University of Texas Press.

Etemad, Bouda. 2007. *Possessing the World: Taking the Measurements of Colonisation from the Eighteenth to the Twentieth Century*. Translated by Andrene Everson. New York: Berghahn Books.

Euben, Roxanne. 1997. "Premodern, Antimodern or Postmodern? Islamic and Western Critiques of Modernity." *Review of Politics* 59 (3): 429–59.

———. 1999. *Enemy in the Mirror: Islamic Fundamentalism and the Limits of Modern Rationalism: A Work of Comparative Political Theory*. Princeton, NJ: Princeton University Press.

———. 2001. "Killing (for) Politics: Jihad, Martyrdom, and Political Action." *Political Theory* 30 (1): 4–35.

Euben, Roxanne, and Muhammad Qasim Zaman, eds. 2009. *Princeton Readings in Islamist Thought: Texts and Contexts from al-Banna to Bin Laden*. Princeton, NJ: Princeton University Press.

Eze, Emmanuel Chukwudi. 1997. "The Color of Reason: The Idea of 'Race' in Kant's Anthropology." In Emmanuel Chukwudi Eze, ed., *Postcolonial African Philosophy: A Critical Reader*. Oxford: Blackwell.

Fanon, Frantz. 1965. *A Dying Colonialism*. Translated by Haakon Chevalier. New York: Grove Weidenfeld.

———. 1967. *Toward the African Revolution*. Translated by Haakon Chevalier. New York: Grove Press.

———. 2004. *The Wretched of the Earth*. Translated by Richard Philcox. New York: Grove Press.

Ferguson, James. 2006. *Global Shadows: Africa in the Neoliberal World Order*. Durham, NC: Duke University Press.

Finlason, W. F. 1868. *The history of the Jamaica Case founded upon official or authentic documents, and containing an account of the debates in Parliament and the Criminal Prosecutions arising out of the case*. London: Chapman and Hall.

Fischer, Michael M. J. 1980. "Becoming Mollah: Reflections on Iranian Clerics in a Revolutionary Age." *Iranian Studies* 13 (1–4): 83–117.

Foucault, Michel. 2005. "What Are the Iranians Dreaming About?" In *Foucault and the Iranian Revolution: Gender and the Seductions of Islamism*, edited by

Janet Afary and Kevin B. Anderson, 203–209. Chicago: University of Chicago Press.

Fox, Richard. 1989. *Gandhian Utopia: Experiments with Culture.* Boston: Beacon Press.

Frank, Jason. 2009. "Publius and Political Imagination." *Political Theory* 37 (1): 69–98.

———. 2010. *Constituent Moments: Enacting the People in Postrevolutionary America.* Durham, NC: Duke University Press.

Fraser, Nancy. 1997. "Recognition and Redistribution." In *Justice Interruptus: Critical Reflections on the "Postsocialist" Condition,* edited by Nancy Fraser, 11–40. New York: Routledge.

Gandhi, Leela. 1998. *Postcolonial Theory: A Critical Introduction.* New York: Columbia University Press.

Gandhi, M. K. 1961. *Democracy, Real and Deceptive.* Ahmedabad: Navajivan.

Gandhi, M. K. 1997. *'Hind Swaraj' and Other Writings.* Edited by Anthony Parel. Cambridge, UK: Cambridge University Press.

Gandhi, M. K. 1997. "Letter to Nehru." In *'Hind Swaraj' and Other Writings,* edited by Anthony Parel. Cambridge: Cambridge University Press.

Gardner, Daniel, trans. 2007. *The Four Books: The Basic Teachings of the Later Confucian Tradition.* Indianapolis, IN: Hackett Publishing.

Gates, Henry Louis, Jr. 1991. "Critical Fanonism." *Critical Inquiry* 17 (3): 457–70.

Geertz, Clifford. 1963. "The Integrative Revolution: Primordial Sentiments and Civil Politics in the New States." In *Old Societies and New States: The Quest for Modernity in Asia and Africa,* edited by Clifford Geertz. New York: The Free Press of Glencoe.

Ghai, Yash P., and P. McAuslan. 1970. *Public Law and Political Change in Kenya: A Study of the Legal Framework of Government from Colonial Times to the Present.* New York and Nairobi: Oxford University Press.

Gibler, John. 2009. *Mexico Unconquered: Chronicles of Power and Revolt.* San Francisco: City Lights Books.

Gibson, Nigel, ed. 1999. *Rethinking Fanon.* Amherst, NY: Humanity Books.

Gilman, Nils. 2004. *Mandarins of the Future: Modernization Theory in Cold War America.* Baltimore: Johns Hopkins University Press.

Gilroy, Paul. 1991. *"There Ain't No Black in the Union Jack": The Cultural Politics of Race and Nation.* Chicago: University of Chicago Press.

———. 1993. *The Black Atlantic: Modernity and Double Consciousness.* New York: Verso Press.

———. 2000. *Against Race: Imagining Political Culture Beyond the Color Line.* Cambridge, MA: Harvard University Press.

———. 2004. *After Empire: Melancholia or Convivial Culture?.* New York: Routledge.

———. 2005. *Postcolonial Melancholia.* New York: Columbia University Press.

Gogol, Eugene. 2002. *The Concept of Other in Latin American Liberation: Fusing Emancipatory Philosophical Thought and Social Revolt.* Lanham, MD: Lexington Books.

Gordon, Lewis R., T. Denean Sharpley-Whiting, and Renée T. White, eds. 1996. *Fanon: A Critical Reader.* Oxford: Basil Blackwell.

Gramsci, Antonio. 1959. "The Southern Question." In *The Modern Prince and Other Writings*. New York: International Publishers.

Guldberg, Horacio Cerutti. 1988–1989. "Actual Situation and Perspectives of Latin American Philosophy for Liberation." *The Philosophical Forum* 20: 43–61.

Haar, Gemma van der. 2007. "Land Reform, the State, and the Zapatista Uprising in Chiapas." In *Rural Chiapas Ten Years After the Zapatista Uprising*, edited by Sarah Washbrook. New York: Routledge. 68–91.

Hall, Stuart, and Bram Gieben, eds. 1992. *Formations of Modernity*. Cambridge, UK: Polity Press.

Hanson, Brad. 1983. "The "Westoxification" of Iran: Depictions and Reactions of Behrangi, Al-e Ahmad, and Shariati." *International Journal of Middle East Studies* 15 (1): 1–23.

Harding, Sandra. 1998. *Is Science Multicultural?: Postcolonialisms, Feminisms, and Epistemologies*. Bloomington: Indiana University Press.

Harring, Sidney L. 1994. *Crow Dog's Case: American Indian Sovereignty, Tribal Law, and United States Law in the Nineteenth Century*. Cambridge: Cambridge University Press.

Hart, H. L. A. 1994. *The Concept of Law*. Oxford: Oxford University Press. First edition published 1961.

Hartstock, Nancy. 1995. "The Feminist Standpoint: Developing the Ground for a Specifically Feminist Historical Materialism." In *Feminism and Philosophy: Essential Readings in Theory, Reinterpretation, and Application*, edited by Nancy Tuana and Rosemarie Tong. Boulder, CO: Westview Press.

———. 1998. *The Feminist Standpoint Revisited and Other Essays*. Boulder, CO: Westview Press.

Harvey, Neil. 1998. *The Chiapas Rebellion: The Struggle for Land and Democracy*. Durham, NC: Duke University Press.

Hashemi, Nader. 2009. *Islam, Secularism, and Liberal Democracy: Toward a Democratic Theory for Muslim Societies*. Oxford: Oxford University Press.

Hay, Stephen N. 1970. *Asian Ideas of East and West: Tagore and His Critics in Japan, China and India*. Cambridge, MA: Harvard University Press.

Hechter, Michael. 1975. *Internal Colonialism: the Celtic Fringe in British National Development*. New York: Taylor and Francis.

Hendrix, Burke A. 2008. *Ownership, Authority, and Self-Determination*. University Park: Pennsylvania State University Press.

Hintjens, Helen. 1995. *Alternatives to Independence: Explorations in Post-colonial Relations*. Aldershot, UK, and Brookfield, VT: Dartmouth.

Hobsbawm, Eric. 1992. "Introduction: Introducing Traditions." In *The Invention of Tradition*, edited by Eric Hobsbawm and Terence Ranger. Cambridge: Cambridge University Press.

Hochschild, Adam. 1998. *King Leopold's Ghost: A Story of Greed, Terror, and Heroism in Colonial Africa*. New York: Houghton Mifflin.

Hofstadter, Richard. 1965. *The Paranoid Style of American Politics and Other Essays*. New York: Alfred A. Knopf.

Honig, Bonnie. 1991. "Declarations of Independence: Arendt and Derrida on the Problem of Founding a Republic." *American Political Science Review* (85) 1: 97–113.

Hourani, Albert. 1962. *Arabic Thought in the Liberal Age: 1798–1939*. London: Oxford University Press.

Hulme, Peter. 1986. *Colonial Encounters: Europe and the Native Caribbean, 1492–1797*. London: Methuen.

Huntington, Patricia. 2000. "Challenging the Colonial Contract: The Zapatistas' Insurgent Imagination." *Rethinking Marxism* 12 (3): 58–80.

Hussain, Nasser. 2003. *The Jurisprudence of Emergency: Colonialism and the Rule of Law*. Ann Arbor: University of Michigan Press.

Issac, Jefferey C. 1998. *Democracy in Dark Times*. Ithaca, NY: Cornell University Press.

Ivison, Duncan, Paul Patton, and Will Sanders, eds. 2000. *Political Theory and the Rights of Indigenous Peoples*. Cambridge: Cambridge University Press.

Jefferess, David. 2008. *Postcolonial Resistance: Culture, Liberation, and Transformation*. Toronto: University of Toronto Press.

Johnson, G. Wesley. 1971. *The Emergence of Black Politics in Senegal: The Struggle for Power in the Four Communes, 1900–1920*. Stanford: Stanford University Press.

July, Robert W. 1967. *The Origins of African Thought*. New York: Frederick A. Praeger.

Jung, Courtney. 2008. *The Moral Force of Indigenous Politics: Critical Liberalism and the Zapatistas*. Cambridge: Cambridge University Press.

Kampwirth, Karen. 2003. "Marching with the Taliban or Dancing with the Zapatistas? Revolution after the Cold War." In *The Future of Revolutions: Rethinking Radical Change in the Age of Globalization*, edited by John Foran, 227–41. London: Zed Books.

Kariuki, Josiah Mwangi. 1975. *Mau Mau Detainee: The Account by a Kenyan African of His Experiences in Detention Camps, 1953–1960*. Nairobi: Oxford University Press.

Keddie, Nikki R. 1968. Sayyid Jamāl ad-Dīn "al-Afghānī": *A Political Biography*. Berkeley: University of California Press.

Keddie, Nikki R. 2003. *Modern Iran: Roots and Results of Revolution*. New Haven, CT: Yale University Press. Updated edition published 2006.

Kedourie, Elie. 1966. *Afghānī and 'Abduh: An Essay on Religious Unbelief and Political Activism in Modern Islam*. London: Cass.

Kelley, Robin D. G. 2000. "A Poetics of Postcolonialism." In Aimé Césaire, *Discourses on Colonialism*, translated by Joan Pinkham. New York: Monthly Review Press.

Kennedy, Ellen. 2004. *Constitutional Failure: Carl Schmitt in Weimar*. Durham, NC: Duke University Press.

Kenyatta, Jomo. 1978. *Facing Mount Kenya: The Tribal Life of the Gikuyu*. Nairobi: Heinemann.

Khoury, Philip. 1983. "Islamic Revivalism and the Crisis of the Secular State in the Arab World: A Historical Appraisal." In *Arab Resources: The Transformation of a Society*, edited by Ibrahim Ibrahim, 213–36. London: Croom Helm.

King, Anthony. 1990. *Urbanism, Colonialism, and the World Economy: Cultural and Spatial Foundations of the World Urban System*. London: Routledge.

Klor de Alva, J. Jorge. 1992. "Colonialism and Postcolonialism as (Latin) American Mirages." *Colonial Latin American Review* 1 (1–2): 233–45.

Kohn, Margaret. 2008. "Empire's Law: Tocqueville on Colonialism and the State of Exception." *Canadian Journal of Political Science* 41 (2): 255–78.

———. 2009. "Afghānī on Empire, Islam and Civilization." *Political Theory* 37 (3): 398–422.

Kohn, Margaret, and Daniel O'Neill. 2006. "A Tale of Two Indias: Burke and Mill on Racism and Slavery in the West Indies and Americas." *Political Theory* 34 (2): 192–228.

Kostal, Rande. 2005. *A Jurisprudence of Power: Victorian Empire and the Rule of Law*. Oxford: Oxford University Press.

Laclau, Ernesto. 1977. *Politics and Marxist Ideology*. London: Verso.

———. 1996. *Emancipation(s)*. London: Verso.

Laclau, Ernesto, and Chantal Mouffe. 1985. *Hegemony and Socialist Strategy: Towards a Radical Democratic Politics*. London: Verso.

Lacouture, Jean. 1968. *Ho Chi Minh*. Translated by Peter Wiles. London: Allen Lane Press.

Lambert, Michael. 1993. "From Citizenship to *Négritude*: Making a Difference in Elite Ideologies of Colonized Francophone West Africa." *Comparative Studies in Society and History* 35 (2): 241–42.

Lefebvre, Henri. 1991. *The Production of Space*. Translated by Donald Nicholson-Smith. Oxford, UK, and Cambridge, MA: Blackwell.

Lenin, V. I. 1956. *The Development of Capitalism in Russia: The Process of the Formation of a Home Market for Large-Scale Industry*. Honolulu: University Press of the Pacific.

Lewis, Bernard. 1990. "The Roots of Muslim Rage." *The Atlantic Monthly* 266 (3): 47–60.

Lewis, Martin D. 1962. "One Hundred Million Frenchmen: The 'Assimilation' Theory in French Colonial Policy." *Comparative Studies in Society and History* 4 (2): 129–43.

Liss, Sheldon B., ed. 1984. *Marxist Thought in Latin America*. Berkeley: University of California Press.

Locke, John. 1980. *Second Treatise of Government*. Edited by C. B. Macpherson. Indianapolis, IN: Hackett. Originally published 1690.

Lonsdale, John. 2000. "Kenyatta's Trials: Breaking and Making an African Nationalist." In *The Moral World of the Law*, edited by Peter Cross, 196–239. Cambridge: Cambridge University Press.

———. 1990. "Mau Maus of the Mind: Making Mau Mau and Remaking Kenya." *The Journal of African History* 31: 393–421.

Lorenzano, Luis. 1998. "Zapatismo: Recomposition of Labour, Radical Democracy and Revolutionary Project." In *Zapatista!: Reinventing Revolution in Mexico*, edited by John Holloway and Eloina Pelaez, 126–58. London: Pluto Press.

Luxemburg, Rosa. 2006. *Reform or Revolution and Other Writings*. Mineola, NY: Dover.

Mahmood, Saba. 2005. *Politics of Piety: The Islamic Revival and the Feminist Subject*. Princeton, NJ: Princeton University Press.

Malley, Robert. 1996. *The Call from Algeria: Third Worldism, Revolution, and the Turn to Islam*. Berkeley: University of California Press.

Mamdani, Mahmood. 1996. *Citizen and Subject: Contemporary Africa and the Legacy of Late Colonialism*. London: James Currey.

———. 2004. *Good Muslim, Bad Muslim: America, the Cold War, and the Roots of Terror*. New York: Pantheon.

———. 2008. "Lessons of Zimbabwe." *London Review of Books* 30 (23): 17–21.

March, Andrew. 2009. *Islam and Liberal Citizenship: The Search for an Overlapping Consensus*. Oxford: Oxford University Press.

Marcos, Subcomandante Insurgente. 2001. *Our Word Is Our Weapon: Selected Writings*. Edited by Juana Ponce de León. New York: Seven Stories Press.

Mariátegui, Jose. 1929. "The Indigenous Question." *Amauta*, July-August.

———. 1979. "El hombre y el mito." *Obra Política*. Colonia La Fama, Tlalpan, Mexico: Ediciones Era: 308–11.

———. 1988. *Seven Imperative Essays on Peruvian Reality*. Translated by Jorge Basadre. Austin: University of Texas Press.

———. 1996. *The Heroic and Creative Meaning of Socialism: Selected Essays of José Carlos Mariátegui*. New York: Humanities Press.

Markovitz, Irving. 1969. *Léopold Sédar Senghor and the Politics of Negritude*. New York: Atheneum.

Marx, Karl. 1853. "The Future Results of British Rule in India." In *Marx and Engels: Collected Works*, 12: 217. New York: International Publishers, 1975–2005. First published in *New-York Daily Tribune* August 8.

Mbembe, Achille. 2001. *On the Postcolony*. Berkeley: University of California Press.

McClintock, Anne. 1992. "The Angel of Progress: Pitfalls of the Term 'Post-Colonialism.'" *Social Text* (31/32): 84–98.

———. 1995. *Imperial Leather: Race, Gender and Sexuality in the Colonial Contest*. New York: Routledge.

Mehta, Uday Singh. 1999. *Liberalism and Empire: A Study in Nineteenth-Century British Liberal Thought*. Chicago: University of Chicago Press.

Mendieta, Eduardo. 1995. "La razón postcolonial: herencias coloniales y teorías postcoloniales." *Revista Chilena de Literatura* 47: 91–141.

———. 1999. "Ethics for an Age of Globalization and Exclusion." *Philosophy and Social Criticism* 25 (2): 115–21.

———. 2005. *The Idea of Latin America*. Malden, MA: Blackwell Publishing.

———. 2007. *Global Fragments: Globalizations, Latinamericanisms, and Critical Theory*. Albany: State University of New York Press.

———. 2008. "The Geopolitics of Knowledge and the Colonial Difference." In *Coloniality at Large: Latin America and the Postcolonial Debate*, edited by Mabel Moraña, Enrique Dussel, and Carlos A. Jáuregui, 225–47. Durham, NC: Duke University Press.

Mentinis, Mihalis. 2006. *Zapatistas: The Chiapas Revolt and What it Means for Radical Politics*. London and Ann Arbor, MI: Pluto Press.

Mignolo, Walter. 1995. *The Darker Side of the Renaissance: Literacy, Territoriality, and Colonization*. Ann Arbor: University of Michigan Press.

Mill, John Stuart. 1977. "Civilisation." In *Essays on Politics and Society*, edited by John M. Robson. Toronto: University of Toronto Press.

Mills, Charles. 1997. *The Racial Contract*. Ithaca, NY: Cornell University Press.

Minh, Ho Chi. 2007. *Down with Colonialism!*. Edited by Walden Bello. London: Verso Books.

Minh-ha, Trinh T. 1991. *When the Moon Waxes Red: Representation, Gender and Cultural Politics*. New York: Routledge.

Mohanty, Chandra Talpade. 1988. "Under Western Eyes: Feminist Scholarship and Colonial Discourses." *Feminist Review* (30): 61–88.

Moore, Barrington, Jr. 1969. *Social Origins of Dictatorship and Democracy: Lord and Peasant in the Making of the Modern World*. New York: Penguin Books.

Moraña, Mabel, Enrique Dussel, and Carlos A. Jáuregui, eds. 2008. *Coloniality at Large: Latin America and the Postcolonial Debate*. Durham, NC: Duke University Press.

Mukumbira, Rodrick. 2008. "White Farmers Win Case Against Zimbabwe Land Grabs." *Associated Press*, November 28.

Munro, Thomas. 1824. "On the Ultimate Aim of British Rule in India." Reprinted in *Indian Constitutional Documents 1757–1947*. 3rd Edition. Edited by Anil Chandra Banerjee. Calcutta: A. Mukherjee and Co., 1961. Vol. 1, 206–207.

Muthu, Sankar. 2003. *Enlightenment Against Empire*. Princeton, NJ: Princeton University Press.

Narayan, Uma, and Sandra Harding, eds. 2000. *Decentering the Center: Philosophy for a Multicultural, Postcolonial, and Feminist World*. Bloomington: Indiana University Press.

Neumann, Franz. 1986. *The Rule of Law: Political Theory and the Legal System in Modern Society*. Heidelberg and Dover: Berg.

Ngugi, James [wa Thiong'o]. 1967. *Weep Not, Child*. London: Heinemann.

Ngugi, wa Thiong'o. 1981. *Detained: A Writer's Prison Diary*. London and Exeter, NH: Heinemann.

Ngugi, wa Thiong'o, and Micere Githae Mugo. 1977. *The Trial of Dedan Kimathi*. London: Heinemann.

Ochoa, Pauline. *The Time of the People*. University Park: Pennsylvania State University Press. Forthcoming.

Okolo, M. S. C. 2007. *African Literature as Political Philosophy*. Dakar, Senegal: CODESRIA Books.

Pagden, Anthony. 2003. "Human Rights, Natural Rights, and Europe's Imperial Legacy." *Political Theory* 31 (2): 171–99.

Pantham, Thomas. 1983. "Thinking with Mahatma Gandhi: Beyond Liberal Democracy." *Political Theory* 11 (2): 165–88.

Parekh, Bhikhu. 1989. *Colonialism, Tradition, and Reform: An Analysis of Gandhi's Political Discourse*. Newbury Park: Sage Publications.

———. 1989. *Gandhi's Political Philosophy: A Critical Examination*. South Bend, IN: University of Notre Dame Press.

Parel, Anthony. 1997. Introduction to *Hind Swaraj*. xiii–lxii. Cambridge: Cambridge University Press.

———. 2006. *Gandhi's Philosophy and the Quest for Harmony*. Cambridge: Cambridge University Press.

Paris, Robert. 1978. "El Marxismo de Mariátegui." In *Mariátegui y los orígenes del Marxismo Latinoamericano*, edited by José Aricó. Mexico: Siglo XXI.

Pateman, Carole. 1988. *The Sexual Contract*. Cambridge, UK: Polity Press.

Pateman, Carole, and Charles Mills. 2007. *Contract and Domination*. Cambridge, UK: Polity Press.

Patterson, Thomas C. 1997. *Inventing Western Civilization*. New York: Monthly Review Press.

Peterson, Charles F. 2007. *DuBois, Fanon, Cabral: The Margins of Elite Anti-Colonial Leadership*. Lanham, MD: Lexington Books.

Pitts, Jennifer. 2000. "Empire and Democracy: Tocqueville and the Algerian Question." *Journal of Political Philosophy* 8 (3): 295–318.

———. 2005. *A Turn to Empire: The Rise of Imperial Liberalism in Britain and France*. Princeton, NJ: Princeton University Press.

Polanyi, Karl. 1944. *The Great Transformation: The Political and Economic Origins of Our Time*. Boston: Beacon Press.

Porter, Bernard. 2007. "Trying to Make Decolonisation Look Good." Review of *Britain's Declining Empire: The Road to Decolonisation* by Ronald Hyam. In *London Review of Books*, August 2.

Prakash, Gyan, ed. 1995. *After Colonialism: Imperial Histories and Postcolonial Displacements*. Princeton, NJ: Princeton University Press.

Prashad, Vijay. 2007. *The Darker Nations: A People's History of the Third World*. New York: The New Press.

Przeworski, Adam. 1986. *Capitalism and Social Democracy*. Cambridge: Cambridge University Press.

Reed, John, and Clive Wake, ed. and trans. 1965. *Senghor: Prose and Poetry*. London: Oxford University Press.

Rodinson, Maxime. 2005. "Islam Insurgent?" In *Foucault and the Iranian Revolution*, edited by Janet Afary and Kevin B. Anderson. Chicago: University of Chicago Press.

Rogin, Michael Paul. 1975. *Fathers and Children: Andrew Jackson and the Subjugation of the American Indian*. New York: Alfred A. Knopf.

———. 1985. *Subversive Genealogy: The Art and Politics of Herman Melville*. Berkeley: University of California Press.

———. 1996. "The Two Declarations of Independence." *Representations* 55: 13–30.

Rudolph, Lloyd, and Susanne Hoeber Rudolph. 2006. *Postmodern Gandhi and Other Essays: Gandhi in the world and at home*. New Dehli: Oxford.

Sáenz, Mario. 2000. "Living Labor and the Materiality of Life." In *Thinking from the Underside of History: Enrique Dussel's Philosophy of Liberation*, edited by Linda Martín Alcoff and Eduardo Mendieta. New York: Rowman and Littlefield.

Said, Edward. 2003. *Orientalism: Western Conceptions of the Orient*. New York: Penguin Modern Classics. Originally published as *Orientalism*, New York: Pantheon, 1978

———. 1993. *Culture and Imperialism*. New York: Alfred A. Knopf.

Sayyid, Bobby. 1997. *A Fundamental Fear: Eurocentrism and the Emergence of Islamism*. London and New York: Zed Books.

Scheuerman, William E. 1997. *Between Norm and Exception: The Frankfurt School and the Rule of Law*. Cambridge, MA: MIT Press.

Schlisser, Hanna, and Yaesmin Soysal, eds. 2005. *The Nation, Europe and the World: Textbooks and Curricula in Transition*. New York: Berghahn Books.

Schmitt, Carl. 2006. *The Nomos of the Earth in the International Law of the Jus Publicum Europaeum*. Translated by G. L. Ulmen. New York: Telos Publishing.

Schutte, Ofelia. 1988. "Nietzsche, Mariátegui, and Socialism: A case of 'Nietzschean Marxism' in Peru?" *Social Thought and Practice* 14 (1): 71–85.

———. 1993. *Cultural Identity and Social Liberation in Latin American Thought*. Albany: State University of New York Press.

Scott, David. 1995. "Colonial Governmentality." *Social Text* (43): 191–220.

Senghor, Léopold S. 1971. *The Foundations of "Africanité" or "Négritude" and "Arabité."* Trans. Mercer Cook. Paris: Présence Africaine.

Seth, Sanjay. 2000. "A 'Postcolonial' World?" In *Contending Images of World Politics*, edited by Greg Fry and Jacinta O'Hagan, 214–26. London: Macmillan, and New York: St. Martin's Press.

Sharabi, Hisham. 1970. *Arab Intellectuals and the West: The Formative Years, 1875–1914*. Baltimore: Johns University Hopkins Press.

Shariati, Ali. 1979. *An Approach to the Understanding of Islam*. Translated by Venus Kaivantash. Tehran: Hamdami Publishers.

———. 1979. *On the Sociology of Islam*. Translated by Hamid Algar. Berkeley, CA: Mizan Press.

———. 1980a. *From Where Shall We Begin and The Machine in the Captivity of Machinism*. Trans. Fatollah Marjani. Houston, TX: Free Islamic Literatures.

———. 1980b. *Marxism and Other Western Fallacies:an Islamic critique*. Translated by R. Campbell. Berkeley: Mizan Press.

Shklar, Judith N. 1987. "Political Theory and the Rule of Law." In *The Rule of Law: Ideal or Ideology*, edited by Allan C. Hutchinson and Patrick Monahan. Toronto: Carswell.

Shulman, George. 2008. *American Prophecy: Race and Redemption in American Political Culture*. Minneapolis: University of Minnesota Press.

Skocpol, Theda. 1979. *States and Social Revolutions: A Comparative Analysis of France, Russia and China*. Cambridge: Cambridge University Press.

Smith, Neil. 2003. *American Empire: Roosevelt's Geographer and the Prelude to Globalization*. Berkeley: University of California Press.

Smith, Rogers. 2003. *Stories of Peoplehood: The Politics and Morals of Group Membership*. Cambridge: Cambridge University Press.

Steeves, Edna L. 1973. "Négritude and the Noble Savage." *The Journal of Modern African Studies* 11 (1): 91–104.

Steger, Manfred. 2000. *Gandhi's Dilemma: Nonviolent Principles and Nationalist Power*. New York: Palgrave Macmillan.

———. 2002. *Globalism: The New Market Ideology*. Lanham, MD: Rowman and Littlefield.

Sternhell, Zeev. 1994. *The Birth of Fascist Ideology: From Cultural Rebellion to Political Revolution*. Princeton, NJ: Princeton University Press.

Stoler, Laura Ann. 2002. *Carnal Knowledge and Imperial Power: Race and the Intimate in Colonial Rule*. Berkeley: University of California Press.

Suleri, Sara. 1992. "Women Skin Deep: Feminism and the Postcolonial Condition." *Critical Inquiry* 18 (4): 756.

Tagore, Rabindranath. 1917. *Nationalism*. Madras, India: Macmillan Press.

Teitelbaum, Joshua, and Meir Litvak. 2006. "Students, Teachers, and Edward Said: Taking Stock of Orientalism." *The Middle East Review of International Affairs* 10 (1): 24–43.

Terchek, Ronald. 1998. *Gandhi: Struggling for Autonomy.* Lanham, MD: Rowman and Littlefield.

Therborn, Göran. 2008. "Roads to Modernity: Revolutionary and Other." In *Revolution in the Making of the Modern World: Social Identities, Globalization and Modernity,* edited by John Foran, David Lane, and Andreja Zivkovic, xiv–xvii. New York: Routledge.

Thomas, Lynn M. 2003. *Politics of the Womb: Women, Reproduction, and the State in Kenya.* Berkeley: University of California Press.

Tibi, Bassam. 1988. *The Crisis of Modern Islam.* Salt Lake City: University of Utah Press.

Tocqueville, Alexis de. 2001. "Essay on Algeria." In *Writings on Empire and Slavery,* edited by Jennifer Pitts, 59–66. Baltimore: Johns Hopkins University Press.

Todorov, Tzvetan. 1984. *The Conquest of America: The Question of the Other.* Translated by Richard Howard. New York: Harper and Row.

Tolstoy, Leo. "A Letter to a Hindu," http://www.gutenberg.org/etext/7176, accessed December 2009.

Toprak, Binnaz. 1981. *Islam and Political Development in Turkey.* Leiden: E. J. Brill.

Tuck, Richard. 1999. *The Rights of War and Peace: Political Thought and the International Order from Grotius to Kant.* Oxford: Oxford University Press.

Tully, James. 2000. "The Struggles of Indigenous Peoples for and of Freedom." In *Political Theory and the Rights of Indigenous Peoples,* edited by Duncan Ivison, Paul Patton, and Will Sanders, 36–59. New York: Cambridge University Press.

———. 2008. *Public Philosophy in a New Key,* vol. 2, *Imperialism and Civic Freedom.* Cambridge: Cambridge University Press.

van Rouveroy van Nieuwaal, Emile Adriaan Benvenuto, and Werner Zips, eds. 1998. *Sovereignty, Legitimacy, and Power in West African Societies: Perspectives from Legal Anthropology.* Hamburg: Lit Verlag.

Walt, Vivienne. 2008. "The Breadbasket of South Korea." *Time.* November 23. http://www.time.com/time/world/article/0,8599,1861145,00.html.

Washbrook, Sarah. 2007. "The Chiapas Uprising of 1994: Historical Antecedents and Political Consequences." In *Rural Chiapas Ten Years After the Zapatista Uprising,* edited by Sarah Washbrook, 1–33. New York: Routledge.

Wedeen, Lisa. 1999. *Ambiguities of Domination: Politics, Rhetoric, and Symbols in Contemporary Syria.* Chicago: University of Chicago Press.

Whelan, Fred. 1997. *Edmund Burke and India: Political Morality and Empire.* Pittsburgh: University of Pittsburgh Press.

Wilder, Gary. 2005. *The French Imperial Nation-State: Colonial Humanism and Negritude Between the Two World Wars.* Chicago: University of Chicago Press.

Williams, Raymond. 1973. *The Country and the City.* New York: Oxford University Press.

Williams, Robert A. 1992. *The American Indian in Western Legal Thought: The Discourses of Conquest.* Oxford: Oxford University Press.

Woodside, Alexander. 1989. "History, Structure and Revolution in Vietnam." *International Political Science Review* 10 (2): 143–57.

Young, Crawford. 1994. *The African Colonial State in Comparative Perspective*. New Haven, CT: Yale University Press.

Young, Robert J. C. 1998. "Editorial: Ideologies of the Postcolonial." *Interventions* 1 (1): 4–8.

———. 2001. *Postcolonialism: An Historical Introduction*. Malden, MA: Blackwell.

Zarobell, John. 2009. *Empire of Landscape: Space and Ideology in Colonial Algeria*. University Park: Pennsylvania State University Press.

Zizek, Slavoj. 2007. *Introductory essay to Mao Tse-Tung, On Practice and Contradiction*. London: Verso Press.

Zubaida, Sami. 2009. *Islam, the People, and the State: Political Ideas and Movements in the Middle East*. Third edition. London: I. B. Tauris, and New York: St. Martin's Press. Originally published London: Routledge, 1989.